Two Against the Tide

Two Against the Tide

A CONSCIENTIOUS OBJECTOR IN WORLD WAR II

Selected Letters, 1941 - 1948

BY ADRIAN WILSON

Edited and with Commentary by Joyce Lancaster Wilson

AUSTIN   W. THOMAS TAYLOR   1990

TABLE OF CONTENTS

PROLOGUE

In two brown cartons beside my desk are the lively, intimate, personal records of the experiences of a young man who refused to fight in World War II. They are revealed in the letters, written weekly or more often, to his parents and his brother. The hundreds of envelopes are yellowed and ragged. Several years ago his mother sent us the boxes of letters, now more than forty years old. His father had pencilled a number in the corner of each envelope and packed them away in chronological order through the years. Very little has been published about what happened to war resisters in America in the 1940s and, with this wealth of fascinating material within my reach, I decided to put together, with clarifications and extensions and with his memories, the story of the war years of my husband Adrian Wilson.

Within the envelopes the sheets of various cheap papers are inscribed in a rapid uneven hand with frequent deletions and substitutions. The letters begin when Adrian left home at age eighteen to go to Wesleyan University in Middletown, Connecticut, in the fall of 1941. They continue through his time in an induction camp for conscientious objectors in New York, his work in a camp for land reclamation in North Dakota, his experiences as a human guinea pig in laboratory experiments in Minneapolis, his activities as a member of the Fine Arts Group in a forestry camp in Oregon, and, after the war, with others from that group, the creation of a theater in San Francisco.

Removed arbitrarily from the outside world, the men in the Fine Arts Group at Waldport, Oregon, developed a loose community that was a creative catalyst for many of its members who went on to distinguished careers in the arts and crafts. It was in producing playbills and programs in the camp, and later for the theater, that Adrian's career as a designer and printer developed. In the epilogue I note what some of the others have done since the war. The writing, printing, publications, and music and theater programs produced in the Fine Arts Group at Waldport, as well as correspondence and editorial records, have been collected by libraries at Berkeley, UCLA, the University of Oregon, Swarthmore, and the Brethren Historical Library at Elgin, Illinois.

War had been raging in Europe for nearly a year when the Selective Service Act of 1940 was enacted in the United States. It mandated the registration and conscription of all American men between the ages of eighteen and forty-five. The status of the registrants was determined by local draft boards acting under very loose guidelines. Classification 1-A was for men eligible for the armed services; 1-AO was for non-combatants to be assigned to medical units; 4-D exempted divinity students from any service; 4-F was for the physically unfit; and 4-E was the classification for conscientious objectors "by reason of religious conviction." Each local draft board had the power to decide whether these last were sincere, and the variations in acceptance were extreme from one board to another even in the same areas.

Men who failed to register, or refused induction outright, and those whose sincerity was not accepted, were sent to prison. Those who were classified 4-E could be assigned to Civilian Public Service (C.P.S.) camps to do "work of national importance." These camps were conceived as a sort of continuation of the Civilian Conservation Corps (C.C.C.), which had been instituted in the depths of the Great Depression of the 1930s to relieve unemployment and provide labor for the preservation of natural resources. Congress abolished the C.C.C. program in 1942, and some of the camp sites and facilities were taken over by the C.P.S. administration.

The three historic pacifist churches, the Quakers (The Religious Society of Friends), The Mennonite Church, and The Church of the Brethren, entered into an agreement with the Selective Service Board to organize and administer the camps. Men of other faiths, notably Jehovah's Witnesses and Methodists, were also assigned to the camps. In the course of the war 151 camps were in operation, only eight of them administered directly by the government. They were all in isolated areas, probably to keep their existence out of the public eye.

Conscientious objectors, or C.O.'s, were also assigned to what was called "alternative service," which included work in mental hospitals, on farms, and as subjects of medical research. Applying for these projects appealed to many C.O.'s, who thought they could thus demonstrate their willingness to submit to discomfort and actual danger in experiments that would help save lives or improve health and living conditions.

All across America, singly or in small groups, men in khaki dotted the roadsides to "thumb" their way from one place to another; there were few hitchhikers in civilian clothes. Gasoline had been rationed since the beginning of the war, and it was almost a patriotic duty to share space in a car or truck with a serviceman. The man in "civvies" was often bypassed. For a conscientious objector it was a risky way to travel. He might find himself dumped, anywhere, when the driver discovered his position. On trains, planes, and busses, servicemen had priority, and at any point on a journey a civilian could lose his seat to a uniform. World War II was a popular war. The outrages of the Axis powers were in the headlines of every newspaper. The train and bus stations and the airports were plastered with posters proclaiming "Uncle Sam Wants You!"

Adrian Wilson was the elder son of emigrants from Holland. As in a classical immigration romance, his parents met on a boat bound for America: Christine van der Goot was on her way to fill a position at the Dutch consulate; Adrian Peter Wezel was returning to America after visiting his family, to seek further employment as a horticulturist. After their marriage and a short period in New York, they moved to Ann Arbor, Michigan, where Adrian Peter was put in charge of the grounds and greenhouses of the University of Michigan. Their first child was born there in 1923 and named after his grandfather, Ubele, and his father. Three years later a brother, Norman, was added to the family.

Only Dutch was spoken in the home until little Adrian began elementary school. He remembered his first year as a frightening struggle with language and foreign ways mitigated by the warmth and support of his parents. The constant flow of mail to and from Holland was all in Dutch, and the weekly letters to the relatives were a family ritual. The walls of the house were decorated with photos of the relatives, Delft tiles, and pictures of tulip fields and windmills. The windowsills were covered with plants, just as one sees everywhere in Holland today. Friends were mostly emigrant Hollanders, many of them in the plant and bulb business. Vacations were often trips to the mountains, where Adrian's father reveled in the awesome natural grandeur of his beloved adopted country.

Eventually, because his Dutch surname Wezel (pronounced Vehzel in Holland) was pronounced here like the name of an unpopular little rodent, Adrian Peter legally changed it to Wilson, in homage to his favorite American president.

The family went to Protestant churches wherever the sermon or the minister attracted them, and they were strictly committed to frugality, to hard work, to achievement, and to a tightly knit family life.

By the time Adrian was in his late teens, Germany had invaded and occupied Holland, and his parents struggled to get CARE packages and money to the relatives there. Adrian's pacifism had begun in childhood, much influenced by his mother's activities in the Women's International League for Peace and Freedom. Despite her feelings for the pitiful plight of Holland, she supported him warmly when he became a conscientious objector. Adrian's father, although he was a deeply patriotic new citizen, respected his son's independence and made no issue of Adrian's stand.

As I went through the letters compiling and deleting, I gradually came to the conclusion that in a subliminal way Adrian had in mind, almost from the earliest ones, their preservation and possible publication. He thought of himself as a poet and writer from his high school days. Years later, from the Minneapolis laboratory, he wrote, "I am beginning to consider all the letter writing I have been doing in C.P.S. as an unconscious preparation for the great novel." For narrative purposes I have inserted episodes and interpolations drawn from his memories and my own recollections.

Joyce Lancaster Wilson

Two Against the Tide

Middletown

The earliest letters from Adrian Wilson to his parents were written in Sep-
tember 1941, three months before Pearl Harbor, when he arrived as a freshman
at Wesleyan University in Middletown, Connecticut. He had graduated from
high school in Beverly, Massachusetts, near his home in Prides Crossing, where
his father was in charge of the grounds of a large estate. His frequent letters
usually began with the salutation Liefe Moesje en Dad, *with en* Norm *when*
his brother was at home. They ended with kusjes *(kisses) or* heel veel stiefs
(very big hugs). They were often signed with the diminutive Adriaantje,
although he was then a strapping six-foot-three. His descriptions were often
slanted toward his parents' love of nature, but sometimes he deliberately aimed
to shock their conservative attitudes.

Adrian had been admitted to Harvard but not granted a scholarship. He
concurrently applied to Amherst College, which offered him a $200 stipend,
and to Wesleyan, where the scholarship was $300. So his family chose
Wesleyan, but the money was not forthcoming until a satisfactory term had
been completed.

Wesleyan was a small ivy league college, which had offered Adrian an
attractive tuition grant because of his fine scholastic record. His first letters
describe the typical freshman rounds of aptitude tests, banquets, speeches,
rushing rituals for the fraternities, and finding friends. He wrote enthusiastically
about his studies, his clarinet, and the spacious tree-lined old campus.

> *Foss House*
> *Middletown, Connecticut*
> *September 11, 1941*

Dear Mom and Dad,

In my mind's eye I often have seen Mom valking to the post office and Dad
riding *op de viets* [on the bicycle] to get the first letter from their son,
U. Adrian, at Wesleyan. At last, here it is. I am writing at my big desk in Foss

House, 20, my black Freshman hat with the big Cardinal red button perched on the back of my head and the sound of a hot boogie-woogie record, filtering through the walls, in my ears. Just now I returned from cashing the ten dollar check and purchasing this classy writing paper in the Downey House. Yesterday, I took the final typhoid shot at the infirmary. To sum it up, everything is working out fine and I am supremely happy. . . .

September 14 & 15, 1941

. . . Saturday saw registration in which I found that Dad had faithfully paid the $95 bill; I signed up for football; I passed in the medical blanks; I passed in the approved list of courses which now consist of English, German, physics, math, economics or classical civilization (to be decided Monday), music, phys. ed. and hygiene, a total of 21 credit hours when the limit is 18; I had my picture taken; I bought a compulsory $1.85 gym suit; and I got my athletic ticket book.

Instead of dining together, the Freshman class lunched together, speeches being given on Dorm rules, Fraternities, and Rushing rules. It was with the last two that we all have been concerned since last evening. At seven, the long awaited rushing started and though I had no intention of joining a frat I nevertheless took part in order to meet fellows and join in the fun. . . .

September 19, 1941

. . . My first day date from 12 noon Monday to the same time Tuesday was spent with the boys of Sigma Chi. . . . After lunch came a jam session with a sax player, then bowling at the "Y," . . . and to top the afternoon off, a glorious sail down the Connecticut and back on a trim cabin cruiser owned by a Sigma Chi whose family lives in Middletown. That evening five upper classmen and I went to a show in Hartford, returning to the house for a community sing. Two of the brothers asked me to come upstairs with them. In the quiet of a cozy study, they told me that I fitted in very well with their group and that they would be very happy to have me become one of their brothers. At this time, as well as many others during the week, a momentary spell of sadness came over me for I realized I would have to turn down these fine, sincere fellows. [Adrian's family could not afford fraternity costs, nor would they approve because the boys drank and entertained girls in the houses.]

. . . Since Wednesday I have been working out with forty-four other Freshmen under Jim Langhurst, last year's Ohio State captain and fullback. In four days we have learned much, engaging in our first scrimmage this afternoon. The two and one-half hour practice sessions have bothered me little. . . . I am down to a mere 169, stripped, and hence have suffered considerable loss of prestige. But I feel in the pink of condition so am sticking until I am dropped or compelled to drop from the squad. . . .

November 29, 1941

. . . Well, kindren, you may dub me a Fifth Columnist if you wish. . . . No, I am not a Fascist, not a Socialist, not a potential saboteur of the East Hartford airplane factory, not a Nazi, not even a Communist. I am a member of the Fellowship of Reconciliation! "Das freut mich sehr," Moesje will say in her best Dutch. "And it pleases me also," I say in my best English. My Senior friends, Art Hoffman and Phil Watters, about whom I spoke Thanksgiving, and with whom I eat lunch at the Garden Restaurant, mentioned an F.O.R. meeting. Of course I perked up my ears, let a few hints drop as to my interest, and was urged to attend the next gathering Friday at 4:30 in the Downey House. We met in the Blue Room . . . with eight in attendance, I the only Freshman. Phil and Art, Pres. and Sec. Treas. respectively, conducted the business meeting. Plans for repairing the dilapidated Negro church and cleaning up the Red Cross headquarters were made. One of the eight earnest fellows was Rev. Darr, a strong pacifist. Two years ago he had been asked to take the pacifist side in a symposium (or something) against two other ministers. . . . Mr. Darr had framed his speech as one of a series of articles appearing in the *Christian Century* on how various ministers' minds had changed concerning war and peace. But Rev. Darr entitled his "Not Changed." . . . He read this speech, the gist of which was that if war was right, then all the teachings of the gospel were false. He wouldn't believe that. He hadn't believed it twenty-five years ago and he wouldn't believe it now. After his deep voice had ceased and we had sat in meditation, Phil thanked Mr. Darr for helping him to better form and express such a creed, for Phil too is going to become a minister. And so with a few more comments and questions, the F.O.R. ended its meeting, as serious and sincere a get-together as I have ever attended. No mention was made of C.O.'s but these fellows seem underneath to have that as an object. Me too. . . .

To economize, Adrian moved out of the dormitory, Foss House, and into a room in the home of the Congregational minister, which he had in exchange for doing the dishes daily, shoveling snow, and other odd jobs.

60 Crescent Street
Middletown, Connecticut
December 7, 1941

My chores, "chowas" as Madame Rollason calls them, are just finished. My stomach is satisfied with some of the mistress's usual Sunday biscuits which I help devour for my supper with the family. My windows are locked tight against the icy blasts which are whipping around the stolid brick corners of 60 Crescent Street, and I feel prepared to write the letter I promised. . . .

This weekend has been all Alden Nicholls. I meandered into the Garden Restaurant about 6:30 yesterday night, saw none of the boys, and hence sat down at the counter for chicken broth and a hamburg. But no sooner had I finished this first part of the meal, than entered Art Hoffman and Eric Martin with a handsome stranger in tow. I knew at the first glimpse that it was Alden. So I joined them in a booth. . . . Of course the prominent C.O. held the spotlight. He asked us upon what points we thought he should touch at the F.O.R. meeting scheduled for 10:00 p.m. We offered some suggestions for his talk and he gave us a few of the many impressions he has gotten at camp [the Petersham Camp for C.O.'s in New Hampshire]. Quite a mind Nicholls has. "I have never read a book or met a person with whom I didn't disagree!" But that doesn't mean Alden isn't friendly. Far from it. He is intelligence, humour, and good fellowship combined. So I was glad to have this intimate supper table preview of the man who was to give us such a splendid talk that evening. . . .

At 10:00, sitting by the globe in the well-filled Blue Room of the Downey House, Alden began his tale of life in the Petersham camp. He didn't know how he came to be a pacifist. Yet he believed it was a combination of a number of things, the Bible teachings, previous war experience, and common sense, which brought him to his present belief. And so when August 8th came he left for his $2^1/_2$ year stay in the woods. When he arrived, the total enrollment swelled to 35 earnest fellows, 11 Methodists, 9 Quakers, 6 Baptists, 2 Jehovah's Witnesses, 1 Pentecostal, and other unheard of sects, ranging in education from a sixth grader to a Ph.D. in organic chemistry—a motley yet unified crew. The C.O.'s welcomed Alden with open arms, and the newcomer was put immediately at ease. Fortunately, each fellow respected the other's ideas and opinions, so Alden found little, if any, straining of relations. Maybe their pacifist leanings contribute to this lack of usual enmity in such a group. At any rate harmony is essential, for the boys live more closely together than they would with their own families at home. They sleep together, eat together, work together, and play together.

Concerning the first, one dormitory, in which the double-decker beds are lined up next to each other, houses the 35 C.O.'s. When one fellow goes to bed with a cold, they all have it by morning. They have a one-bed infirmary, two privies, a wash house and tool house, and, of course, the mess hall. At present they are carting sawed-up sections of permanent C.C.C. buildings from a nearby camp to their own grounds to make a new infirmary and recreation headquarters. Soon the camp should be pretty well outfitted.

Eating together is carried on in the mess hall; breakfast is from 6 to 6:30, followed by a 20-minute Quaker-style meditation period which only half the fellows stay for; lunch is usually eaten at the working spot; dinner, a sumptuous meal, is eaten back at camp. Alden says the food is marvelous, which makes me happy.

Working together consumes most of the time. When Alden first came, ten water holes 25′ x 30′ x 6′ had to be dug as part of the forest fire fighting program. Just now the C.O.'s are waiting for more material to continue their construction of a telephone line up Mt. Toby. . . . Conversation in the water-hole digging is very lively, but when the fellows are some 60 feet apart digging telephone pole holes, conversation is rather dull. When this latter project is completed, clearing up of more hurricane timber will take over. Despite the meniality of the tasks, especially for Ph.D.'s, the fellows feel that they are doing something *constructive*, not *destructive*. For example, for a whole week they fought a forest fire 30 miles from their camp, a far more profitable occupation than fighting cannon fire.

Playing together consumes less time since "lights out" is sounded at 9:30. However, they have discussions, sings, softball games, reading in the well-stocked library, and listening to records, which help pass the relaxation hours.

The staff of the camp consists of a main director who supervises the Royalston and Ashburnham camps as well as the Petersham group; an Army sergeant, a Quaker assistant director, a dietitian, a nurse, one of the boys who acts as night watchman, and four K.P.'s who prepare all meals under Miss Dietitian's direction. According to the Draft Commission, the American Friends Committee is responsible for all discipline, but this organization hands everything over to the boys. When one fellow overstayed his special furlough, the whole camp worked an extra hour to make up for the time the naughty boy had missed. There is no guard house or brig as in the Army.

Alden feels that the Quakers are under a severe burden in having taken on the whole C.O. program. Whereas the Mennonite camps have just Mennonites, the Am. Friends have all sorts of denominations. In Petersham only 9 are Quakers so they are supporting 4 times as many fellows as they could normally be expected to. In addition, most of the fellows are unable to pay their $35 per month, so the Quakers lose both ways.

Liberty is granted to the boys from Saturday noon to Sunday night. Hence Alden was able to be here in Middletown. Of course the fellows get furloughs which can add up to as many as 15 days. Alden recently took a week off, so the C.O.'s certainly aren't in prison.

The C.O.'s have been giving service to two surrounding communities. Some of the boys form a Baptist Church choir, others supplied entertainment at a church show, and some pulled a stump out of a parsonage lawn.

Incidentally, Prof. Harlow's sociology class from Smith [College] visited the camp for study of C.O. life and some other reasons even more obvious. In turn the C.O.'s have attended Smith and Mt. Holyoke dances and F.O.R. meetings. Not bad at all. Before Alden had finished with this information and a lot more, it was past midnight and so the F.O.R. adjourned. . . .

I have purchased a $5.00 meal ticket for $4.50 at the Garden Restaurant, Phil, Art, Eric, and Stu Bush's hangout. On this amount I expect to eat handsomely for a whole week. At any rate, don't worry. I don't tolerate hunger.

Classes are much the same as ever. Physics is now concerned with sound and music, most interesting. I talked with [Professor] Eaton for an hour about the possibility of designing a machine to copy solos off records. "Very difficult," he said. Yet it's such a discussion which makes college a valuable experience.

That Sunday afternoon Adrian was at the college pastor's house listening to the Philharmonic broadcast when the program was interrupted by the announcement that the Japanese had bombed Pearl Harbor. We were in the war.

In May 1941 the first camp for C.O.'s had been opened in Maryland, and others soon followed. After Pearl Harbor and the declaration of war on Japan, a bill was passed in Congress to draft men between eighteen and sixty-five years old. Across the country, Civil Defense volunteers and rescue corps were organized, and air raid sirens were set up.

At Wesleyan every gathering of students seethed with excitement. The little cadre who ate together in the downtown Garden Restaurant (since none of them was a member of a fraternity) discussed with intensity the government's moves to build a conscripted army. They argued about civil rights, religion, resistance, and pacifism. They called themselves the Heretics Club.

December 14, 1941

. . . Of course the war has had a marked effect on the attitudes and life of the college body. Out of the so-called "emergency" have grown a few definite types of college men. There is the "what-the-hell" group which, because of likely compulsory service soon, has decided to quit school and volunteer, preferably in the Navy. There is a group which makes its home within ten feet of a blaring radio, intensely interested. "Nuts to Nippon!" Another bunch takes this war as the greatest excuse for not studying since the hurricane. And then there are the C.O.'s, still firm. Upon the announcement that special first aid courses were to replace the regular physical education and that the campus was to be divided into 4 parts with rescue corps and air raid wardens, we F.O.R. boys held a meeting. It was decided to support the program as long as it had no military implications, no drilling or army command. A statement was drawn up to be presented to Prexy. Briefly, it said that the college had our full cooperation but the minute the program stepped over the pacifist and military boundary line, the C.O.'s would drop out.

The new 18-65 selective service bill has caused much discussion around our Garden lunch and supper tables. Art sees himself in jail, Phil in Yale Divinity School, Eric as a "local preacher." As for myself I don't know. Perhaps I'll join Alden Nicholls in Petersham, but more likely I'll stay here in Wesleyan where I belong. I had a loud "haw-haw" over Norm's air raid precautions. In fact, I don't think there has ever been so much nonsensical chaos in this land.

When the fire engine siren shrills, ten boys say it's an air-raid and when a barn a few miles away burns so that the sky over by Foss House is bathed in a reddish glow, the boys say it's sabotage. What a mess! And Roosevelt says that we'll lick the axis so that we'll never have to face such a crisis again. He just as well might have said, "Let's make the world safe for Democracy." With Phil, Art, and Eric, I utter a mournful, "O, me." . . .

December 18, 1941

. . . At this very moment a drastic plan of action is being discussed by the faculty. Seeking to emulate Dartmouth and some others in their patriotic moves, some of the profs have suggested that this semester be shortened and the spring vacation be omitted so that college may close by May 7. Thus, draftees will have a better chance to gain a deferment since the Army won't have to wait so long. By suppertime I should know the decision for I'll be with Phil, Art, Eric, and Stu, the first two of whom seem to be on the "inside" of everything. The plan seems to me pretty good from a personal point of view, since I'll be able to earn money . . . for an extra month and a half this summer. . . .

January 11, 1942

. . . Friday night I journeyed with Phil and Art and another forceful pacifist, Dale Cunningham, in Simeon [the nickname of Phil's old car] to Hartford to hear A. J. Muste, who, as you know, is one of the F.O.R. leaders. After a late start because of filling up on anti-freeze we were further delayed when good Samaritan Phil stopped to help a lady whose chain had caught on the inside of the car wheel. So when we putted into the Y.M.C.A. Muste was just finishing his talk. You'll be surprised to know that the room was so crowded that we were forced to stand outside the door. What I remember of the actual talk most was Muste's claim that if the U.S. were to sink the fifty-nine million the President just asked for, into an active peace effort, the move would sweep the world. In this war as contrasted with the last, the people are reluctant to engage in hostilities. Although he was sure the world would accept such a proposal for peace, it would cause such disastrous revolutionary effects as to be impractical. In the question period, Phil, who managed to squeeze in the door, asked about dealing with certain F.O.R. leaders who went about displaying their pacifist leanings in aggressive almost belligerent fashion. Muste said that to get any reaction out of the members of the "cells" leaders had to resort to wielding a big stick instead of sticking to strictly pacifist measures. Afterward when we four from Wes met Muste we discussed the issue a little more. It happened that Phil was referring to your John Swomley, Mom. Muste, who considers Swomley almost a son, said that this dynamic fellow was the organizational type of leader, the field general who saw a cell here and a cell there and wanted to bring them together in a big powerful unit. All the way home after soup in the Waldorf we conversed on what we had heard. Mrs. Rollason had done all the dishes when I returned at midnight. . . .

I have solved the problem of joining a church to back up my conscientious objection all by myself with advice from no one. . . . I have decided not to join at all. To me it seems such an artificial way of going about it. "The spirit hasn't moved me" to join up. Alden Nicholls told of C.O.'s at his camp who think Christianity is the biggest hoax that ever hit this universe, and most of all it seems to be such an easy way of getting out of the mess that I would actually feel guilty for having become a Quaker. Becoming a Friend looks to me like running home to Mother for protection. I want to fight this battle alone. Of course I talked to Phil and Art about it. If I were to join they would advise the Quakers. But I ain't gonna. . . .

January 14, 1942

. . . Grünbaum ate with us again this evening and kept our supper party going until twenty of eight. This time he gave the psychological reasons why Phil Watters says he is a social reformer. Adolph says Phil has been frustrated in some way, which, according to Freud, has probably been sexual. There has never been a genius who was not frustrated in some way. Grünbaum cited Goethe, Beethoven, Shakespeare, and many more. He made a statement to the effect that the only reason we love our parents as children is because they give us what we want and thus help us to orientate ourselves to the world.

Naturally, with my close relationship with you two, I was struck by this
statement and so added that as we get older and less dependent on the mother
and father this love changes to one of admiration and appreciation. And so
the conversation raged. I picked up the fact that Grünbaum is writing a
sixty-page typed paper on the "Psychology of Sex" in addition to his book.
As a personality Adolph is likeable but as you would say in Holländsche, "een
beetje eigenweis" [a bit conceited]. But, gosh, he has a right to be. He knows
everything! (Just an impression, not a literal fact.)

What delights me particularly when I am with Phil, Art, and Eric, are the
constant flashes of humour, gags, jests, and jollity. For instance Eric is the
constant butt of our jibes with his varied jobs. He now has a cadaverous glint
in his eye from associating with the Doolittle Funeral Home where he lives.
The boys say he prepares the floral pieces for Fountain [the local flower shop],
drives the hearse to the funeral for Doolittle, and performs the last rights
[sic] in his capacity of local preacher. "How's business, Eric?" "Pretty *dead*,"
comes the reply. Then the billboard on the First Congregational Church is
an object of our amusement. Today's words of wisdom from the pen of Rev.
Christie are, "No matter what your lot in life, build a service station on it."
We'll go around hating gas dispensaries for the rest of our days. Once Christie
had up, "In crossing the street look sharp or you'll be flat." Likewise the
theater marquee, "Errol Flynn and Marlene Dietrich, They Died with Their
Boots On," or, "Wed. Night Only, Hold Back the Dawn." So from this
letter and my last you can well see that my most enjoyable hours in college
are spent with the Garden group. . . .

January 22, 1942

. . . Last night Phil, Art, and I executed another "escape." None of us had
an exam on the morrow, Simeon was full of gas, and our wallets were full of
money so how about coming to New Haven with us, Ade? Simeon oozed out
of the mud by Foss House under his own power and we were off. A pretty
intelligent discussion, considering the subject, waged in the cubicle of
Simeon's midsection. Art posed the question which remained for the most
part unanswered, "If science were to eliminate all consequences of sexual
intercourse would relations on a high plane outside of marriage be considered
immoral?" . . . It takes fellows like Phil and Art to bring my thoughts onto
the table. We wished Grünbaum had been there to enlighten us on Art's
perplexing puzzle. . . .

. . . I was startled to hear potential ministers Sibley and Watters condemn
the Protestant organization and state that if all the churches collapsed it would
be a stroke of good fortune. The only reason these fellows want to be preachers

is because they believe in the Christian principles. I gave a dissertation on what I had observed while living with the Rollasons concerning this matter. The church for them has lost all its basic meaning; it is just a big social organization by which this family earns its livelihood just as the Sigma Chi executive makes his daily bread by giving a talk to each of the Sigma Chi fraternities the country over; you're a *good person* if you come to church and the sewing circle and help out with the Red Cross; I have never heard the real meaning of Christianity discussed in this Christian home; only, "You'd never get Lucy Smith to come!" or, "Isn't it wonderful she comes to church every Sunday." Rollason's sermons are just a job, not an inspirational task. You can see why I didn't join up with any religious denomination. I wonder if the Quakers are different? This false front of the church makes me boil within. When Eric Martin (or I even) can get a local preacher's license by just signing his name, something must be radically wrong with the organization. I have one consolation, however. At last, I am *thinking*.

On our way home Art, who is quite brilliant, gave us his theory of the conflict between institutional and individual ethics. It is evident especially in that a group thinks mass killing, commonly known as war, is all right, but murder is all wrong. . . .

In a lull in the conversation I asked, "What would you say if someone told you, 'No matter who wins this war, God will be the loser'?" Phil said without hesitation, "That guy's disillusioned." Art went into more detail, saying that the statement was true in a sense, that because man is the image of God, and humanity as a whole will suffer from war, God would be the loser. . . .

. . . In Jack's Lunch across from the Garden (closed) about 2 a.m. we decided upon some other topics to talk over, for we always omit politics, sports, daily news, and women, sticking to psychology, religion, and philosophy in the main. By two-thirty I was immersed in the dishpan and so ended a grand day for the "escapists." . . .

January 30, 1942
. . . At lunch today we discussed church organization again. The Quakers are *the* denomination. Phil and Art stand on different sides of the fence with respect to improving what we have. Phil stays a Methodist because he feels he can help the church by reforming the rotten structure which is left. Art, a Lutheran, wants the whole thing to collapse with only the Quakers remaining. Only when he feels the Quaker doctrine a part of himself will he join. For the same reason, lack of Quaker conviction, have I refrained from joining. . . .

Tomorrow at 8:15 a.m., Dale Cunningham and I are going to get ladders and painting materials to start work on the Negro church. I started a short-lived argument about this subject with Phil and Art after reading Fosdick's splendid sermon on "Man's Greatest Need—Communal Living." The inference I drew from this talk was that segregation of Negroes from whites in matters of religion is all wrong. "Since you, Phil and Art, think likewise, why are we helping to entrench this separation by fixing up the place where they worship," I asked. Both said that elimination of segregation was a slow process and that all we could do was help make things pleasant as they were. "Still—" I mumbled. . . .

February 8, 1942

. . . We had a lively F.O.R. meeting Friday despite the presence of only six out of (I found out from the record books) twenty-three members. Dale Cunningham and the gentle philosophy Prof. Reynolds reviewed chapters 1 and 2 respectively of A. J. Muste's *Non-Violence in an Aggressive World.* I found an answer to Johnny Rollason's trump card "What if Hitler were over-running this country and—" We should give love no matter in what circumstances we find ourselves. Did not God keep on giving love despite the sins of man and finally sacrifice his only begotten son? We should do likewise. The deaf Miss Bryant wondered why Muste always resorted to Christianity for backing for his statements when Einstein used no backing (except what he had proved correct by himself) to discover his truths? Couldn't pacifism arise from any religion, Buddhism, for instance? Art said that religion in his idea was "reverence for the truth." . . .

February 15, 1942

. . . Grünbaum lived in Germany until six years ago. He still has "more black and blue spots from the blows of the Nazis than we have spent dollars in college." He has seen Lutheran pacifists, kind, loving men, turn into blood-thirsty murderers in a year under the Nazi education. . . . Living among the bourgeoisie in Berlin, he saw the greatest intellectuals and thinkers turn right about into the Nazi machine. How can he be a pacifist after seeing all that? . . .

Grünbaum advises psychology is the field. He remarked about my diversity of interests, one of which I should choose for a career. He will go into physics, probably to study electronics. Research in this field should lead him to some discoveries in airplane and submarine interception. Says Adolph, "Thus only a few lives would be lost instead of thousands, were the attackers to drop their loads." Bang Bang! The Argument begins, two and one-eighth guys to one. I am the one-eighth.

I won't have to register tomorrow as this day is for the 20-44 age group. The blanks of the college boys will be sent to their local draft boards. Art will register as a C.O., and Sandy Cutler, a Sigma Chi, one of our "cell," plans not even to fill out a sheet. Trial and jail for him. He is a strange fellow to say the least. He was engaged to marry in his freshman year, but then thought better of it. I hope he changes his mind before twenty-four hours elapse. Messrs. Darr and Krusé [head of the Philosophy Department] are working on him. . . .

February 22, 1942

. . . Sandy Cutler didn't register and so on Wednesday the gendarmes slapped him in the klink. His guardian paid the $1,000 bail, so Sandy was back in class Saturday morning. I think if he had parents he would have taken a different course of action. Everyone, even we F.O.R.'s, condemns him.

March 2, 1942

. . . The mediocre Round Table Discussion was taken apart in a follow-up talk by Sinclair Lewis. He slammed everyone of the undergraduate and graduate participants, except the lone girl. These students hadn't found any ideal in the war to fight for. Lewis thought he gave them the key with his "learn, learn, learn." Lewis is too fast on the trigger, too witty, too flippant to have put any thought into his statements. He is amazingly entertaining but his cracks seem almost automatic. Ideas, not wit, will get us out of this mess. If Hoffman had been there, he would have frowned on Sinclair. The trivial has no place in Art's make-up. . . .

From 11 to 12 we had a cozy coffee party at the Garden. . . . Censorship of college newspapers was our topic. It happened, strangely enough, that Sandy Cutler's non-registering didn't get one line of type in the *Argus* [the college newspaper], while the Hartford paper made it a "scoop." We suspect that Prexy put on the ban. I think it probably helped Sandy, though an honest statement of his reasons for not registering would have spared a lot of unwarranted criticism. Sandy is back on campus after three days in the Hartford jail. . . .

March 7, 1942

. . . Yesterday evening at 9:00 we had an interesting F.O.R. meeting which included two Wesleyan C.O.'s about whom we had never heard before. Art and I reviewed chapters 3 and 4 of Muste's *Non-Violence in an Aggressive World*. My review went quite well despite the entrance of several latecomers. . . . After Art's splendid review of his chapter I spoke up out of a dead silence for the first time in my life to precipitate a discussion. It felt good to have an audience at my command even if it was rather small (twelve).

My question was "Does pacifism outlaw the use of force, and if so, how do you explain Christ's driving the money changers from the temple?" Mr. Darr and Mr. Reynolds gave good answers and brilliant Art gave one that was even better. Art gave us historian's facts that stated it wouldn't have been possible for Jesus to use force because the court of the temple was so big and the money changers so many. Moreover, the money changers were hesitant of the righteousness of working in the temple, a little show of verbal indignation would have sent them scurrying. As for the first question, force is permissible when it is of a redemptive nature. Would you support the American penal system? A long discussion. Dale Cunningham, more absolute than the others, says he would not.

March 12, 1942

. . . Monday afternoon Tom Waring, whom I knew best from our work on the Negro church, came all the way down here to ask me to come up to his house, Sigma Chi, for a visit with Naomi Binford, a representative of the Quaker work camps, which number about fifteen now. Of course she told me what you already know from reading "The Camp at Westlands." But I wasn't so much interested in the camps as in Naomi, so relaxed, poised, and sensible. Her voice was so mellow, so soft, so soothing I almost fell in love with it. Perhaps she was twenty-five. For the first time I realized what unusual depth a Quaker can have. . . . After a while I began to think a bit more about the camps than I had been. I had some sort of revelation—if I worked in a camp I would be actively benefitting a whole community of common people; if I went to work [on a Prides Crossing estate] I would be raking a drive so a Countess's shiny limousine could roll down and leave tracks in my day's work. From a theoretical point of view, there is no question which would be my choice—a work camp. But, as I told Naomi, my problem is money—cold, hard cash. I have to earn during the summer instead of spend. As I see it now, I will do both. This year's camps start June 19th and run to August 21st. Thus I could earn for five or six weeks before camp and maybe a week or two afterward. As you know, however, camps cost money ($100). How to manage that and still have enough for college stumped me. The next morning Prof. Reynolds, our active F.O.R. member of the Philosophy Department, hailed me with his "Hey, *Professor!*" (because I always carry Norm's satchel around the campus). When he had pulled abreast of me and given me a hefty slap on the back he said, "I hear you are interested in the Quaker work camps." "More or less," I replied, "but of course it's out of the question because of the money angle." "Well," he lowered his voice, "I have a faint suspicion the Christian Association can help you out with that part of it." "Yeah?" my eyes opened wide. "That's off the record, but I have an idea—," and Reynolds turned in to Fisk Hall. So maybe next summer will see me in a Tennessee Work Camp, at work in a Social Agency, in a Civilian Training Seminar, in a Peace Service Seminar, or even in Mexico, whichever I choose. The personal advantages will be many—experience in a new part of the U.S., body-building labor, girls, and most important, a cooperative community spirit. I'll bring the application blank home so we can fill it out just as we did the college forms a year ago.

And here is another metamorphosis in my thinking. We used to laugh at your Peace movement, Mom. Now I am an ardent pacifist. We ridiculed psychology. I almost have decided to major in it. I refused to listen to talk of the Quaker camps and read "The Camp at Westlands." Here I find myself almost going to a work camp. I wonder if you used an incorrect approach in bringing these subjects before me. Now when someone from the outside uses a more effective method I turn right about. I think it goes beyond that, however. A few years ago every idea and opinion of mine was biased. Today, prejudice means nothing to me. All I want is reasons and proofs to make me believe in the worth of an idea. Once, I was too immature to comprehend any logic you might offer me. Things have changed.

March 24, 1942

... Last night we had a surprise blackout. They ought to have such a twenty-minute session of darkness and quiet every night so people could relax and think for awhile. They'd soon get over the stage of peering out of windows to see if all the neighbors were complying with the regulations. Then they could do some serious meditating.

Yesterday afternoon when football was over and I had joined Phil and Art in their suite we took a walk along the river and up onto the Portland Bridge. Phil pointed out a nearby hill from which the Mt. Tom and Holyoke ranges are visible on clear days. Hard to believe. The bridge has a big bronze plaque on the first girder designating the tremendous structure as "the most beautiful steel bridge in America for 1938." I was surprised to feel the bridge floor tremble with the passing of each automobile. What a height down to the turbulent water. No flood will ever reach this colossus. The brisk breeze whetted our appetites as much as the delightful fragrance of some hole-in-the-wall bakeries that we passed on our way to the Garden. Walks like this make true companionship.

Well, Norm, you *have* to come to Middletown now. Yesterday evening a friend of Grünbaum's joined our Heretics Club. He is one Hugh Staples, Andover '40 [Norm was attending Andover], who started his tenure with us

by stating that all prep schools are "bunk." "I went to Andover and I know."
So I told him you'd be willing to contest his ideas any time. You are scheduled
for a verbal battle over this next weekend. If you don't show up "yer yaller.". . .

April 5, 1942

. . . Yesterday afternoon we finished the whole paint job on the walls and
ceiling of the Negro church just in time for Easter. It took plenty of labor
but now we rest in peace. In fact we were almost as surprised when it was
finished as was the skeptical Mrs. Green, wife of the "pygmy" preacher (he
is that small), who worried tremendously over sitting in a half-painted church
on Easter Sunday. We got considerable cooperation from non-F.O.R. fellows
who helped to keep at least four brushes going at a time. When someone
wasn't entertaining us on the dilapidated piano, the rest were telling riddles
and jokes (clean) or Hoffman was expounding his theories and explaining
religious doctrines. . . .

May 11, 1942

. . . You seem to have your authors mixed, Moesje; T. S. Eliot is a poet of
some note who wrote *The Wasteland*—a terrific poem characterizing the
tumult of the twenties. He uses concrete images which are designed to stir the
conscious, subconscious, and even unconscious minds of the reader.
D.H. Lawrence wrote *Sons and Lovers* and *The Rainbow*. Every time I wander
into Art's room I pick the latter up and drink it in. You would, too. Lawrence
goes right into the minds of his characters and brings out the deepest feelings
with violent vividness. His portrayal of the emotions of both sides of a
married couple (of which you get three pairs) are really amazing. I have an
idea you two would revel in his sensual descriptions of feelings I am sure you
have experienced. And incidentally the writing is so good I told Art he might
have underlined every row of type instead of only the half to which he applied
his pencil. The writing is really overwhelming in its incandescent brilliance.
"They walked on opposite horizons with their hands touching across the
dusk." It's the "goods"—the way I want to write. Read *The Rainbow*
if anything. . . .

*In late May three of the inner circle members of the Heretics Club received
their degrees and left Wesleyan, so the stimulating discussions at the Garden
Restaurant came to an end. As it developed, Wesleyan did not omit the spring
vacation to shorten the semester. Adrian went home to Prides Crossing and
announced, to his parents' dismay, that he would not spend the summer there
with them working as a lifeguard or a gardener's helper on one of the estates.*

*He returned to Middletown to look for a job, and was hired by the state
hospital. Probably in his favor was the fact that he was a sturdy six-foot-three,
190-pound, eighteen-year-old. The conditions and experiences he describes in
the following letters were probably analogous to those of the five hundred
conscientious objectors who were assigned to work in mental hospitals during
the war.*

Connecticut State Hospital for the Insane
Middletown, Connecticut
June 5, 1942

The heading tells most of the story since my card yesterday morning. After
lunch in the Garden and some manual labor in the Red Cross with Art, I
puffed up the hill to the Asylum. I saw a doctor out strolling so I inquired
about summer work and the whereabouts of the administration building. He
told me about both and then introduced me to some doctors and secretaries
in the main office building. Before long I was in the presence of one Miss
Noone who told me to report for work at 8:30 this morning. She handed me
six pages of typed instructions. It took me two hours to read them because
she persisted in reiterating and giving anecdotes for each rule.

Finally I found out my work would consist of being an attendant in the
reception hospital where all types of cases come for thirty days probation.
Miss Noone thought that with such a variety of mental disorders this place
would prove most interesting to a college student whose primary object is
knowledge. . . . Well, knowledge was my least concern in looking for work.
I felt that a state hospital provides most opportunity for use of the pacifist
technique and the betterment of my fellow men. Where else could I find more
material for writing than among these men from all walks of life? I realized
beforehand that I was sure of a job because of the great shortage of help, and
also that the pay was $60 per month plus room, board, and laundry. . . . When
I read the instructions I was impressed with their rigidity. This morning
when I went to work I was impressed with their laxness—all except for the
closing of doors, very important.

A globose Miss Stofford, jolly as Santa Claus, is supervisor. She wasted a
couple of hours by telling me inane stories of the hospital life while droops
shuffled around us with floor polishers ever polishing, polishing, polishing.
I met some of my fellow attendants, who were hard to distinguish from the
patients. I was shown every closet, store room, bathroom, etc., in the ward.
Being an attendant I have a pass key to everything. Life here is an endless
opening and closing of doors.

My first job was manhandling one stupe of an Italian to whom it seemed advisable to give some undesired medicine. . . . By use of violence (in the redemptive sense of course) I got him to his destination. Some of the other attendants seem to enjoy bullying the patients, most of whom are too far gone to take offense. It seemed to me, although they claim a labor shortage (11 in normal times, 8 now for 22 patients), there are too many [attendants] as it is. Even if it was my first day I don't think I loafed as much as the other guys did. For about an hour I pushed a polisher around. The rest of the time I walked around as aimlessly as did the patients—I wonder if four months here are going to affect me adversely. Of course, I have to wait on the patients at meals. Mom, you'd have a nightmare at the table manners. One fellow, about my own age, is so dumb I have to feed him with a spoon. After dinner, the patients who want fresh air or a smoke can go outside for a couple of hours. Four of us attendants just sat and watched them to see that no one "escaped." We attendants eat in two shifts an hour before the patients. Thus half the staff is always on the ward even at mealtimes. The patients pay so little attention to themselves, us attendants, or the others that I was quite amazed.

When Miss Noone said there would be patients of every type here she was right. We have a kleptomaniac, two syphilitics, three alcoholics, a guy who has hallucinations, an attempted suicide, a guy strong as a bull but too dumb to use his strength, a graduate dentist gone off, a young fellow of college age, good looking, and with the smooth talk of a man from a good home . . . , a meticulous fellow gifted for housework who had a brain tumor which was removed and some plates inserted in his skull which has made him depressed, a gaunt skeleton who broke his hip and was allowed to lie in bed for seven years without the bones being properly set, a deaf plump eighty-one-year-old considerably saner than his colleagues, a seventeen-year-old who stands rigid and stares blankly for hours on end, a fellow who won't say a word or even look up, ad infinitum and ad nauseam. I played cards ("casino") with the kleptomaniac, his red head shaved right down to the skull. The cards belonged to him so he couldn't steal them. People already ask me if I like it here after one day. I haven't decided yet whether I am sane or not.

All the attendants talk about the wonders of the metrazol treatments which will be used tomorrow with me on the patient-holding end. But my co-workers moan about the situation that will confront the hospital after the war when thousands of broken soldiers will pour in. . . .

June 13, 1942

Of the correctness of the above date I have been trying to convince a new patient all day. When I went off duty at 4:30 he still insisted it was Tuesday, June 16. Well, that is just one of the many things that happens to an alcoholic or "over-boozer." Last night, when I was on till 9:30, this same fellow contributed to making [the ward] a real madhouse for the first time since my advent. He thought he was at a party and that racketeers were horning in. He went screaming all over the place, seeing gangsters with guns behind every door, shouting to his "Brother Eddy" to watch out for the crooks, jumping on the sleeping patients, and finally tearing the blankets off eighty-one-year-old Simon DeLong and delivering the plump old Canadian a mighty kick in the ribs, before we grabbed him. Five minutes of bellowing "bloody murder" followed from the tremendous-voiced DeLong. Meanwhile another young fellow wrapped in a wet pack of sheets to soothe his nerves continued as he had all day yelling at the top of his lungs, "The shit on my ass is *not* the color of the president's" and also, "I want to see Senator Dana-her, I want to see Senator Danaher, I do *not* want to see Senator Danaher." Earlier in the day he had asked me if I thought the Danahers were nice people. I asked, "Do you mean Senator Danaher?" The above outburst continued all day. Of course our Italian friend, Biagio Pluchino, continued his gruff grating that seems to rise from the depths of his stomach. We had him in the strait jacket affair called a camisole for the third day this week. Pluchino would rasp, "Lemme out! Ah si si, Batoun! Sonnamabitch *!#*," and then glare at me with eyes far worse than the sorcerer's in *Fantasia*—a true mad-man's stare of hate. By 9:30 when the night shift of two men comes on, Kro-pack (a Polack of fifty-three with some twenty years' experience off and on at this place and knowing less than I do about it) and I had the alcoholic in a camisole, Pluchino tied to his bed, and the young fellow quieted down.

Leaving the thundering building and looking out over a twinkling Middle-town with the string of steady yellow sodium lamps a little higher than the rest was like opening a door from the inferno to heaven. And I laughed. Pluchino's eyes, or the maniac's screamings hadn't touched me a bit. Never for a moment in that tumult had I felt a tinge of fear. That is what amazes me most about this new life I have undertaken. There is never any feeling of terror at the hateful bellowing and hideous grimacing. These men are idiots, full of sound and fury, signifying nothing—not real people who have the power to reason and appreciate. And so I let insults and blows bounce off me as if I wore armorplate. If I took offense at the ranting of the patients as the other attendants do, I should be as unhappy as most of them are. In that I think I have proved for myself one aspect of pacifism. Of course it is more difficult to get the patient to respond to the pacifist approach, but it works even with them, including Pluchino, sometimes. At least I don't have to go around threatening to take the unfortunates' ears off if they refuse to comply with my demands. Sincerity goes a lot further than brute force (excuse me, Norm), even with maniacs.

One thing that impresses me more and more is that the patients would rarely get violent if they weren't aggravated by us attendants. Pluchino has never done anything really bad when allowed to roam about the whole ward, yet the staff insists that he wear a torturing camisole and stay by force in the sun porch because perhaps he got more angry than he should have when teased by an attendant. Many of the restrictions are so unnecessary and so indefinite. On the whole, the only treatment is restraint and pills. It should be love, out of concern for the patient's plight, and psycho-analysis, both utterly forgotten here and in any other state hospital I suppose.

The only real *treatment*, and at that I don't approve of it, is the metrazol "shock." When a hypodermic needle is injected into the patient, he gets a "seizure." The doctor taps the patient's head with a rubber tube. The five attendants stand tense, hands pressing straight down on the patient's body, prepared for— And then it comes, one tremendous, convulsive jerk, a contraction of every muscle in the patient's body. The attendants press, tighten, and exert every ounce of pressure to hold those knobby limbs firm to the bed— a moment's pause—and with the drive of a high pressure air drill, jerk, jerk, jerk, the whole straining form on the bed freezes rigid, relaxes, rigid again, in a mounting crescendo of muscular frenzy until all the energy is spent in one last convulsion to be free. Breathing resumes in a ghastly metallic rasping about the thick roll of cotton placed in the mouth to prevent decapitation of the tongue and dislocation of the jaw. Half an hour later the patient is walking around again. What is this startling treatment supposed to do?—Blot out that part of the memory which is troubling the patient most. To me, the treatment doesn't seem to get at the root of things. All it does, or so I understand it, is knock out physically a part of the brain function. It seems to me that psycho-analysis would bring out from the patient's subconscious the troublesome memory. Then, of course, its foolishness could be shown. With these "shock" treatments the patient has to return in a few months or so and take the shots all over again, three a week, for five weeks—a nuisance and then some. . . .

June 17, 1942

This morning I myself faced that great problem of sacrificing my principles for expediency. Just behind this state hospital hill on the slope toward the river a new housing development is well underway. By fall it will house the families of 198 defense workers. I don't go on duty till noon today so I thought I'd take a walk down and see the buildings. A bespectacled negro whom I had been watching sawing beams with a circular power saw commented on my 1945 (on the t-shirt) and then asked if I was going to work here. "Perhaps," I said. "Well if you go down there and see the man with the beach wagon I betcha he'll put you right on." So I went down to another building, spied a snappily dressed official, and asked about summer work. He ushered me into a frame structure and asked the head plasterer if he needed "a good man." "In about a week." The snappy dresser, who was an Inspector, took a great interest in me because his nephew is in my class. . . . To fill the gap in between today and the beginning of the plastering he told me to go to the main office. See Vince, the carpenter foreman. I couldn't find Vince, so I went back to the head plasterer for more information about the job. He couldn't tell me anything except that I'd have to join the union. Scare No. 1. Then I read the big sign which said, "This project is part of the defense—" Scare No. 2. I debated on how much I would be helping the war effort by working here. I decided that I would be capitalizing on the war as much as munitions makers, for I would be receiving government cash. So after pondering awhile I came back to my room consoled by the fact that I was needed here at the hospital much more. . . .

A tempting or persuasive factor in urging me to leave this job is my own conviction that I have learned all I am going to learn in this hospital. No mention is ever made of what is really wrong with the patients, what maladjustment of the cells in the cerebral cortex makes the maniacs act the way they do. The only thing we learn about them is what they have done, not what made them do it. I doubt if the nurses and doctors know either. But then the fellow I thought a week ago was the worst off in the bunch, bedridden and hallucinating, has snapped out of it beautifully and now has the honor of dishing out the food to the other sick (bed) patients. Pluchino, the fiery Italian, has been transferred, thank God, to another part of the hospital.

Yesterday, being my day off, I rambled down this hill and trudged up the undulation opposite to the Downey House. In the "Book Nook" I read considerable of Joyce (*Dubliners*) and *The Strangest Places*, a book about New York, until Dave Clark, Art's old roommate, came. We browsed around for awhile and then sauntered up to Clark Hall. For two hours we discussed pacifism and the draft. I sent for some info sheets from the N.C.C.O. [National Committee for Conscientious Objectors] which will tell all about the registration and its consequences on us guys. I will see Krusé tomorrow, I think, about whether to register as willing to do non-combatant service or not. The only such service under military control which I would accept is the medical corps. I looked over Form 47 and read Dave's adequate and frank answers to the questions. I feel I can give suitable testimony also. . . .

June 21, 1942
It is a rainy Sunday up here on the hill where the thunder makes the

windows rattle. . . . Your letter came yesterday, Mom, with the card from
Eddie Holmes in La. I suppose supper with Brad and the subsequent F.O.R.
meeting were pleasant and interesting. But I wonder if you realized at this
meeting, as I have at all ours and elsewhere, that pacifism has a tendency to
become just a number of words and trite phrases that anyone might recite.
Pacifism may be a criticism of life and society, but more strongly it is a way
of life. How many of the group at Brad's meeting realized that? What did a
statement like, "You can't combat one evil with another evil," mean to them
in terms of life? Have they ever tried to see if the principle works in reality
or are they merely repeating the words of a higher authority? Not until
pacifists live their doctrine can we hope for the future. I met Adolph Friday
evening at the Downey House waiting for the bus to Meriden (and then to
New York via train for a weekend of sin). Somehow the bus didn't come and
so we talked for an hour till the next one came. Among other things we remarked that Art is too much of an "armchair philosopher." What does he
know about life in the raw as Dave Clark saw it in Harlem and I am seeing
it here? Grünbaum thinks that if Art went to Europe or any other place where
people are of a different temperament from his own he would immediately
see that pacifism doesn't work. Here I disagree.

Why, when pacifism and everlasting peace seem to be the final goals . . .
do people use just the opposite methods in gaining those ends? Because
people are hypocrites. The human psychology as now constituted loves a
fight. That is why the most frequently posed question, "What if we all were
pacifists?" is utterly ridiculous. Everybody couldn't be a pacifist. . . .

June 23, 1942

It is another miserably moist morning as I write to you on my wide
window sill that serves just like the desk on a college classroom seat. "Grati-
fying" was the first word that came to mind after my wonderful hour-and-a-
half talk with Kruse. The spirit of the conversation meant more to me than
what we said—and we said plenty. In the "Colonel's" thickly carpeted office
with a whole wall of filled bookshelves, expansive windows that look out on
the lovely Honors College Garden . . . and a desk littered with books bearing
the word "philosophy" in different languages, we began our conference at
5:15. I posed the most immediately important question first. "Should I
register as a non-combatant C.O. or just as a C.O. ?" Of course I only consider
the medical corps as giving enough good to outweigh the evil of its militaristic
control. Kruse pointed out that non-combatant service has been given such
a wide interpretation by the draft commission as to include everything except
actually pulling the trigger. There is no guarantee that I will get into the

medical corps if I do register in the non-combatant class. Krusé said that if he were powerful enough the whole C.O. program would be changed to include work in hospitals and asylums, where help is so badly needed, especially help of the C.O. caliber. . . .

. . . It was nearly 6:45 when Mrs. Krusé, looking very buoyant, bounced in to take the professor and Uncle Fred Millett [head of the English Department] across the hall, to supper. Her first statement was that Sandy Cutler was sentenced that morning to eighteen months in a federal pen for not registering. No profound comment from anyone; not even a note of sadness. Millett and the Krusés joked with me about asylum life and the quantities I am eating up there as we went down the Russell House (Honors College) stairs and out to the car. I skipped with joy down the hill to the Garden.

After gassing a few moments with Grünbaum and Walter Simon, who were just finishing their meals, I joined Dave Clark in his booth in back. Dave's big news, as big as if he had gotten married, was that he had gone to his local draft board Friday night and had withdrawn his registration, although he had already filled out his questionnaire. What a dramatic step to take! He is still a free man, however, but expectant of the arrival of [the] gendarmes. To make a long story short, we talked for six and a quarter hours straight . . . on registration, the ashram, the asylum, Reed College, our philosophies of life, religion, women, consideration for parents in not registering, literature, Krusé's conference, roommates, and music. Just at dusk, we walked through the beautiful Honors College garden on the way to the library from the restaurant. We stood outside of Rev. Darr's home for some time listening to the beautiful recording of an unfamiliar symphony. Dave has taken the place of Art, if that's possible.

Adriaantje

[P.S.] Your most interesting letter came yesterday morning, Moesje. I read the story of Brad's 15,000-mile trip to Dave after he had told extensively about an absolute pacifist named Lutweiler who had traveled all over the country starting conferences and cooperative movements, and had lived a week at the ashram. The problem is pressing more and more upon my mind whether to go back to college next year or to devote myself to some cause like the C.P.S. camps or the ashram, or cooperatives, etc. Or is all this too idealistic for even me? Should I continue in the rut worn by tradition? I don't think so. But it is early yet, we'll see.

June 26, 1942

To me your last paragraph of the June 24 letter was disgusting and re-volting because it was motivated by fear. You are afraid that I'll be making trouble for myself that isn't necessary, that I'll call down upon myself the wrath of all Beverly Farms and Prides Crossing (about which I don't give a hoot), and perhaps even that my C.O. registration will hurt the rest of the family. I ask you, as I have before, if an idea ever got anywhere without being transmitted to others or at least brought to light. How can Bradford Gale base his main objection to registering as a C.O. on the undesirability of getting a martyr complex when he is the minister of a church of martyrs? Don't you think Jesus knew he was doing something worthwhile? And how about the others, St. Francis, Gandhi, Kagawa? Of course Brad doesn't think I'll make as good a martyr. And besides Brad can easily register in the conventional form because he knows as a minister he won't ever be called on the carpet. The only time wrath or anger means anything to me is when it comes from someone from whom I desire respect. The people whom I consider worthy of giving me respect won't be angry if I register as a C.O. There is no such person in Beverly Farms. If you have brought me up to the point where I am convinced that registering as a C.O. is the only way, I can't understand your objection now. And even if you still don't agree with me, your own strength of character should be sufficient to withstand any onslaughts and reflections because I registered as a C.O. *Pacifism based on fear is worthless.* . . .

June 28, 1942

. . . I have been considering quite seriously going into the ministry. But I am nauseated by responsive readings, most of the hymns, the prayers, in fact anything that relates to what Rev. Rollason calls "testimony." I doubt if I ever could believe half the junk in the theology textbooks I have seen. God is only a figment of the imagination. Who is going to tell me what to believe about Him when my conception of Him rises from my own personal experience of what is good? My God is Christian personality. I don't believe in singing to it, reading to it, or praying to it. I believe in living it. If I knew of a church that believes this I should be willing to be its minister. But a church that really believes this doesn't need a minister. The Quakers? However, I believe a theological seminary might be just the thing for me. Perhaps I could stand the years of straight theology I'd have to take and really profit by the rest of the experience. Unfortunately, I feel emotionally prepared for it now with three years before my plan can be realized.

My reactions to your writing Prof. Krusé were as follows: (1)? (2). (3)! I am very glad you wrote for I think he will tell you just what I said so flagrantly in my last letter. And being a higher authority than yours truly, he'll make a bigger impression. To sit in the security of a physical deferment would be intolerable. It would be the greatest perversion of good imaginable.

I think that a desire to go to theological seminary would gain me a deferment and thus allay some of your fears. But I stick with my plan of registering as a C.O. on Tuesday. I did not realize until today that "the notation 'I am a Conscientious Objector' (on the registration card) will have no legal effect and that the registrant will be given a full opportunity to make any claim that he desires at a later date." But it doesn't change my mind. I want to get this thing off my chest.

Friday evening Dave Clark and I had a final pow-wow, for it was the last day of summer school on our campus. . . . I arrived at his room at 10:03 p.m. after the late shift, 12-9:30. We went down to the Red Wing Show Grounds just below the Portland Bridge to take a look at humanity in Coleman's "Clean" Shows, a carnival affair with two ferris wheels, etc., and several "exotic" stripteasers. We felt poor in purse and clean in heart so we patronized the penny arcade instead of the latter (price 30 cents). After enjoying the punching bags and strength testers we watched the impassive faces of the Italians interspaced by college boys coming out of the striptease show. They tried to look so unconcerned over what they had just seen and did such a bad job of it. But an hour gazing at the faded paintings on cracked canvas of "The Hideous Two-Faced Baby" and "Ugly Mexican Lizard" was too much for us so we climbed up the embankment to the approach to the bridge.

It was midnight as we reached the center. The lighted face of the Wesleyan chapel clock floated above the murk of the hill. The Main Street lamps cast weird shadows on the upper stories of the buildings. I looked at my tie. The brilliant Scotch plaid was completely yellow, every color taken out, in the steady sodium light. All along the way to the Portland side we smelled the intriguing, satiating odor of baking bread. "Kelly's Bakery" I said. "We smelled it the last time we were up here, Phil, Art, and I." We agreed to go down there to the source of the wonderful fragrance. Like two thieves we peered into the windows of the bakery, converted from an old car garage. In front of one of the windows a fellow was handling a wire-mesh tray of jelly doughnuts just out of the vat of fat. We both grinned and rolled our eyes, they looked so tempting. We stole into the half-lighted storeroom stacked high with the loaves Middletown's population would eat on the morrow. Three white-clad fellows stood around watching a fourth turn over the crunchy brown biscuits in the bubbling grease. They were willing to do business with us, so Dave asked for a dozen of the morsels of dough that had just ceased their bobbing and rolling in the fat. While the doughnuts were being individually injected (at last I found out how they do it) and sugared in a tremendous wooden bowl, Dave and I wandered about in the warm, fragrant atmosphere. We gazed into the cavernous oven that held snugly rows of brown pillows of bread that undulated faintly in the glowing, diaphanous vapor. When our doughnuts were wrapped the bakers came over to the oven and rapidly slid pan after pan of hot bread on a shapeless oar out of the grinning door to a solid table. From there the loaves were righted and shifted to large rubber-wheeled racks. We bought the first steaming loaf that came sliding out. It was warm and soft as a baby in the paper bag in which I carried it to the Garden.

It took six slabs of butter each to finish the moist loaf that I had broken squarely in half. We felt like little Kagawas, though more greedy, eating mere bread and butter while those around us smiled and sipped fancy cocktails. I think we both felt a little guilty for having been such gluttons. "This is almost overdoing it," I thought cramming in another hunk of the delicious stuff. Oh, but you should have tasted those doughnuts, the most tantalizing concoctions imaginable, stuffed with cool jelly that was a perfect contrast to the tasty warm exteriors. "We'll visit Kelly's Bakery again," I said to Dave as he left me midway up my hill.

I got my first paycheck this week, $23.15 (84 cents taken off for retirement fund; haw, haw) for working half a month less three days. Very generously they took off only $2.00 for each day I failed to work. . . .

[postmarked July 8, 1942]
. . . I went to Hartford Sunday night for a visit with Dave Clark at Trinity, really a lovely college, much more English in architecture and plan than Wes. I hardly knew what to make of Dave when he told me he had, after going three times to the Draft Board and coming back each time undecided, to submit his registration after all. He sacrificed his principles for expediency, as I pointed out to him; he had read that non-registrants who had been paroled were all going back to jail. That seemed not too tasty to Dave, so he took a physical exam at the same time he re-registered. The results haven't come out yet. Also a pamphlet on delinquency from the Seymour police got him scared. Apparently they would bring that charge against him. After talking for an hour we took the bus into town and saw a corny attempt at answering the question of the C.O. in *Sergeant York*.

July 19, 1942
. . . I went to mass this morning with three patients. Of all the foolishness this Catholic service takes the cake. It is more insane and meaningless than the antics of the patients. The unpolished priest gave a sermon which surpassed even Rollason's preaching for simple-mindedness. If Rollason spent twenty minutes writing out his great culmination of a week's thought and study, this

guy didn't even bother writing his out. And then all this kissing of the Bible and drinking of wine at least twice during the service seems to me to be custom arising from superstition. They ring a bell and you stand up. They ring it again and you sit down. Mumble, mumble, hokus, pokus, and then the raucous voices of insane women burst into an endless chant that nearly stupefies you. If God is beauty the churches are doing a pretty poor job of giving it to us. . . .

July 23, 1942

The ignorance of the average American is appalling. In the first place he couldn't even pronounce the word "pacifism." . . . My argument with 250-pound Mr. Fahey, the latest bruiser on our staff of attendants, started out with a comment on the new soldier-boy patient. Fahey said, "Now if that guy had some money he could have gotten into—" I filled in with, "a good place like the Hartford Retreat."—No, into a camp for conscientious objectors." "But is he a conscientious objector?" "I don't know," Fahey answered, "but it takes money to get into one." "Yes, $35 a month," I told him. Then he blurted, "Those guys are whacky just like the nuts upstairs, except in a religious way."

I thought I just as well might enlighten the blustery gorilla opposite me so I said, "I am a conscientious objector." He laid off the insanity stuff but told me that this government upheld Christianity, that the U.S. was a Christian nation, and that therefore we C.O.'s should fight for it. I couldn't remember Middleton Murry's argument about this *not* being a Christian nation, so I let Fahey unleash his next bolt: "What if we were all pacifists?" I smiled that one by, too, handing him a spoon with which to eat his peaches. He said that this country was his heritage, etc., and that it was his duty to fight for it as the majority saw fit.

That is where we differed fundamentally. I am a citizen of the world and bound to every man in the world as a brother, even to Fahey. He told me of a magazine article that proposed to put the C.O.'s on the front lines as ammunition carriers without rifles to defend themselves. I said that the sincere C.O. would not carry ammunition. Fahey said he would then be shot, he would be a martyr which would be foolish. Fahey only grunted when I informed him that this country and the church were founded by martyrs. Fahey said the reason the Japs stabbed us in the back was that we (the U.S.) had fostered too many organizations like the C.O.'s. Fahey said that jealousy, hatred, etc., would never be wiped out in a million years. (Of course not, by the method he proposes) and that a strict police force was the only way to insure permanent peace. "Then there is no hope whatsoever for humanity," I said firmly. But he bellowed on, hearing nothing. In the corridor as he rushed up to the ward and I ambled back here I shouted after him, "Isolationism is not part of pacifism." And so the discussion ended for the evening. I wonder if it will continue tomorrow. The idea that C.O.'s are religious maniacs who pay some money to get out of the army was revelatory. . . .

July 28, 1942

The transition from day to night duty has been rather difficult to make because it is so hard to sleep through the noise and heat of the day. I wake up countless times at the shouts of the matrons giving orders to the patients who clean this attendants' home and at the rumble of trucks going to the housing project. But I haven't fallen asleep on the job yet, which is more than I can say for the other attendants. . . . Well, "midnight in a madhouse," contrary to all ideas of songwriters and the public, is nothing but snores and muffled coughs. So most of the night is free for reading and in my case writing. As I perhaps have written I am writing a book of poems called *The Asylum* in which I am characterizing the society of this war period in concrete images that have a deeper relationship to another asylum, the world, than to this Connecticut state hospital. When my seventeen days of night duty are over a good part of this work should be written. Of course all the poems won't be expressions of disillusionment. There are bright sides of this institutional life just as there are to this life of the forties.

I am writing much in the style of T. S. Eliot if that is at all possible. His compression is remarkable—the thing I admire most in his poetry. I have been reading in two volumes of the poems of D. H. Lawrence, most sensual love lyrics but superb for that type of writing. James Joyce has a volume of poems that were written, I think, to show the contrast between poor poetry and good prose. The poems are corny but his writing in *Dubliners*, *Portrait of the Artist As a Young Man*, and *Ulysses*, which I am just starting, is marvelous. I finished Joe Conrad's *Victory*, a book filled with exquisite description, my second night on duty. I am three-quarters of the way through the *Future of an Illusion* in which Freud is proving the absurdity of religion based on the presence of a divine being. He comes to the conclusions I wrote a few letters back. . . .

July 30, 1942

The enclosed tag was forgotten in the rush to cart John Smarzeniec's body to the morgue last night at 9:45. The following poem tells most of the rest of the story.

Epitaph

Laid out there upon the table
Like shrivelled orange peelings,
Thirty-five pieces of cranium
Impress my detached feelings
As being quite a few
For a man to bash a skull into
So they gave him the chair.

Laid out there upon the bed
His mouth a frothy, bloody crater,
In too great a hurry to die
To bother closing his eyes, he looks far greater
In death than he ever did in life. He died
Master of himself, a suicide.
He sleeps so peaceful there.

John Smarzeniec, from mumbled reports, killed his aunt and landlady and was sentenced to death. In prison he went on a hunger strike leading the authorities to question his sanity. The board of three psychiatrists, working under the new Connecticut law that permits a condemned man to go to an insane asylum if he has a psychosis, found something wrong with John and sent him to us. He arrived at 1 p.m. yesterday and was dead six hours later, very strange. His still warm corpse, waiting to be wrapped, greeted Jennings, Melien, and me at 9:30. We did our joyful job hastily since the body was wanted for an autopsy, the circumstances of the sudden death, the bloody frothing at the mouth indicating internal hemorrhages, and the fact that he had made several suicide attempts, being suspicious.

So I wrote my poem. Jennings suggested we pin it to the corpse. This afternoon at supper, however, Paul Bushman, who had done the autopsy, told me death was from natural causes. I was sorry to hear that because my poem was wrong in its best line. "He died master of himself, a suicide." Paul was the one who told me of the skull shattered into thirty-five pieces since he does the state police autopsy jobs also. Perhaps it is just as well the patient died so soon. We attendants would have been living in mortal terror of having our skulls bashed in at any minute.

Night work otherwise has been very pleasant. I try to write one poem a night but somehow slipped up the second and third nights on so that in six days I have written only four poems. The first cheerful little ditty follows:

The Living Dead

Whittled sideshow dummies
Drifting by on oiled gears
Waiting for someone to shatter
The teacups that dangle from their ears.
Fools! They're in for life,
The last twist of the knife.

Herein I use the same sort of symbolic device T. S. Eliot uses in *Rhapsody on a Windy Night* when he says:

And through the spaces of the dark
midnight shakes the memory
As a madman shakes a dead geranium.

Each of the concrete images symbolizes something important. If you wish you may analyze the poem, discover what "gears" and "teacups" symbolize, and write me what you think. My other poems concern women and would probably need lengthy analysis for your comprehension. Women mean a lot more to me than you would think seeing me "dateless" at home.

[Attendants] Jennings and Carr are proving very interesting from an objective point of view. They are direct opposites in their ways of thinking. Jennings is very free (or thinks he is) at 52. Carr is a puritan at 43. When Jennings informed Carr that he had been swimming nude with a woman, Carr was furious and threatened to break off relations with his senior. Carr absolutely refuses to go over to the women's ward and help with the wet packs since it involves seeing naked females. He is a confirmed bachelor. Jennings on the other hand talks as if he played around with women even in his old age. *However*, both couldn't recall ever having seen the very lovely attendants' dining room waitress . . . about whom I wrote a poem of six stanzas. They eat breakfast there every morning. Queer guys!

I was reading Jennings' *Negro Quarterly*, a review of negro culture and life, last night. The racial prejudice was apparent in every article and poem. Slavery still is an issue. I was amazed to see articles on *Anti-Negroism Among the Jews and Anti-Semitism Among the Negroes*, which is drawing it to a pretty fine point. The poetry was all modern and pretty good. But to see in every article bitterness over the racial prejudice becomes irritating. The argument on every page was that racial prejudice is destroying national unity to defeat fascism. This is a people's war and the negroes must be given an equal share of the fighting and fruits of victory. At any rate, a very informative magazine. . . .

August 10, 1942

... Three weeks ago [Dave Clark] appealed to his local Seymour, Connecticut, draft board to have his 1-A classification changed to 4-E on the grounds of conscientious objection. Dave came to the hearing all prepared with proofs of his sincerity, signed references, articles he had written, a newspaper clipping about a sermon on pacifism he had preached, and a composition written in the seventh grade on the foolishness of war. Well, you know the American way of conducting these hearings or interviews. The same police commissioner who was talking steadily when Dave came in, kept on his steady stream all during the hearing and as Dave was being ushered out. Dave was asked one question, the gist of which was, as Phil always put it, "What would you do if the Germans came in and began kicking your grandmother in the belly?" Dave, of course, gave the theoretically correct answer ["Step between them"] and left without showing all his proofs and the 4,000-word statement he had prepared. His 4-E appeal was granted. In a month he expects to go to a C.P.S. camp. . . .

During the summer an ocean storm struck the private estate of which Adrian's father was superintendent. The waves threw up a salt spray which inundated the green semi-circular terrace lawn on a cliff ninety feet above the sea. When the mistress of the estate looked out from her mansion she saw to her horror that the grass had turned yellow, and she fired Adrian's father on the spot. He went to Middletown in search of work in the nearby "defense" plants, and visited his son at the state hospital.

September 7, 1942

... I wonder what the mail brought to Prides—something favorable I hope. About taking a job at Colt's [Armory] or Pratt & Whitney I have some vague premonition, some subconscious hunch that such work is not for you, Dad. . . .

With the death of John J. Byrnes, 92, the first night you were here, I thought my troubles on that score were over. But when I came on the ward after leaving you at the bus, Hjalmer Salstrom was on his way to the great beyond. Ever since he arrived three days before on a stretcher he had looked more dead than most dead men do, with his pale eyes rolling up under his lids. And besides, he had one tremendous black eye that had bruised over most of his face. When I took his temperature for the last time at 8 p.m., it was 107. He was burning up. You could hear his hoarse breathing interspaced suddenly by dreadful lapses, at the other end of the corridor. It is comical the way we day people try to shove matters of this sort on the night men and vice versa. So we gave him an alcohol sponge bath in an effort to cool him off.

Afterward, Hubbs, the other attendant on with me, admitted every time he had gone into the room he had sprinkled a little water on the man's lips and forehead. At any rate we saved him through a nerve-wracking hour and a half until 9:30. In fact he didn't die until two hours later. . . .

John Fields, a colored gentleman of excellent breeding, was badly battered when I came back Friday. The X-ray showed his upper [and] lower jawbone broken in two places beside the ear. The report said he had become nasty in the dining room and in struggling with attendants Lee Smith and Ginty had fallen, hitting his head against the door and floor. But John tells quite a different story and John is an *honest* man. But what can you do when three sane attendants concur perfectly on the story? Why was the stronger and far more troublesome Carrignan never molested when he was here? I seem to recall a blow struck by Smith that put a hole through a patient's lower lip so that he could blow pieces of food through it. . . . And to them Fields is just "a damn nigger." . . .

September 12, 1942

Three and three-quarter hours before I go on duty for the last time. . . . Your letter with the clippings came Monday along with an Occupational Questionnaire from the Beverly Draft Board to which my case has apparently been transferred. . . . The fact that my case had been shifted to Beverly was puzzling after I had registered here with the idea of having my case taken up with Middletown in order to eliminate sudden trips to Beverly for advice and hearings when Middletown is my year-around home. I have asked for a re-transfer. How wise this move is I am hesitant to say after spending Thursday with Professor Reynolds. He told of the Ben Richards case. After being accepted by the Field Service to go abroad he needed the draft board's O.K. In a hearing a week before your visit his request for 4-E classification was denied. Ben was put in 1-A. Ben is at a dreadful fork in the road. When his induction order comes will he refuse to go, and take the road to jail, or will he join the army and try to use C.O. tactics in camp and on the battlefield? Furthermore his father, a shell-shocked world war veteran, and his mother, are very much against his stand. The way Reynolds talked it would break their hearts to see Ben in jail instead of the army. But if Ben is firm in his stand he will take the former road.

Now that the Middletown board is denying many of its requests for C.O. rating, even to fellows as sincere as Ben is, it might be better to vie with the probably untested Beverly board. The statement in the "Arcadian Bliss" article that C.O.'s get their rating by merely proving they have not had a fist fight for the past ten years is obviously untrue. . . .

*In early September Adrian left the state hospital and after a visit to his parents
he resumed his studies at Wesleyan University as a sophomore. He lived again
at the Congregational minister's home. One weekend he hitchhiked to Boston to
visit a schoolmate in a hospital there and first mentions his draft card in the
following letter.*

September 21, 1942

. . . Because someone had seen a parachute land in Rocky Hill on the road
from Hartford to Middletown, we were stopped three times by State Police
and made to show our draft registration cards. Though I was able to fill out
my [Wesleyan] registration blanks at school I couldn't hand them in because
the offices were closed. This means I have to register tomorrow and will be
assessed $5 (fine). In addition they tell me I have to pay my college bill of
$245 at the same time. I should have registered between 11 and 12 this morning.
Why don't people tell me these things, or better why didn't I read my catalogue? What a mess! I hope it is straightened out by tomorrow when I'll
write again. . . .

September 27, 1942

School has plodded on into another year continuing right where it left off
last spring. This is no flaming introduction to a new life as it was last fall—
this beginning of a second year. There is none of the hand-shaking and back-
slapping, none of the class dinners and speeches, none of the glowing letters
home filled with wide-eyed description of fabulous frat entertainments and
such "sincere" pleas for my pledging. The profs don't hold me spell-bound
with their first-day witticisms and scholarliness. I am a sophomore—a bit
aloof, unaffected, detached. . . .

When Eric proposed that we take Phylis and Marian to the Coast Guard
game in New London on Saturday I thought it an excellent idea. Rather than
give up Phil for lost after only two dates I decided to take another try. At
least we'd do something different from sitting in Eric's car listening to the
radio or going to the movies. . . .

The problem of kissing a girl Good Night is a very delicate one—far more
delicate than Dorothy Dix, etc., would imply. The day before, Eric and I had
talked this matter over. He says he kisses them Good-Night every time; he
thinks they expect it as much as he considers it a reward for time and money
spent. Yesterday cost me $7.00 and I didn't feel any more like kissing Phil
than if I had spent 70 cents. To me the Good Night kiss is the climax that all
the little trivialities and what-not of the evening lead to. It is like the sexual
intercourse that ends a courtship in true marriage. Eric advised me to go

ahead and kiss her; it would let her hair down; it was just what she needed. But for me nothing led up to it, just as in the other two dates nothing had led up to it. And how could anything have, when I had more fun with Eric's girl? These displays of affection should and for me *do* come naturally. So I didn't kiss her. . . .

From October 9, 1942, until his first letter from the Civilian Public Service induction camp at Big Flats, New York, there are no letters from Adrian to his parents because his father was put in charge of the war gardens in nearby Hartford and his mother had taken a position at a reform school for girls in Middletown, so they were often together.

While continuing his courses at Wesleyan, Adrian was also working as night cook at the Middlesex Hospital, a job which required no gourmet training but simply the heating up of dishes left by the day crew for the night nurses. Most of his stimulating Heretics Club members had graduated and others were eating in the college facilities instead of the Garden Restaurant. His schedule allowed time for only classes in music, English literature, German, physics, and the required one in physical education, where he felt he proved the strength of his pacifist convictions. The coach urged the boys to get in top shape because they would all be in the army soon. Adrian felt immediate rebellion to this assumption. He left the gymnasium without a word and went to the head of the department. The man was flabbergasted, became livid with anger, and directed the "conchie" to report to the Dean's office. Here Adrian and the Dean had a heart-to-heart talk. The Dean's attitude was that Adrian should learn, in Dante's words, to "bend like the reed." Adrian decided he was getting enough exercise in his daily rounds and didn't show up for the class again.

In January 1943, Adrian was called for induction, and for physical examination in Hartford. He found himself in a room filled with hundreds of men of all types who were told to strip, and were then herded naked into the examination room, where all day they took their turns with the examining physicians. They were allowed to dress before lining up to swear the Oath of Allegiance to the flag. All men who were willing to serve in the armed forces were told to step forward, place their right hands over their hearts, and repeat the Oath. Adrian had heard that this was the moment at which one declared one's refusal to join the fight. He was the only one who stood in place. He was immediately grabbed by a uniformed soldier who said, "What's the matter with you, Buster?" Adrian replied, "I'm a conscientious objector." The response was, "Oh, yeah? You're nuts. You're going to the psychiatrist." He was interviewed by a doctor who seemed to bear no malice, and his report on

Adrian's sanity was apparently positive. A few weeks later his 4-E classification came in the mail.

By April the Quaker administration notified Adrian that he was to report to the C.P.S. induction camp at Big Flats, New York, and sent him a train ticket to Elmira. On arrival he was met by the camp director and taken to the camp. The induction center was a dreary row of barracks on a dusty plain.

Big Flats

C.P.S. Camp No. 46, Big Flats, New York
April 14, 1943

Liefe Moesje,

What am I here for? That was the question that struck me last night when I snuggled into my bed in Dorm 2 here at Big Flats. The wind was roaring in the black tin chimney of the pot-bellied stove and all about me I could hear the heavy breathing of the C.O.'s. Why were all these fellows plucked out of their work and set down here in this level plain surrounded by these rolling mountains? Outwardly there seemed no reason whatsoever. But in my own mind I had the deep faith that I was here to grow and that these sleepers whose presence I so keenly felt were here to grow also. In the surety that I am here at Big Flats to become a better man I rest my hope for a profitable experience in C.P.S.

... The camp work project [is] breeding grasses and trees with an eye toward making them hold soil firm so that it cannot wash or blow away. But the work is of the farm variety—pure drudgery.

My whole trip to Elmira was marvelous. Of course I saw Dad in Hartford and we had a very wonderful visit. Only when I saw him standing on the platform searching for my face in the train windows (I was sitting on the other side of the car) did I feel in my heart that I was going and that my going must mean a lot to Dad and you. Phil [Watters] was at the train gate in Grand Central. After coffee and much conversation we found the Lackawanna ferry. Both of us took the marvelous five cent ride across to Hoboken. I thought then how I might very well be on the bow of a troop transport facing into the roaring wind, plunging toward some European battlefield. ...

This morning at 5:30 I saw Dave Clark, who had made all the arrangements that I bunk near him. I didn't realize he was only four beds away. After breakfasting and meeting hundreds of fellows (all surprisingly "sincere") we went to chapel, where James Stevens, a Colby grad, read about Brother

Lawrence, a man who was spiritually aware even while taking orders for
food in the monastery kitchen. (I don't believe it!)

These first three days at camp are for "conditioning." I don't have to do a
thing but take a physical exam in a very few minutes. I went out on the
project with Dave anyway, just to see what the fellows are doing. Somehow
all orders for grass seed and little trees had been filled so the project was
ditch digging. For the hour I watched seven fellows paddle with their shovels
in the ice and mud while twice as many just sat in a warm pile of hay out of
the wind that roars across these flatlands. As far as I know they are still sitting
there. This is work of "national importance"? . . .

April 16, 1943

Dear Dad,

Realizing that your trip to the West was the happiest of your life I wonder
how you will take the news that I am scheduled to transfer to Elkton, Oregon,
in about two weeks. This Big Flats camp has been asked to supply one carload
of thirty-eight fellows to the Oregon camp. I was one of nine volunteers.
The others will have to be selected in some manner. The reasons I volunteered
are three-fold. First, the train trip all the way across the country is paid for
by the government. Second, the scenery of Oregon is more beautiful on the
whole than that of California—and certainly New York—according to Dave.
Third, the work project seems more interesting than raising grass seed and
little trees, for it consists of surveying in "spike" camps of six to ten men,
that operate from the main camp with mobile kitchens, etc. Another angle to
the project is more dangerous, fighting forest fires. There are also opportunities for fellows with drafting experience to make maps, and perhaps I
might qualify for that.

There is one big disadvantage to this Oregon venture of course. It will be
so long, maybe seven or eight months, before I can see you again. My only
hope is that the advantages of the project will compensate for this loss. With
these things in mind I feel that I'll perhaps never have a similar opportunity
to see the West. By the time the war is over I'll want to have a quiet home life
or perhaps more college education. This seems to me a rare chance to see the
country free. I hope you do not object too strenuously.

Dave Clark, Mike Janier, a mystic, and I are sitting around a little stove in
the camp pumphouse, the only quiet place in the vicinity except when the
pump is going. Outside it is snowing—spring in Big Flats. No one could
think of any project for the fellows to do today, even before the snow started,
so they all have the day off. And even yesterday no one went to work until
9:30. I have been chopping more logs voluntarily, but tomorrow I am

officially required to work on the project—whatever it will be.

And so it is tomorrow and the project was mopping the dormitories and squeezing a few hundred Florida oranges for the punch we are going to drink at the party tonight. The boys have invited down twenty-five girls from Elmira College and a hospital, for whom we shall have square dancing and entertainment. . . .

Of all the things in this camp, the fellows are most interesting. Yet many impress me today as not being pacifist personalities at all. So many are here on purely political or intellectual grounds. They have not made pacifism a part of their lives nor have they tested for themselves the pacifist technique. Dave is still the finest fellow I have come across here at camp. He has been wonderful in getting me adjusted to this life. But now for baked beans and brown bread. . . .

April 21, 1943

To have seen the peace of this valley yesterday evening as I walked across the little foot bridge over the quiet brook to the pumphouse, you could have never understood why I wanted to go to Oregon. I could hardly understand it myself. I really did not want to go. So yesterday after supper when a telegram came saying that there was room for only nine of the eleven volunteers, I quickly crossed off my name. Dave felt as relieved as I did about my staying in Big Flats. "Lafayette, we stay here!" I said.

Already I am quite attached to this camp, especially its population. Dave has been a wonderful companion all along. . . .

So occupied have been my evenings that I haven't had a chance to finish this letter. Of course I don't need to tell you what my evenings have been occupied with when I tell you another of the interesting birds here is Jackson Wilcher, a negro from deep in Georgia, who plays a solid boogie piano.

If you thought that I would escape some of the horrors of war by going to C.P.S. camp you were very much mistaken. All this week I have been alternating between pulling stumps out of what was once a forest, and breaking up the concrete floor, 3,500 feet square, of a barn across the tracks. I am official chain-man of the stump pulling crew. I work in a frenzy wrapping the big link chain, links about four inches long, around the trunk stump or the roots if I can work the hook underneath them. Then fat MacGinnis lurches ahead on top of his tremendous bulldozer; the chain snaps tight, the tractor grunts and whines, roots snap; and with a sudden burst the stump flies free. Very often things don't go so easily; and MacGinnis has to roar backwards and forwards bumping and jerking at the stumps. We have broken three big chains so far on stumps that seem impossible to get out. By the end of the morning the field is a checkerboard of tank treads spotted with shell holes and rooted distortions of trees. A blue haze of wood smoke from the fire where the chief fire watcher and his twenty assistants are burning the stumps hovers over all. We trudge off through the mud and grass to lunch, the war over and armistice declared for an hour at least. . . .

April 25, 1943

. . . As for the rest of the horrors of war, the banging of the high-pressure air-drill on the concrete floor is like machine gun fire. The pigeonness who has a nest with two eggs on a beam in the barn always flaps away through a broken window pane when we begin blasting at the stone. John Yanger, a brewery worker, thirty-four years old, usually handles the ninety-pound air-hammer for he did that in the three other camps he's been in. The compressor motor roars and air hisses out of loose connections in the rubber hose to the drill. John pulls the black goggles over his eyes, raises the drill to a vertical position and blasts away. Stones and old cement spatter in all directions as if the drill point banging at the floor were a stream of machine gun bullets. Soon the concrete begins to crack into blocks and John pries them up with the drill point if they aren't so heavy that Bob Scion (Dutch name) has to loosen them with a pick. I pounce on them as if they were wounded soldiers, throw them into my steel wheelbarrow-ambulance and haul them off to the stone pile behind the lines.

The roar of the drill is like a gun being pointed at me. I work like fury all day, even when the others are taking it easy. In this work, monotonous as it is, I am consciously trying to throw everything into a task, to re-form the habit I somehow lost this last year in college. And secondly I am trying to *run*, not walk, the second mile for Selective Service and the A.F.S.C., trying to *turn* the other cheek, not to let them just hit it. Of course, the work we are doing is just pure wasted labor, as John so often explains. Even now the Agriculture Department men don't know just what they want. All the old concrete and stone which we have been hauling outside is sure to be needed inside the barn when they decide to lay the floor in another part, John says. I have hauled out at least two hundred loads this week. Just now we are leveling off the stone four inches below the level at which the new concrete is to be poured. When I look forward to smoothing off the new floor I feel sure that it *is constructive* work even if it has no pragmatic value, the old floor (five years) being perfectly good for many more years. At least we are creating, and I am sure no matter how insignificant the work may seem, it has much value. After all true "success is engaged to effort, not married to attainment.". . .

. . . For me there is music. Gene Schroeder, who played first clarinet in the

Massachusetts N.Y.A. Symphony under Arthur Fiedler, while teaching and going to the New England Conservatory, and who would have gone to the Indianapolis Symphony had not the draft come, is here and very willing to teach me. His own instruments are at home just now but he'll get them soon. Then there is Jackson Wilcher with whom I have been jamming nightly. He has a real feeling for swing music. I have never seen a fellow who knows fewer tunes yet with greater ability. He is catching on to my repertoire quickly and has already doubled his of about ten songs. . . .

I read the clipping about Lockman's sermon. Personally I think he is wrong when he says, "God is merely working out a problem" and "God is going someplace and we're going with him." I see no goal or great solution toward which God is carrying humanity. All I see is a great creative drive working through man that flows on into eternity, without heed of wars or good and evil. Good and evil are not absolute and objective but only subjective. God is not "good" in the sense we think of it, but only God. Christ's life was the best example of man reconciling God with man. But don't take this seriously, I'll change my theory tomorrow. . . .

May 5, 1943

The next time you hear from me I may be on my way to Williston, North Dakota. Big Flats has been asked to select thirty-three to thirty-nine men for shipment to this irrigation ditch-digging project. . . . Since I do not have any real reasons for staying east like others have, I am as eligible as any for transfer. But I am not eager to go. The location is near nothing. The project is ditch digging. The country is flat. The climate is hot in summer, freezing in winter (coldest in the U.S.). The camp is newly organized. The trip is nothing in comparison to Oregon or California. . . . If I am selected for North Dakota should I refuse to go as some here have stated they will do? No, I will go and have faith that the natural course of events will smooth the way. . . .

. . . Please send my watch. Dave and I have great need of it in the pump-house for we can only hear the dinner bell there when the wind is right. . . .

The school of non-violence began here Monday evening with John Nevin Sayre. He gave a general background to the course, using Gandhi and Christ as specific examples. Yesterday evening he lectured to the class of thirty on the various types of non-violent techniques and examples of their application. Sayre was just the kind of man I had expected. Small, bald, kindly yes, a David Robinson grown-up. He worked on project with us, hammering slats on the same frame I did. Howard Brinton from Pendle Hill [the Quaker Graduate Study Center in Pennsylvania] is here tonight and for the rest of

the week. Then come Jim Farmer, Bayard Rustin, and finally A. J. [Muste]
himself; also one M. K. Alexander. I think this school is the most marvelous
thing I could have found at Big Flats. I am so interested in the non-violent
technique that I well might make its study my life work.

In between working on the project making seed beds today and going to
non-violence sessions I have been jamming with Jackson. Jackson has a
greater love for jive than has any man I have ever seen, including Murray
Surrette. Right now he is hovering over my cot, his white teeth flashing and
his southern drawl imploring me to join him in another session. We had
reports that a very good tenor sax player was coming, just what we needed
since we now have a trumpet besides myself. Yesterday he arrived. Jackson
asked him to jam awhile. The fellow insisted upon going into the chapel to
play. He bid Jackson raise up a prayer, played a few nauseating hymns, and
prayed himself. Jackson, after all the anticipation, is so sad that he'll play the
blues until midnight. . . .

*The orders to transfer to North Dakota came through for thirty-three men,
among them Adrian and his friend Dave Clark. Adrian paid a visit to his
parents in Middletown before leaving for the Trenton camp. During the long
train ride across the country he mailed several postcards to his parents at
every one of the four stops.*

May 9, 1943
. . . It was wonderful being back in Middletown again. There is the same
wholesome spirit pervading Paul's [Prof. Reynolds'] home as there was in
ours, and being there gives me peace and confidence. Everything worked out
so nicely getting to Meriden [to the train station]. Paul's hospitality seems
without bounds. Don't take my being in North Dakota too hard. I really look
forward to it with great relish. Thank you for all the darning. Seeing you cry
at the station makes me feel I don't appreciate your concern for me half
enough. . . .

[postmarked May 10, 1943]
Six p.m. Sitting in the green plush seats of our private pullman car we are
being rocketed through the hazy countryside to Buffalo. Bob Meyer is sleeping
beside me. Dave is writing a letter across the aisle, down which Bonner is
lurching. When we get into Buffalo we will perhaps take an excursion to
Niagara Falls. We had a fine chop suey supper in the diner. . . . Walking up
the aisle was like being in a circus parade, everybody gawking at the "C.O.'s".
My only regret: The windows are so dirty.

[*postmarked May 10, 1943*]
The flat tree-studded landscape of western New York is wheeling by us
as we knife into the forty-five minutes that remain between us and Buffalo.
Our stomachs are well satisfied with a chop suey supper served by negroes in
the diner. Only one of the thirty-three refused to go. With glee he saw us off
at the station—Selective Service will deal with him later. Hoping that Niagara
is still illuminated and viewable, we plan an excursion this evening when we
pull in to Buffalo at 7:05. Looking around the pullman car at all the wonderful
fellows makes leaving Big Flats less painful.

May 11, 1943
We are lurching into South Bend, Indiana, after a night in the sleeper.
The boys are all writing cards in the modernistic smoking lounge which takes
up one half of the dining car in which we had a scrambled egg breakfast.
Niagara was on the rampage last night, very misty, deep-roaring. Then the
blackout sirens began screaming. Everything became dark and still, pre-
occupied with war. But the mighty falls plunged on into the depths, with the
indifference of the Gods in its throaty rumble.

May 13, 1943
All this sunny day it has been fields of yellow and dark brown stretching
clear to the horizon. In Minnesota there were farmhouses, spindly windmills
and domed silos protruding from clumps of trees. But now there are only
occasionally trees against the horizon and the farms are wider apart. These
are the great plains I had always imagined. Since childhood I have thought of
lying in their airy spaciousness surrounded by the ripe wheat. That would
seem supreme bliss. I will always love the plains for that alone.

C.P.S. Camp No. 94, Trenton, North Dakota
May 15, 1943

Liefe Moesje en Dad,

All the romance of this Lone Ranger Country, this Great Grain Belt, this Coldest Place in the United States, this Great West, this North Dakota has vanished. All is like Big Flats, the dormitories, the food, the water tower, the weather, even the mud are the same. The Chemung may have changed its name to Missouri, the Erie and Lackawanna may have consolidated into the Great Northern, and Big Flats may have been rechristened Trenton, North Dakota, but in this third day at C.P.S. Camp No. 94 I might as well be back at No. 46.

To convey an idea of the country hereabouts I can at the same time tell you of the project on which we are busy. For this summer, twenty farm units on tract No. 2 are planned, involving surveying, leveling, and prefabricating of houses, barns, granaries, pens, etc. The soil is very good, but in the droughts we had in the thirties did not produce. Hence most of the farmers moved away. But for the last two years tremendous crops of wheat have been raised. When another drought comes, good crops will be assured by the irrigation system. There is no fear of poor crops this year. John Mardis, project superintendent, predicted Thursday that if we had one more rainfall between now and harvest time, the farmers would get thirty-five to forty bushels an acre, the soil being wet clear to the bottom. It rained yesterday and today.

On the basis of my experience in the Middlesex Hospital I was made one of the eight cooks in the camp kitchen. I would much rather work outside on the project, however, for the shifts in the kitchen are split and the work builds only the stomach muscles. Today I am pot-washer, which makes me like the work even less, so I think I'll talk to Director Tom Potts about getting out in the field. . . .

It was interesting to note how we Big Flats men grouped when we were allowed to choose our own cots. The thirty-three of us split distinctly into two factions, one, the cultured, the other, the uncultured. Into dorm No. 2 the painters, musicians, poets, and literature men naturally came. Into dorm No. 4 the uneducated, unthinking, common men came. I am very nicely situated in dorm No. 2.

This change of atmosphere has made me a "fast worker." I already have a girlfriend in North Dakota, one Stella Aalgaard. Coming into Hannaford, North Dakota, on the train, Wednesday, a house close to the station drifted into view. Suddenly a very pretty, dark-haired girl emerged and stood on the porch looking at the train. I quickly raised Dave's candid camera, which I had hanging on its strap around my neck, for a shot. Before I could flick the shutter another equally pretty girl stepped out and took the arm of the other girl. Both caught sight of my up-raised camera and smiled. I snapped two pictures of them before the train chugged out again. One blew me a very delectable kiss as we rolled away—and that, in the wilds of North Dakota! So impressed was I that I hastily penned them a card offering prints of the pictures and a copy of a poem I thought of writing to them. How to address it took ingenuity, however. The following was the result of my cogitations:

Two very pretty auburn-haired girls
First house east of the station, north of the tracks,
Hannaford, North Dakota

Well, amazingly enough, yesterday came an answer. One of the girls was married; the writer was "the one with the apron on." The postmaster was puzzled, all right, but when the girl came in she claimed the mystery envelope. She gave no other pertinent information besides her name. Hannaford is only two hundred miles away (just below Minot) so I may wander down that way some evening. . . .

May 16, 1943

I took a fine walk with Dave into the wind and the hills that lie behind Trenton, this afternoon. They are weirdly shaped, some knobs, ridges, and steep cliffs, one flat-topped Aztec pyramid all colored in tan and yellow with here and there some green. From their long-rolling tops, real ranges, we could see all the immense curves of the Missouri in whose embrace stretches the land we are irrigating. The distance across the valley (ten to fifteen miles) made the hills far opposite blend flat into the landscape. Below us lay the rubble of Trenton with its two tall red grain elevators standing watch.

Telephone poles and wires thrown like a net over the town. Across the tracks, the gray sheds of C.P.S. No. 94.

It seems that I always take special note of these large sweeps of landscape dotted with the houses and farms and railroads and towns, these creations of God and of God working in man. Dave always is calling my attention to something small, the tiny flowers, certain colorful rocks, orange moss on boulders, and the sudden flights of birds. He pointed out all the different varieties of grasses and plants and I remarked how completely unlike the vegetation back east this plant-life was—sagebrush, tumbleweed, thistles, and large clumps of stubby many-needled cactus. When we were climbing the path up the steep meadow we both spied a horse on a ridge way off to our right. Suddenly the horse broke into a gallop along the hill's backbone, its mane and tail flying. It made a turn and plunged down across the stubbled wheat field on the large yellow slope to the farmyard down below us. Then with a mighty whinny it came to a stop and waited for its master to open the gate. Later when we had gained the range a white mare and a black horse and a black colt with a white star on its forehead were grazing on the wind-blown grass. I looked back at them after we had passed and slapped my hands against my trousers. Instantly they dashed away, wheeling off into the open prairie, then looking back simultaneously and finally stopping in a row over by the fence, white mother, black, white-starred son, and black father eyeing us very cautiously. This *is* the Great West, the Lone Ranger country, full of romance and exhilaration, after all.

May 20, 1943

"We are not interested in pick and shovel workers but only in men who can handle heavy machinery." That is how the bulletin describing this North Dakota project read, as posted on the Big Flats bulletin board two weeks ago. So today no one was interested in me, for we dug all day with pick and shovel, and for that matter all day yesterday, too. But I loved it. Of course the wind was blowing in just the direction that made half of every shovel-full you pitched out of the hole blow back at you in the form of grit and dust; and the sun was scorching; and "from the dry rock no sound of water"; our canteens were empty; and the other fellows were griping and disagreeable. But all the same I loved the feeling of sweat rolling off my forehead and its taste on my lips and the sight of the concrete become bare and clean and the smell of the insulating tar and the sound of the long-handled shovel stabbing straight into the soil. We were digging out the big half-culvert that tapers in to the tin aqueduct across a small valley in the prairie. The aqueduct or "flume" as the bosses call it, was demolished when the Missouri, flooding, threw cakes of ice against the wooden underpinnings this spring.

Tuesday we tore down the remains. Wednesday and today four of us dug all around the concrete culvert. . . . If the digging is tedious work, it is yet constructive and must be done for the irrigating to go on. Out of that fact I might get some satisfaction. But I get my real satisfaction out of the work itself. Very often I work very hard to impress the other fellows and the foreman—on this job a snappy red-headed man who says "Shit!" every time he misses the nail with his hammer. But when my efforts aren't recognized by the fellows I begin to have misgivings. Every time I come to a moment like that I realize that my endless pitching up of dirt is really not unrecognized. I feel that there is some divine presence watching and recording what I do. That divine presence is perhaps in me, as my conscience; by working hard my conscience is satisfied. And with a satisfied conscience comes the peace that for me follows each work day.

. . . The more I talk with Quakers and read their literature, the more I want to join a yearly meeting. My seeing eye to eye with Howard Brinton was a great encouragement to such a move. Don't worry about my "possessions," a word I am trying to eliminate from my vocabulary. You may keep the records and books and everything else. If I ever need anything I'll write for it. I am not practicing voluntary poverty as yet, though daily I feel how cluttered my life is by certain things I own—my watch, at which I look and am asked to look too often during work hours, my books, which have remained in the box in which they were sent, and my swing records, which bother my conscience more and more. I still treasure my clarinet, for with that I can create, my work shoes, the good ones I bought in Elmira just before leaving [Big Flats], and my work clothes, for with those I can work, and my glasses, for with those I can "look into the hills," my greatest joy at lunch time. When I look at my Sunday clothes I wish I could dispense with those. But without them I could not travel—to Yellowstone perhaps, or later, home. I have already asked to have my name removed from the Book of the Month Club and Book Coupon Exchange mailing lists and have decided to spend no more than the $2.50 wages a month—that for writing paper and stamped envelopes.

I am happy, Dad, that you are finding instructing the Victory Gardeners so enjoyable. With the right approach you can do much to breed not only good vegetables, but good community spirit. In fact you are building "Friendships, not Warships, for Defense" and in so doing you are building the only real defense—believe me. . . .

May 23, 1943

. . . The west wind is howling across the prairie and roaring in the chimneys today. All week it was very hot with only a soft breeze to cool us at our shoveling. But yesterday clouds began coming out of the west and before we left work it was sprinkling. Everything out west seems larger and longer. The clouds travel slower, the clear blue sky lasts longer, and the storms take forever to break. This past week has lasted an eastern month. The landscape is infinitely more vast and we travel more than ten miles every day to go to work. My days seem less full. Time and Space have far less significance than they did in Connecticut. As Dave described it, this country gives the observer the illusion that he is looking through the ends of a telescope. Coming from the East he looks through the eyepiece and finds everything is more spacious. But coming from the West back east he looks through the lens end and finds New England more cramped and stifling than he had ever expected. As evidence of my waning awareness of time, I have cast aside my watch in my first move toward voluntary poverty. I found on project that it is always earlier than one thinks and hopes. What is the use of disappointing yourself every fifteen minutes by finding that you still have longer to work than you thought? Friday and Saturday without my watch I found that my day went more quickly and with fewer interruptions by fellows wanting to know the time. . . .

I have been playing clarinet every now and then, this morning duets with trombonist Charley Lord. Monday evening Gene Schroeder, the symphony player, and I took cracks at Chopin's *Second Nocturne*. There are no devotees of le hot around here, for which I am thankful, so I hope to stick to classical music. I have been doing little in poetry except thinking about it while I work and coming to the realization that much modern poetry does not say a thing beautifully but only puts it in the form of a riddle that guys like Millett take pleasure in deciphering. Some of the stuff Dave and I have been reading seems now to be a perversion. But not T. S. Eliot.

May 27, 1943

. . . The question came up this week about our desires concerning C.P.S.— do we wish to remain with the Friends or do we wish to transfer to the government camp that is being opened July 2 at Mancos, Colorado? Sixteen fellows signified their intentions of going to government camp where the pay is fifty cents more a month—$3.00—and where we do not accept Quaker charity. I am so much in agreement with the Service Committee's original purposes for C.P.S. and feel so much loyalty to the Friends who have carried this program so far, that I plan to stay with them. Furthermore I like the freedom they advocate and allow and appreciate their shock-absorbing action to the orders of Selective Service. Now comes the question of whether we are willing to raise potatoes for the open market on project time. There are a hundred angles and considerations so I have not yet made up my mind whether I can or cannot plant spuds "conscientiously.". . .

I play my clarinet almost every day now. Often Gene Schroeder comes over and sits down beside me on the bed and points out my mistakes and indicates where I can make improvements. . . .

As of tonight I am secretary of the Worship Committee. I feel more religious every day, more aware of the "divine immediacy," a phrase that recurs often during my working hours. . . .

Adrian's mystical feelings about voluntary poverty led him to post a declaration on the camp bulletin board announcing that all his possessions were to be community property. It was entitled "Denial of Ownership." He placed his books and bookends in the camp library, his phonograph records, scores, and clarinet in the music room, his clothes in the dormitory common closet, and his wristwatch in the supply room, "in hope that they will be used freely and without hesitation by all campers and staff members who so desire." He stated that he also hoped that his faith that he was "acting on the will of God" would induce other campers "who have the maturity" to do likewise. The general reaction of his fellow campers was amusement.

June 2, 1943

Since the night before I had to make a speech to the sophomore class ('43) of Beverly High on the *Aegis*, I have not had such a restless sleep as I did after posting my "Denial of Ownership" notice Monday at 9:50 p.m. For all my faith that I was doing as God had willed I feared the dawn when I would have to face the fellows. Instead of feeling suddenly free when I felt that green thumb tack . . . sink into the bulletin board, my soul seemed rent apart. All the instinct that had been built up through the years for possession and material gain was in that action being ripped out of me. It left me torn and bruised. The night was feverish, full of doubts and misgivings. Yet that conscience had me stuck through with a pin, like a beetle, and I could only obey.

When I think back on that moment Monday morning, working out in the field with Roy Thurman, a colored man whom I like so much, and looking into the hills to have those two words "community ownership" smack into my consciousness, I feel that the moment had the quality of a mystical experience. Never have I felt my conscience moving me more strongly than it did for the rest of that day. "This I *must* do," it said. "I can do nothing else."

Whether the solution is right or wrong, whether or not it will work matters little to me. An experience as powerful as the one I had is out of the plane of pragmatic, authoritarian and rational right and wrong. The only right is that I act upon it with all my strength. With the confidence that I was right with God, if with no one else, I entered voluntary poverty. . . .

Here are three of the comments that have been written on the notice by unsigned campers:

"After nineteen months in C.P.S. . . . I have nothing to give away."

"Don't think it will work, pal."

"You're the one that's not mature."

And yesterday while cutting up seed potatoes for planting on 200 acres, we talked about some of the queers we had met in C.P.S., grass-eaters, etc. The fellow cutting next to me (he didn't know my name) asked the group, "Who's this U. Adrian Wilson?" I quickly said, "That's me." We didn't talk about queers anymore. The question left me with a good idea how my plan was being taken—as the brainchild of some unstable radical, not as the dictate of direct revelation in a very serious minded thinker. And, as I had expected, the plan itself was misunderstood by even my closest friends. . . .

Perhaps I have made mistakes in my presentation of my plan. Perhaps I should have disposed of each of my possessions slowly. Perhaps I should have refrained from putting up a notice, especially since it was generally misunderstood anyhow. Going about this business of getting poor quietly would have been more effective and less straining. But that conscience and a boundless enthusiasm for the new undertaking barred all hesitation. Kermit has the watch, I notice. He drives the lunches out to the crews and so supposedly needs it. I hope it will make his life happier as I thought it would mine. I don't think it will. My clarinet was taken out of the music room because a case of trench mouth has popped up in camp, making its use by a number of fellows inadvisable. No one has needed my clothes more than I have, so I have been wearing them as I always did. Here in the library I sit facing my books, twelve of them, and above them, the bookends. It is hard to believe that they are not mine. . . .

Adrian recounted later some of the reactions of the men that he did not include in letters to his parents.

Gene Schroeder came to his bunk when he was putting on his bluejeans and said, "Do you realize that you are an insult to your Creator? Look how you dress and what a mess your hair is. Now you have given your clarinet away. I have no more respect for you."

Adrian decided to take a shower and wash his hair. Another naked C.O. came into the bath-house and turned on the next shower. "Aren't you the guy who posted that notice about giving everything away? What if everybody did

*that? No one would take care of anything! Man, you don't even know how to
dress right."*

"How do you mean?"

*"Look at your pecker. It hangs to the right. If you knew how to dress it
would hang left," and he slapped Adrian's penis across his crotch. But it flopped
right back. It wouldn't stay.*

"See what I mean," he said, "you're a screwball."

*Naturally, Adrian's parents and brother were distressed by his increasing
piety and the voluntary poverty program, but at the outset they assumed he was
having "growing pains" and would soon recover.*

June 8, 1943

... This Quaker idealism is hard to take—and do I know it. For the
Catholic boys ... it is the most insufferable piece of tommy-rot ever contrived.
Work for no pay, huh, and become a slave! Be shipped off to a god-forsaken
place like this and become a slave! They fought the Civil War and look what
it got them, slavery, white slavery! The indignation at the inhumanity of the
Quakers has resulted in tremendous bitterness, frightful cursing and damning
of the A.F.S.C. and the S.S., and drunken orgies in the dorms. . . . Charley
Lord and I went into Dorm 1 the other night to carry out a cabinet that had
been designated for our Dorm 2. We were met with a barrage of boos, hisses,
shoes, rubbers, and galoshes. It was consistent with the sign the Catholic
boys put up on their door:

CASBAH

Abandon all hope, ye who enter here

4th milers,

200%ers,

and

conscientious

objectors

Keep Out

per order Pépé Fitzsimmons.

Such disunity and actual hatred for those who work hard I never expected
to find in C.P.S. My conception of a Catholic C.O. was a fellow who lived the
life of Saint Francis, their favorite saint, meaning complete pacifism,
humility, and voluntary poverty. I find not one who even professes the
slightest doctrine of pacifism. They are as rowdy a bunch as you would find
in any army. To us who believe in making C.P.S. No. 94 a true pacifist com-

munity, they cause much concern. Some of us like to think that when they go to the new government camp the problem will be straightened out. But the men themselves are the problem and it is up to us to change them if we can. How? I talked with Fitzsimmons for a long time last night, swing music being our springboard as usual. He is used to the New York life in which he went to a jam session or night club at least two nights a week. In this wilderness he finds nothing to do after work hours except griping. There is no phonograph on which he can play his and the camp's (my old ones) records. There is no ice cream parlor where he can guzzle sodas. He doesn't like to read, write, or meditate. And so it is with the others of his Casbah clan. What we must do is supply some evening recreation. . . .

June 11, 1943

. . . Potato cutting was delightful today. I was supplier, meaning that I kept the cutting table at which ten men work, filled with spuds. I brought them over in bunches of five bags (100 pounds each) one by one and in between times read aloud *My Name Is Aram* by William Saroyan. The book held the attention of the fellows through the last 215th page. And afterwards I conducted a good literary discussion on its merits. The reason we read this book was that it was recommended by the *Pissoir Book Reviews*, a series inaugurated by Bob Rathburn, hung over the urinal for reading by the piddling public.

For many weeks ten or more campers devoted all their project time to cutting up seed potatoes for planting. Evidently the scruples about supporting the war were overcome. Adrian initiated readings aloud of contemporary literature to fight the boredom of potato cutting.

At the other end of the entertainment spectrum, all the camp men were invited to a dance in the town of Trenton, which was primarily Indian. Adrian was asked to play some jazz clarinet. Despite the trench-mouth ruling he retrieved his clarinet, cleaned it carefully, and went with some of the men to the dance. Naturally they were all eager to meet girls.

June 14, so they tell me

There was to be a dance in Trenton Saturday night, all C.O.'s invited. . . . We went up to the dance hall Saturday evening about 7:30. You couldn't see the place until you came right up to it for it is the roofed-over basement of a church that was never built. We heard a fiddle scratching out "Home Sweet Home" above the singing of men's voices down in the cellar. Most of the fellows were still outside, dressed in their Sunday suits, lolling on the corrugated tin roof. By eight not one girl had shown up except for Florrie Potts [the camp director's wife], who was singing inside. And by nine no fem had yet arrived. A few of the fellows were standing on the dirt road thumbing the one-car-every-half-hour to Williston. But by ten a few girls trickled in. They were snatched up quickly by some of the bolder (and more frustrated) C.O.'s who sat, fifty of them, in a row along the wall opposite the bandstand, waiting to pounce. No local fiddlers had arrived, so Plettau, or "Pluto," and I were bid to knock out a few numbers. . . . By the time we had played ten numbers the place was packed. Women had been bringing in cakes, pies, and other delicacies, obviously for refreshment. Mothers had been bringing in babies bundled in pink and pastel blue blankets. Five of them lay in a row on a table in the side kitchen. A few toddlers scampered around below the bandstand until they were squelched by their mothers or big sisters.

Later on their fathers tottered in, big cowboy hats cocked on their heads, red and blue silk shirts, and big brown bottles of liquor jammed into their back pockets. Every last one of them was an Indian, modern style. There wasn't a white man or woman in the place besides the C.O.'s. . . . There was the drunken "cat" driver. When the spirit seized him he would yell out something incomprehensible. His wife in her white silk shirt, red necktie, and black skirt, would break off dancing, pounce upon the man, slap her hand across his mouth and kick him in the shins with her black cowboy boots. "Shut up, you damn fool." The Indian only grinned and smacked his lips. When the "old lady" had gone to dance some more, another tipsy Injun came over and proffered his gin. The cat-driver couldn't resist. Two little Indian girls, twins dressed in red gingham, dangled their feet over the edge of a bench. They were half asleep. The dancers whirled madly below me, a seething sea of color, dreamy eyes, and arms entwined. . . . Indians and white men, farmers, drunks, and Ph.D.'s, the rhythms of Chicago, Kansas City, St. Louis, New Orleans, New York pouring out of my instrument, melting, fusing, boiling, all in the cauldron of that basement. What a melting pot this nation is!

After a while the local talent thought we needed a rest so they took over for several Norwegian waltzes and a whole string of square dance tunes that lasted past midnight. The band consisted of guitar, fiddle, and piano, all in ten-gallon hats. The pianist knew two chords, C and G7th, that he played boom, boom, boom, through every piece no matter what the melody was. It didn't matter much because you could not hear the tunes anyhow. The violinist concentrated more on stamping his feet than playing notes. He had the most amazing gallop, with which he set the pace for each number. I have never heard anything quite like it except in a horse, notably the Lone Ranger's. When they were finished it was time—no, not to go home—but for an auction: An Indian cowboy in a white-braided, black silk shirt, sweat rolling off his head, was auctioneer for several boxes of cakes, cigars, cookies, and bottles of whiskey. The bids went up to $5 on some items. The Catholic church collected $19.75 in all. Then everyone lined up for lunch at fifteen cents a plate. From a distance it looked like sandwiches and buns. I didn't buy any, so poor, you know. "Pluto" had mysteriously disappeared from the premises when it was time for us to take the stand again—and so had Frank, Louis, and Charley. So I recruited the local guitarist and Canby Jones, son of the president of Fisk University in Nashville, Tennessee, to beat a wooden chair, and jumped into an hour of Benny Goodman rides uninterrupted. I kept thirty couples stomping almost to exhaustion with my hot licks. Never have I felt such control over a crowd. No matter how poorly I played (and how wrong the guitarist's chords were) they loved it for its fire and spontaneity. The C.O.'s who were standing in the stag line slapped their hands in rhythm. Canby, beating the chair for all he was worth behind me, yelled out all the jitterbug howls he had learned from the negroes at his father's university. "Now you're talkin', Brother," "Never dun heard such talkin', Yeah!" "You sure do send me, man. Sho' nuf." About a quarter of two when the guitarist's father began beckoning for him to come home, I figured it was about time to quit too. The piano player wanted me to stay, but I knew I wouldn't be able to play anything with his two-chord background. So I quietly left despite his entreaties. . . .

June 23, 1943

. . .You ask about the Catholic boys and how they ever got 4-E. Their position is simply this: the Pope has never proclaimed this a *just* war. Therefore, it must be bad. Catholics will not participate in an unjust war. They believe in self-defense and righteous indignation, evidenced by the shoe and swear barrage that greets every man who enters the Casbah. . . .

July 4, 1943

The night watchman had the clever idea of awakening us by blowing off a firecracker in each dorm. His revolutionized reveille had the desired effect and it made me aware, too, that this was the glorious Fourth. I looked at the last issue of *Life*, the one that listed the war dead. If that list was intended to stir us to "avenge (O Lord) thy slaughtered saints," it had a far different effect on me. It filled me with an overwhelming grief. Some say that the sense of futility you get in C.P.S. is unbearable—but, God, when you contrast it to the futility of this war. . . . As I so strongly felt seeing the naval pre-flight cadets marching around the Wesleyan campus, those boys are no more my brothers than the boys in the German army, for they are all my brothers. When they say they are fighting to preserve the things I love, they lie. In their very fighting they preserve the thing I hate, the real enemy, war. I cannot hate any man. I can only hate the things men do. The only way to destroy those things is through infinite and constant love of that which is of God in the men themselves. . . .

July 18, 1943

. . . You relayed an interesting question from Mrs. Tootsie-twinkle [Mrs. Te Winkle, a Dutch friend], Moes. Has my voluntary poverty affected anyone in camp. Until last night I wouldn't have been able to give you a concrete answer. But now I can give you a definite "yes." After meditation (vespers) Monday evening, Canby told me he was in the "doghouse," his temper short, his initiative lacking. Later that evening when the band was blasting out "Softly as in a Morning Sunrise" . . . and "Indian Love Call," with me as Artie Shaw, Canby whispered that he was out of the Doghouse. I didn't know what he meant. I said, "Good," and swung into another solo. Yesterday, Tuesday, after meditation I sat down [with him]. "Well, I've given my stuff away," he said. It was as if a ray of sunshine had entered into the room and fallen full upon me. For a moment as I grasped his knee and looked into his eyes we were one. Then Canby went on to tell me what he had done. He had given his clothes and $75 to the Camp General Service Fund. He had done it out of a feeling that he didn't need most of the things he owned. . . .

July 25, 1943

. . . The mosquitoes around here are thriving on this camp. I had considered them annoying, to say the least, but I never thought they would become actually destructive. The mosquitoes were whining around the laundry Friday. One came close to my ear. I swung wildly at him. My hand hit my glasses, knocking them to the cement floor. When I had chased the mosquito until he was flattened against my palm I came back to look for my glasses. The left lens was shattered. So Saturday morning I went into Williston with the station wagon to get a new lens fitted. It took the doctor so long before he could take me, that the station wagon had gone when I left the office. . . . Instead of waiting for the station wagon to come in again in the afternoon I thumbed home. It was a bright warm afternoon with a brisk west wind blowing across the rolling yellow grain fields. The road to Williston takes you out of the valley onto the plateau. From almost any point you can turn to see an unbroken circle of horizon. . . . I could watch the moving of the wind in the fields as I used to watch the myriads of waves drifting shoreward at

Prides Crossing. . . . Every few moments I would realize that this was how I always had thought the West would be. There was the fusion of the preconception and the perception making moments of joy and satisfaction. I suppose my preconception of the West has been molded more than anything by those marvelous Billy Whiskers stories. Let me remember—crossing the Sierra Nevada in a boxcar—walking the trestle across the Great Salt Lake— San Francisco and the earthquake—Billy butting the bad characters—the happy reunions of Billy and Nanie on the farm—sleeping in haystacks— Chinamen with queues—and the sun setting over the great plains. . . .

Tuesday evening after Canby had told me of his giving his things away, we went on a mission of social service. . . . There is an Indian in West Bottom who has his house on one side of the irrigation ditch and his barn and land on the other, with the nearest bridge half a mile west. As one of the projects for the camp F.O.R., building a bridge for this man was suggested. Canby and I went to ask the fellow what he wanted as to size. I caught sight of the barn before we jumped over the mud in the ditch bottom. . . . The green fields of flax stretched south to the river. As we scrambled over the other side of the ditch we could see the house, long, low, logs chinked with mud, one window, grass growing on the roof, the old man and his woman sitting on a bench in the front yard watching the shadows creep across the valley floor to the red palisades just across the river. He had a big knob on his forehead, I observed as we crawled under the barbed wire fence into the yard. The woman yelled at Towser, the tan mongrel dog, to shut up when he started growling and slinking in an arc around us. Her voice deep, and gruff, far gruffer than the man's, more like the dog's.

Canby sat down on the ground and I leaned against a fencepost. We learned that the Indian really wanted a bridge big enough to run a team on—but anything would be better than what he had now. The sides of the ditch got icy in winter and you had to slide down and try to work your way up the other side. There were minutes of silence, not long and full of tension as in city life, but full of meaning and understanding, more refreshing than words could ever be.

A moron son came out of the door—and stood silent. He smiled when we smiled, he laughed when we laughed, yet he never said a word. The old man said he had been out here forty-four years and this was the best crop he could remember. He didn't own the land though. The owner wasn't interested in putting a bridge across so that was why. . . . Canby wanted to know the time since we wanted to catch the "cat" crew transport back at 9:30. The son went in and came out with the alarm clock. Ten minutes of ten. We knew it wasn't really more than quarter past nine. We didn't say anything. What

difference did it make? So we said, "So long"—nothing ceremonious, just
like leaving the room for a moment—crawled through the fence, plunged
down into the ditch, hurdled the mud, and, having scaled the dike on the
other side, trudged on toward the road. . . .

The dance last night was a pretty dead affair, until around midnight. By
that time the Indians who had been bounced out of Williston night clubs
arrived. Within half an hour the number of couples on the floor doubled, the
dancing grew wilder, my licorice stick grew hotter, the old dining hall really
steamed. I saw a white cap in the sea of heads rolling below the bell of the
clarinet. It was a sailor. When he and his clumsy partner wheeled in front of
[us] he shouted something at me, unintelligible, but plenty vicious. I wondered
if I wasn't playing hot enough. . . . Orm Greene, who was M.C., thought we
ought to quit at 1:30 as scheduled. But seeing that so many had just come I
put the deadline at 2:00. Of course, we went over that. But finally I announced
our last number, our theme "Toselli's Serenade." Everyone left very quickly
and peacefully. It was only after I had come back from the latrine that I
caught garbled accounts of a brawl that had just occurred. The sailor had
lashed out at Ogden Hannaford and knocked him flat. Ogden being a good
pacifist merely got up and walked away. Outside the sailor laid into Canby,
hurling epithets about C.O.'s having a good time when a war was going on.
Canby put his hands over his face and backed away from the flying fists. But
before the sailor could do much damage Johnny Mack, one of the Casbah
men, lifted the sailor off his feet with a haymaker and ran away. A battle
started between the Casbah and some of the big drunken Indians from
Trenton. A fat Indian was sitting on Duane Whelan, batting him on the head
and trying to gouge his eyes out. Somehow the brawl petered out, but the
camp has talked of nothing else all day. And it was all my fault for keeping
the dance going. . . .

July 30, 1943

Your vivid account of Norm Gessner's trial and conviction came today. . . .
If I went to jail so that I might spare my will from enslavement in conscription,
I would have to carry out that demand for complete freedom of conscience
and will to its logical conclusion, fasting until death or exemption. It seemed
to me that I could make a more effective testimony by working toward the
good life in the compromise of a C.P.S. camp, than by dying on a fast in
Danbury jail. I suppose Norm considered all this and came to the conclusion
that jail was the only honest testimony. Perhaps I will come to that conclusion, too.

Bayard Rustin's interest in the trial surprised me. That fellow really gets around between situations requiring use of the non-violent technique, trials, and talks to C.P.S. camps and F.O.R. groups. I think he too refused induction into C.P.S. camp, but the courts have so far taken no action. . . .

I was looking at some literature Frank Donovan had on Glacier National Park and its Canadian extension, Waterton Lakes Park. For their glaciated peaks, ice fields, meadows of flowers, chalets, and deep blue lakes, these parks seem all that Switzerland could ever be. How I long to go to them! Remember Mr. Chips' experience in the mountains? *There* is *one* motive! I am hesitant about going into Canada for presidential decree has it that no man classified 4-E may leave the country. . . . Charley Lord, Bob Meyers, and three others have been approved to catch jaundice at the Philly Mental Hospital as part of an experiment. They would be leaving immediately were it not for the smallness of our population. Unfortunately (for the band and myself as well as Dorm 2) that fly in the ointment will soon be removed and the boys will leave to get the color associated with C.O.'s—yellow! . . .

August 5, 1943

. . . George [Barbarow] and I thumbed into Williston Saturday afternoon, bought some phonograph needles, four bottles of beer, a Silex coffee maker, and four cakes of soap and walked toward Eighth Street, east. A vivacious babe came running after us. It was George's wife, Toni, coming home from work at the U.S. Department of Agriculture office. We presently skipped into their one-room basement apartment through the garage and George started playing records. He indicated to Toni that she was supposed to feed me. . . . George and Toni seem always at odds with one another, as if each was the last thing in the world the other needed. They argued over the way to use the coffee maker with the new filter rod, when neither had read the directions. They decided to go to different places when George had furlough, he to the Black Hills, she to the Badlands. They are the two most independent people I have ever met. Her whole appearance speaks defiance. . . . We took time out for spaghetti and meat balls, milk, coffee, brownies, grapes, and dusting the furniture, undone since last weekend. . . . Harless Kinzer, an unhappy intellectual from Duke who knows more about T. S. Eliot than I do, dropped in, making it time for beer. A big bowl of stale pretzels appeared from underneath the studio couch. Harless and I followed along the words of the blues songs George had typed out while Bessie Smith shouted them. It was stupendous! Harless informed me that our band was supposed to play at one of the Indian dances in Trenton that night. I figured I had better go since the band couldn't possibly get along without me. . . .

By twelve I was stamping the dais in the gas-lamp lighted church basement

buried in the hills behind Trenton. The dance had just started. They
auctioned off several beautifully decorated baskets and sold plate lunches. . . .
There weren't any brawls, except a short scrap between two girls who suddenly flew at each other like two jealous hens, scratching and slapping, until
their escorts separated them. Yes, Moes, playing at these dances is hardly
consistent with my theories but then, inconsistency is the spice of life. . . .

August 14, 1943

. . . Yesterday with a crew of twelve we poured the basement for a farmhouse
in three hours, when the previous record had been four and a quarter and
the ordinary time, six or seven hours. . . . For us, heaving gravel and breaking
bags of cement into the outstretched paw of the mixer, it was a steady grind
without one moment's rest. But through the clang of our shovels and the roar
of the mixer and the hiss of the cement pouring from the wheelbarrow into
the wooden forms, and the chop chop chop of the tamping rods, a note of
mysterious fellowship grew from piano to double forte. We all felt it and
reveled in it. Even those who criticize the Quakers for their emphasis on work
felt in those hours of hard constructive labor the binding fellowship. . . .

August 18, 1943

Here is a handful of wheat kernels grown by Pete Honeb of Williston. A
bushel of these kernels weighs sixty-four pounds, the heaviest grain brought
into the Farmers Union Grand Terminal Elevator yesterday. The handful was
given to me as payment for some work I did there last night. The station
wagon was going into Williston. . . . Purely out of "whim" I signed up to
go. . . . I couldn't think of anything to do, no money, no friends. . . . I had
seen the trucks lined up, piled high with yellow grain, waiting to be unloaded
in the enormous four-stack elevator. Perhaps they could use a little help for
a few hours. I stood outside of the elevator for a long time wondering if I
should ask the farmers, talking outside of their trucks, or the blackhaired
man sitting in the office where I could see him through the window. "Could
anyone use some help—free?" or "May I do some work around here?
Pay? Nothing." No, too ridiculous, and besides I might be destroying the
economic order, too revolutionary. . . . There was a line of trucks all the way
out to the street, waiting for the signal to plunge into the bright, yawning
door of the great stacks. After standing around for awhile, that door, into
which a truck would disappear every few moments, began to attract me. I
stuck my head in, watched them empty two trucks, and then asked a fellow
they called Harless, flour-faced in striped overalls and a snappy straw hat if
I might help. "You lookin' for work?" "No, just want to help for a couple of

hours." "O.K. Sure." So each time a truck would roll in I would help him take off the back and watch the wheat kernels stream golden yellow like a heavenly waterfall through the floorgrate. The whole truck stood on a big scale. Besides weighing the truck full then empty, the scale tipped up the front end of the truck to about thirty degrees so that all the grain slid out. My job was to help the avalanche along with a big shovel, a broom, and an enlargement of the little silver food pusher I always used to use. All the farmers had conversation with Harless as they drove in. Harless would reach into the truck, grab a handful of the stuff, feel of it, lick it with his tongue, put a few kernels in his mouth as if they were chewing tobacco, and chew, looking very appraising. "Who the hell grew this stuff?" "Olie." "How much he gettin'?" "Forty-five" (bushels an acre). "Christ, these farmers are gonna have too damn much money this year." And so they went, truck after truck, each with a new character for a driver. All the while there was the roar of the four lickety-split conveyor belts zipping the wheat and barley from the cellar to the top of the bins. . . . By 10:30 the last truck had gone through. Harless said there wasn't anything more to do; they cleaned up the place in the morning. So I asked if I might have a sample of the sixty-four wheat to send home to you. He gave me a handful and showed the scales by which they tell how much the wheat weighs per bushel, though they measure out only a cupful. Happy with my pay, I left the place, but not before Harless was upon me, waving two quarters which he wanted me to take. I absolutely refused, but when he chased me halfway out of the driveway and I saw that the money was offered more in love than as a payment, I couldn't refuse any longer. I walked toward Main Street almost crying with joy, singing "Eternal Are Thy Mercies Lord."

The station wagon was scheduled to leave at midnight so I headed for the railroad station hoping to find some way to help out there. A man was loading milk cans into a white and blue Land O' Lakes Butter truck. I explained that I had an hour or so to spend, so couldn't I help him. . . . It took us an hour to carry six Railway Express truckloads of full five-, eight-, and ten-gallon milk cans into the truck. . . . When we were done he said, "Yumpin' Yimminy, this is the first time anyone ever helped me out." He sounded as if he had a new faith in humanity. He said he would treat me, except that he never carried any money to work with him. And so my evening of playing St. Francis came to a close. If he gained a new faith in humanity, I gained a new faith in God.

The fifty cents from the elevator came just at a time when I was beginning to worry about stamps, envelopes, and paper. But now I have been able to buy a hundred sheets of this snappy stationery for a dime and have purchased more envelopes without any qualms of conscience. You see, the situation was ideal almost. The money was given in love and what I buy with it I share and give away in love. . . .

Guess what, I have ten days of furlough saved up already and by Sept. 13 I will have twelve and a half. If your trip runs through October 13, I will have earned another two and a half days which I am allowed to take. But you undoubtedly won't wait that long. . . .

[*c. October 29, 1943*]

. . . When I rode Walt's horse the other day after writing to you I met up with the best display of non-violent direct action, or civil disobedience. At the first crossing of the irrigation ditch, I wasn't insistent or firm enough in my reining and from then on "Silver" knew he could have his way with me. Before we had gotten a quarter of a mile from camp he started balking and pretty soon refused to go at all. Being a very non-violent sort of fellow myself I decided to see if I could out-balk him. But I lost patience long before Silver did and got off the horse to lead him. He agreed to that, however sulkily he followed. For a time I thought maybe *he* had better ride *me*. So Silver won over me simply by his humility and his non-violent resistance. Now I ask you, to be a good pacifist does one have to be part horse? I also discovered on that trip that I still have pride, that I am not completely unselfish, humble, that I don't want to subordinate myself to a horse. When a car full of Indians (all expert horsemen I suppose) came along the road, I had to scramble back on the horse to give a little hint that the horse was not completely master. But Silver stood solid in the middle of the road even when the car approached within twenty feet. I couldn't make him budge. Did my face burn! . . .

Adrian's parents traveled across the country to visit the camp and to take a trip to the Canadian Rockies with him during his furlough. In fact the vacation was spent in Glacier National Park rather than in Canada, for there was some question about the legality of a C.O. leaving the country. They had an extremely happy time in Glacier, fishing in the mountain torrents with rods lent them by the kindly proprietor of the tourist cabin where they stayed. They cooked their trout in the cabin kitchenette.

Discussions of Adrian's attitudes and actions seemed to have reassured his father and mother that he was still normal. They probably led to his application, after his return to camp, for reclassification as a divinity student, which would exempt him from military service or C.P.S. He actually applied to The Hartford Seminary Foundation, and was promised acceptance if Selective Service would reclassify him as a 4-D. That was refused, and Adrian settled down to making the most of his life in the Trenton camp.

The senior Wilsons returned to Connecticut, and soon afterward Adrian's father was hired by Wesleyan University to work in the greenhouse of the laboratory. Adrian's mother took a position in the school's library. Adrian's first letter after this development expresses dismay; he assumed that he would return to Wesleyan as a student after the war.

December 2, 1943

The news of your employment at Wesleyan gave me the strangest sensation I have had since you taught us how to plant bulbs at the [Smith College] Day School. In our society, school and home are so separated that to have one's parents in his school seems an intrusion and an encroachment on his freedom. I remember how queer it seemed to me that Earl Shaw's mother should be one of the janitoresses at Beverly High as if she couldn't let her son live a life without her presence being felt. Now, if you were professors I might feel quite different. This lurking in the background with well-swept floors in Shanklin [Laboratory] and dusted and neatly catalogued books in Olin [Library], this giving your time and your energies but never yourselves disturbs me. . . .

January 2, 1944

. . . What Brother French has to say about more detached service is quite true: a tuberculosis hospital at Wallum, R.I., a thirteen-man "guinea pig" project at the Mass General Hosp, and a C.P.S. project on the effect on healthy men of malaria vaccines at the U of Minnesota for which three to six men from this camp will be recruited when one Dr. Keys comes next week. They all appeal to me especially the latter, for the possibility of study at the University. Of course, the first two are out on the score of [the ruling that the project must be at least] a hundred miles from [the C.O.'s] draft board and home. . . .

. . . So here comes the story of Wednesday night's session of L'Académie de Café et Culture of Trenton, North Dakota. The art studio of Thomas Steger, with its general confusion of tubes of paint, twisted and dried, its messy palettes and unwashed brushes, its unfinished paintings, and its one soft modernistic light, was an ideal setting for Beloof's poetry. I had gotten the stove going an hour before so the room was very cozy in the below-zero night and the fifteen chairs I had brought over were all filled soon after nine. Bob followed an outline of "suggestions for a poetry reading" I had made up which included tracing his life, pointing out influences, and sketching his method of working. But it was Bob's poetry that made the impression and gave us *Bob Beloof* as he himself could never have given us Bob Beloof. The

poems were well received with the same reverence and delight an audience
might receive Robert Frost's work. I got more kick out of it than out of an
Honor's college program. The coffee afterwards was thirty-seven cents a
pound, co-op brand, which I had specially ordered from Williston. Its wonderful flavor lingered with me and recalled the famous Garden meetings. . . .

January 5, 1944

This has been a day of momentous decision for me. You will recall a
sentence in my last letter saying that one Dr. Keys of the University of
Minnesota was coming here to recruit men for a guinea pig experiment.
Instead of Dr. Keys, Dr. Harold Guetzgow and Dr. Henry Taylor arrived
here yesterday morning to do the work. I met them in the dining hall as I was
beginning my daily transmission [transposition] of the English suites of Bach.
I joined them in their late breakfast and, being curious, had them tell me of
the experiment. I learned this: "The Department of Physiological Hygiene
is occupying a thirty-five-room former athletic locker building under the seats
of the Minnesota stadium to conduct experiments in vitamin deficiency and
bed rest: In one of the rooms are two treadmills on which the men walk a
quarter of their forty-eight-hour week while they take tests in 'coordination'
etc. The rest of their time is spent on work like tabulating research data,
scheduling experiment hours, cleaning up the labs, working in the diet
kitchen from which meals of exactly measured vitamin content are served, or
as librarian (the job which would appeal to me most because it entails going
to the Minnesota [University] library and getting out books for the profs).

In this experiment the doctors are trying to prove that the minimum vitamin
requirements set by the National Research Council are too high. The way
to prove it is to give them first the council's quota of vitamins and make tests
on efficiency, and then to give smaller amounts and to test efficiency again.
For the first five weeks beginning January 22 men in this experiment will be
fed a special diet of only lard, casein, and something else mixed into various
dishes to tear them down. Some days men will live on a starvation diet—
nothing at all. Then men will be built up again as fast as possible. All the time
they will be expected to do their regular work no matter how badly they feel.

The bed rest experiment involves lying in bed for a month with one or
more limbs immobilized in a cast as if they were broken. All this is being
done under a staff headed by Dr. Ancel Keys and including two psychologists,
two physiologists, seventeen paid employees and twenty C.P.S. men who
get $12.50 per month plus maintenance. The project is under the Brethren
Service Committee and eight men from the Brethren camps have been there
since May. Besides the general interest of the project there are the cultural

advantages of the Twin Cities and the certainty of being able to study at the University. One man is taking full-time work for a degree at the Seminary and another is taking almost full-time at the Ag school. The campus and city are alive with the arts and two lab assistants play in the University symphony orchestra in which many Minneapolis Symphony players perform. There are no after-hours restrictions and men can arrange the work and experiment schedules to permit going to classes."

So I submitted to a one-hour official interview and then was given a personnel inventory test. I gave no final answer about my willingness to go; all last night my mind wavered between yes and no, and again this morning. But tonight at supper I gave the doctors my "yes." They left tonight for Minneapolis. On the train they will discuss and decide upon the six or so out of the twenty they interviewed who will go. For doctors to take such pains about selecting mere guinea pigs is quite remarkable and gives me the idea that this experiment is really worthwhile. Their apparent special interest in me makes me suspect I will be chosen. By Friday noon, even before you will get this letter, I will know, for they promised to telegraph selections when they arrive at the University. . . .

Minneapolis
JANUARY / JULY 1944

Laboratory of Physiological Hygiene, Stadium South Tower
University of Minnesota, Minneapolis, Minnesota
January 22, 1944
Liefe Moesje en Dad,
   A new situation and it looks as if I am going to lose all my independence, self-sufficiency, and resolution—in a word be institutionalized. But what an institution! I am writing in our sitting room that adjoins the eight-man dorm where I slept last night. On the table stands a tall Bausch & Lomb apparatus for measuring field of vision. My paper is illuminated by long fluorescent tubes attached to the twelve-foot ceiling. The scratchings of my pen (now pencil) are absorbed by two inches of soundproofing. I sit on a green leather steel-tube chair. Outside I can faintly hear what sounds like the drum beat of the University band in the stadium. In the corridor is the voice of an un-doubtedly pretty girl. What more do I want? Ink.
   Don Martinson of the cows and hogs was on hand at the Minneapolis station when the Empire Builder pulled in at 11:45, an hour and a half late. We crowded into a streetcar pleasantly jammed with sunny-faced co-eds and in half an hour were at the dark stadium. We followed along the portalled stadium wall to the positive (yes) pole of the horseshoe. We met some fellows of the unit in tuxes coming back from the symphony. Their talk was im-mediately of culture, the relation of knowledge to happiness and appreciation, not of D-8 cats. Don having given me a bunk below his in the steel double-decker, showed me around the place. If Guetzgow had told the boys at Trenton it was going to be this royal he would have had twenty more vol-unteers. It felt very strange to walk on solid in-laid linoleum floors, breathe conditioned air, have every footstep deadened by insulation, open thick sturdy doors, and flick on daylight with the movement of a finger. I am afraid it's all too civilized for this barbarian. The equipment here is tremendous—two elaborate treadmills, giant X-ray and fluoroscope machines, a long lab of

bottles, tubes, refrigerators and sterilizers, and a kitchen that is as different from Trenton as dark from light. . . .

This morning, having slept rather poorly on account of the difference in temperature between this building, constant 68 degrees, and my dorm at Trenton, close to freezing, I was pleasantly awakened, not by Canby for meditation, but by a hollow voice. "Good morning, fellows, it's seven fifteen. Don't forget your laundry and urine specimens." It came over the inter-communication system. . . . The drumbeat of the band is now returning and with it the blare of trumpets and the indistinct syllables of a thousand men singing. Trevor Sandness tells me we have the Army Air Corps above us and they are making the music. . . .

January 24, 1944

I feel extremely well-stuffed this evening, the last thing I expected in a vitamin deficiency experiment. The reason is that we six in the bed-rest experiment are, for the present, getting one third more food than the nutrition boys. But it feels as if we are only being fattened for the slaughter. On the schedule until June 30th when our experiment ends are two sets of a week of starvation, a couple of weeks of tearing down, three weeks in bed, and then "recovery." Today Czechoslovakian Dr. Jaschka Brozek demonstrated the treadmills and the psycho-motor tests to be performed while walking on it— a trace maze, a pipe down which one slips a metal ball and catches before it falls out, lights to switch out when they snap on, back pulls and hand grips, and two electrified plates to be banged alternately with a brass pencil as fast as possible. We will be tested on these to find just what effect bed rest has on our efficiency. For half an hour four of us walked on the large treadmill with the friction sparks banging between us whenever we touched. When I got off and moved around, the walls seemed to float past, for while I was on the treadmill they had stayed in the same place. The wonderful thing about the treadmill is that you can read as you walk. I got through several newspaper articles for lack of anything better at the moment. Such reading is an indication of degradation but in this mechanical atmosphere I feel helplessly drawn to it. I am beginning to fear that it was the environment at Trenton that let me self-abnegate myself in these matters, and not any great inner discipline I had developed. . . .

This place is a submarine, clean, compact, bristling with apparatus. We never see daylight and never know the weather, but I am convinced we are going somewhere. Dr. Ancel Keys, dark-eyed, driving . . . captains an alive staff of seventeen, all under forty. Their concern is intense. They give all to their work. The lab moves like clockwork. Every man knows his station. . . .

February 2, 1944

I may be the biggest man in this unit now, surface area 2.12 sq. meters against Gene Sunnen's 2.10, but they're whittling me down fast. When I came I weighed 195, this morning 187^1/$_2$. Apparently I am burning a few more than the 4,500 calories I am being fed daily. But I am getting in fine condition and even if Jaschka is displeased with my speed on the psycho-motor tests, my dynamometer readings get higher and higher. This week we are doing fifteen minutes on the small treadmill as we take the tests, stretches of forty-five minutes and an hour on the large treadmill (3^1/$_2$ mph, 10% grade), and five minutes of running (6^1/$_2$ mph, 10% grade). All in all it makes an afternoon as tiring as football. But then the exhilaration of the shower and the luxury of clean socks.

February 4, 1944

... I went to the Extension School office in the Administration Building last night and found out that the five weeks of the semester I am to be in bed would be too many for me to miss. Of course I could do the work in bed but tests would be on the things that were said in class as much as on textbooks. The lady at the desk recommended correspondence courses with my residence in Minneapolis making it possible to have occasional conferences with the professors. I am skeptical, however, that this sort of arrangement would be much more valuable than study on my own, even if not for college credit.

... Dr. Keys, suave, confident, let his shifty brown eyes wander over us bed-rest boys as he gave the whats and whys of our experiment yesterday morning. Briefly: "Everyone recommends going to bed for all sorts of ailments yet no one knows just what happens physiologically and psychologically —what adjustments the heart and kidneys make to the supine position, what happens to the density of the bones, what happens to muscle tissue, to efficiency, strength, and mental processes like learning. The answers to these questions will be determined in the first three weeks of your lying-in through X-rays, comparing the amount of calcium and protein taken in and excreted, and the psycho-motor tests. In the second three weeks we will see if tissue deterioration can be prevented by extra feeding of protein and calcium, exercise in bed, and tilting the bed to stimulate circulation. It makes a hard job for the lab, all you have to do is eat and excrete."

Judging by the way the staff is going about it, I expect to see some very significant results published by the beginning of next year. One thing this lab conclusively proved in the 1943 experiments on C.O.'s is that vitamins taken in excess of those received in the normal diet people like you eat, are more likely to have a toxic than a beneficial effect. . . . Last night Guetzgow,

Jaschka, and Dr. Keys spoke before a physiological association on the work being done here. In the question period someone asked if the results of experiments done on such unusual people as C.O.'s could be considered valid. Guetzgow replied, "If they take in thiamin they give out thiamin."

February 23, 1944

... Today on the treadmill I culminated the greatest reading achievement of my career, James Joyce's *Ulysses*. The erotic excitation of the concluding stream of consciousness record of Mrs. Bloom, supposedly the greatest revelation of the psychology of a woman in print, kept me pounding to the end. I hope Mrs. Bloom's thought-train is not that of woman *per se*, for if it is I'll join John Plott in vows of celibacy. Joyce, I concluded, is the greatest writer the world has produced. He could write anything, from Lydia Pinkham ads to Chaucer. Like the people he portrays, he dwelt too much on the Lydia Pinkham angle. But this is man, though we hate to admit it. . . .

February 29, 1944

... Alexander Brailowsky, black Mephistopheles, flipped the tails of his coat over the back of the bench, scraped the seat to the correct distance from the keyboard, drew his arms out of the sleeves of his coat as if to plunge them into water (hot), and struck the keyboard. The concert was magnificent and while my thoughts often strayed from the music I was at times transfixed by the throbbing notes. . . . Afterwards we went over to Annabelle's house . . . to hear the NBC Symphony play Robert [sic] Cordero's composition . . . but Brailowsky's encores made us too late.

... Anyway we stayed talking to Dick Zumwinkel, who walked out of the Terry, Montana, C.P.S. camp. What does a man who is momentarily free of the clutches of Selective Service do? He putters around as janitor of the Wesley Foundation, a sort of Minnesota Christian Association; he goes to all the meetings where Christian young men and women and would-be saints gather and makes his presence felt; he talks over his position with others; he goes to parties; he lives in the same room with a young married couple, a highly immoral situation; and he generally acts as a man who has committed no crime at all, who is in fact entirely in the right. Is it sane for the government to send a man like this to prison? . . .

Most of the men in C.P.S. camps and "alternate service" cooperated with the administration by the government and the peace churches, of course. But there were individuals who rebelled against the unpaid "work of national importance," against government control, against conscription itself, and against confinement in the camps. The most drastic demonstration was "walking out," or simply leaving the camp and moving about freely until apprehended by the F.B.I. A man was then imprisoned, often released on bail and then tried and imprisoned again.

March 12, 1944

This being my last day on earth, the warden has been very kind to grant my last request that I be permitted to scribble an 'umble note to those loved ones I leave behind. Tomorrow at dawn I shall trudge down the long corridor into the dim chamber where lie the shattered bodies of those who have gone before, namely Brothers Martinson and Michener. My last duty will be to assist these two out of the room in the event they wobble too much to maintain equilibrium. Then I shall climb into bed, feel myself buoyed on a warm cloud of inner spring Beauty Rest, and drift into the arms of Morpheus. . . .

Of all the concerts this week I liked best "the abstruse ramblings of fevered brains, braiding the brittle clarinet with the plastic voice and an arched violin, so daring, arresting, exciting, shocking, so fresh in their non-conformity, the rebels." I refer to the original modern compositions of the students of Ernst Krenek Thursday night at Hamline University, for which I am enclosing the program. Here, at least, were young people who were doing something besides murdering or waiting. The atmosphere was definitely chamber society, a hundred or so in attendance, including Dmitri Mitropoulos, a lot of the symphony musicians, intellectual college girls, with a lot of foreign accent being slung around.

Representative was the song "Jesus Wept"—a few weird chords, boom, boom, boom, a girl screaming, soaring the words "Jesus wept!" another chord, boom. Applause. But with my ear for jazz I could take it. It was highly refreshing, inspiring, and revolutionary. Roque Cordero, whose sonatina for piano had made a big hit, rode home with Lauris [Guetzgow's girl], Getz, and me. The negro talked intensely of his music. Of the second movement of his sonatina: "Sometimes in Panama we have much rain. The drops go ping ping ping, the single note and below it the somber theme of nature." He is studying under Krenek as a prodigy of Mitropoulos who is financing his education. He writes very fast and is now experimenting with the twelve-tone scale, very weird to our unaccustomed ears. . . .

March 13, 1944

Here I lie in the same position in which I used to write my journal, on my left side, my head propped on my left hand, my right pen-hand casting a shadow to the bottom of the paper from the bed lamp perched on the head of the bed. A hoarse tenor sax is telling a loud smutty story out of the radio over by Gene's bed. The atmosphere is that of the Wesleyan Infirmary. But judging from today I won't get as much work done here in a day as I did there. The lights are off thirteen and a half hours a day; meals and nursing service (bath in bed, etc.) take two hours, tests and other medical attention an hour or two more, visitors in the evening (we hope) will consume an hour; so we really don't have as much time for reading and writing as when we were treadmilling and free after 6 p.m. . . . .

When I lie in the dark the novel on the effects of conscription on various personalities takes shape. I think I will dispense with the dialogues at the beginning and the end and make it just a series of letters. . . . Why I think the letter form is particularly apt is that through it men who find various "escapes" or "solutions" to the C.P.S. problem (jail, 1-AO, insanity, simple waiting, or violent expressionism) can show their reactions to the same events, to various personalities, and to new policies. . . . The whole shift of a man's attitude can be very subtly traced. Think of the way my letters changed in emphasis from when I first came to Trenton to when I left. I don't know whether this novel will have a pessimistic or optimistic spirit. It is more likely to show how one individual can conquer his environment while another falls a slave to it. Whether or not this conquest is an illusion is the question.

The sad story of your exams came this morning, Norm. I never took them very seriously in high school and college. I always considered my papers far more important since they involved adding something of my own creative ability to the simple reproduction of information. In the end I forgot most of the facts anyhow. But I do not forget the way to produce art or to use the scientific empirical, analytical, and introspective methods. So don't feel depressed.

Your stand on conscription answers the question I pose in the novel. Ultimately you are a slave anyhow. Even in jail you cannot escape from the oppression of the government so you just as well might take the most expedient way, colored of course with a bit of righteousness and justice. This is essentially what you did, Dad, in the last mess, saying, "But my heart wasn't in it." This is just what our society does. Then it goes ahead and rationalizes the ultimate good of its cause, using slogans, atrocity stories, and misrepresentations of the enemy. It never considers "that love is the effective force for overcoming evil and transforming society into a creative fellowship"— the platform of the F.O.R. Please do not say that my attitudes toward war are "stereotyped" when you mean "consistent." I realize the flat-on-my-back testimony I am now making isn't what I should be doing. Lauris Steere's younger brother was here in Navy uniform the other day. He wasn't much impressed by this luxurious set-up or what we were doing. He *was* impressed by Dick Zumwinkel, who is still waiting for the F.B.I., for Dick has been willing to go all-out for his stand. At least here is a man who is not a victim of expediency. . . .

March 14, 1944

It has been good to have such jolly mail from you these first two days in bed, Brute Force [Norm]. I only hope you will keep it up. So far they have been the only exciting things that have happened. . . .

I am sick of arguing about your going into the Navy, so where I started writing more hackneyed statements on freedom and pacifism in the other letter I began, I will apply my pen to something else. I read your arguments against my suggestion that you ignore the draft to Gene and Jack O'Leary, who was in jail four weeks before deciding to submit to a physical exam after all. Reading your words aloud I first realized how clear and to the point your writing is, something like Hoffman's. If you wrote as earthy prose for your English class you would get an A. Jack thought your arguments were pretty good even if they were concerned with consequences. He found that even in four weeks he got a bad martyr complex. As Bill Simpson maintains, Christ's teachings were meant for the few. It is only the few who, like Christ, can keep from getting this martyr complex. . . .

March 16, 1944

Oh, what I wouldn't do for an hour on the nice treadmill! This lying in bed under orders to move as little as possible, and a recorder under one caster to check up on how much we do, is worse than any Freudian sexual frustration. My imagination works at a great rate, especially from ten p.m. to one a.m., fired by all sorts of schemes, projects, and ideas. But then the lights are out and I won't be getting up for over two weeks. Why don't I do something now? The days are so broken up with blood-pressures, rectal temperatures, baths in bed, meals, doctors and all sorts of visitors that you can never really concentrate for more than a minute. Then the lights go out again. No phonograph has been procured as yet so when it is dark we listen to the most perverted American institution (next to the movies), the radio. If we were only enough animal to excuse this as hibernation! . . .

March 22, 1944

. . . The last hour of rest, ten to eleven, during which the lights are out and the bed flat, has been about the first I have felt I haven't wasted. Getz toted Lauris' fine Phonola electric phonograph over. During the hour it boomed

out in beautiful tones some of Wilbur Held's records made during his organ
broadcasts, *Introduction and Allegro* for string quartet, harp, flute, and
clarinet by Ravel, *Scapino* a lively comedy overture by Walton, and Weber's
Concertina for Clarinet as played by Reginald Kell. . . .

I am beginning to consider all the letter writing I have been doing in C.P.S.
as an unconscious preparation for the great novel. . . .

March 26, 1944

How much we take on faith, on hearsay! I dream of the sex experience,
which I am told is the most wonderful that can happen to a man. But how do
I know? For me it might be a great disappointment, and only an "experience,"
nothing more. If I had not been told of death I would have no inkling that
someday I might lose this consciousness for good. If I had not seen men die
and prepared their bodies for the autopsy table, if I had not carried Anna
Walton's coffin out of the Star of the Sea Church and let it slowly descend
into the yellow earth overlooking a woolen mill in Lawrence, Mass., I would
be able to live on and grow naturally, finding in each day something new,
discovering more about where I was going and what I was becoming. I might
live with the faith that I would have consciousness eternal. Bob Emeott
sincerely thinks that the reason he kept free of the draft for two and a half
years was his belief in freedom, that freedom was the only thing for him. Only
in a weak moment when he was convinced by a friend that C.P.S. was the
only decent thing did he lose his belief in freedom. Then he was drafted. His
old faith resembled mine in using the non-violent technique with patients at
the state hospital, that if I acted always with love and with "soul force" I
would be "untouchable"—and, as it happened, I was. In contemplating
walking out of C.P.S. I sense a danger: I dream more about what I shall do
in jail than about what I shall do while I am "free." I should not have a
moment's doubt that I will be left completely free, especially if I justify that
freedom with a more significant life than I am living here. I am not leaving
C.P.S. for jail as the F.O.R., *Reporter*, and *Christian Century* writers say, I am
leaving it for liberty. Of course I realize that real freedom comes only in the
individual creative experience. Is this an admission that I have failed in
C.P.S. to demand more freedom than I am given in this set up? Shouldn't I
be able to be as creative in all my tasks here as I would anywhere, even though
lying in bed or carrying urine doesn't seem at first as meaningful as writing?
Wouldn't I be open to the charge that I have "gone sour on C.P.S."?
Wouldn't it show ingratitude to the Service Committee? Inconsideration for
the government? "No," I say to all these, provided I make walking out only
a means, not an end, a point of integration. I must believe heart and soul in

what I am to do with freedom, and never consider the consequences. Question: "If the penalty for walking out of C.P.S. were like the penalty for desertion from the Army would I depart? Is what I am to do worth death?" As it is, even the maximum of five years in prison doesn't scare me much—a nice time to write and think and reform. But this is something which I must never admit possible. My imagining what I will say to the judge and premeditating how I shall act when accosted by the F.B.I. puts the emphasis in just the wrong place. All my thoughts should be on the vision for which I must have freedom—farming, ministering, and writing. I am not quite ready yet.

After three fine days of records during our four hours of rest period Henry Taylor decided he had pulled a boner. Changing records caused the circulatory system to make too much of an adjustment. It might make the results fuzzy. I would be in better condition from the exercise than I was supposed to be. Now we are trying to contract people, pretty girls preferred, to sit with us in the dark and turn platters. . . .

The breath of spring Lauris sent over soon faded but Eleanor Lindeman came over with roses and carnations. They too became droopy and withered and have been disposed of. How I long to get outside, out of the city, into the hills where I can feel as close to nature as in Big Flats and during the summer at Trenton. . . .

April 1, 1944

After responding to this bed rest experience with a tremendous desire to get up and out of this prison, the realization that tomorrow is my last day in bed has caused the reverse reaction to set in. When you come down to it, this isn't a bad life at all. Never have I been so completely cared for, never have I felt so well rested, so physically comfortable. Having to expend energy, to think what I am supposed to do next, to make decisions, is going to be a novel experience. It might be a rebirth. But of course I will follow in the old patterns because they are the easiest, the most natural, the best I know and maybe not so bad after all. . . .

I asked Henry Taylor if our experiment had borne any positive results. "There was no decrease in the amount of work one could do, only in the effort it took. Apparently no cell tissue deterioration. Only the cardiovascular system went to hell. After three weeks out of bed Don and Ralph are three-fourths recovered. The next quarter will take as long. Weights have remained the same." Monday come the pains of rebirth.

April 4, 1944

Monday morning, my first day on earth, and I was raring to go. "Let me at that treadmill." Twenty minutes later I thought I would collapse. If I looked sick then, you should see me now. I hobble around like [a cripple], muscles jabbing me all over with every move as I drag myself up stairs and shuffle through the corridors. But no one notices my misery. They all remark about my haircut, the first one in Minneapolis! What I wrote about the cardiovascular system was very true. It couldn't make the postural adjustment. When my legs were moving the blood kept circulating, but when I stood still it all stagnated in my legs until I thought I would keel over. The old heart tapped along weakly, "I think I can, I think I can," 168 per minute, but I wasn't so sure. Anyway I walked half an hour at 10%, $3^1/_2$ mph, ran two minutes at 10%, 7 mph, and did forty-five minutes of psychomotors. This is no hospital where nurses wheel you around in chairs and guide your newly learned babysteps. This is an experiment to get data for the glory of Science and suffering just has no meaning. So today with my legs so stiff, particularly in the inside upper thigh, that I have to pick them up with my hands and place them on the next step to climb stairs, I was required to run two minutes at 15%, 7 mph, which I had done with difficulty before going to bed. Well, I made all but five seconds of it. My legs just wouldn't go fast enough and I kept sliding back. When things got hazy and I started to stumble they dragged me off, puffing and snorting into the drooling mouthpiece through which I was blowing all my air into a Tissot tank. My exhalations had been so hard the diaphragm in the mouthpiece valve closed off again. It was a terrific battle blowing out as fast as I could to get in another breath and then having my exhalation stopped abruptly. I couldn't slow up or blow more gently. I wondered how these yogis who take one breath a minute would do on this run. Well, by now I am pretty well recovered except for the stiff legs. Tomorrow we go at it again. . . .

. . . We were amazed to see Dick Zumwinkel who had been picked up finally by the F.B.I. and put in the St. Paul jail Friday morning. Of course, the newspapers had the story all garbled. He was an Army deserter, the headlines said. They gave his address on University Avenue, 1209, which happens to be the First Methodist Church where Dick has been staying. The American Civil Liberties Union had put up bail and he had been released at 3:00 that afternoon. . . . His trial will be held in Billings, Montana, sometime in June. He still has a long time to wait and forget about it.

April 9, 1944

. . . All the moaning I did in my last letter is forgotten. By Friday I reached the base line on psychomotors established before bed, and most of the stiffness had drained out of my legs. Even Wednesday night I felt good enough to walk all the way downtown. It being Holy Week, Wilbur Held [a C.O. who worked in the lab kitchen], the pious organist of the First Baptist Church in St. Paul, and I went to the Alvin Burlesque Theater. We had a hilarious and relaxing evening being objective, analytical, and critical of the whole business. . . .

Gene and I went to bed just this night three weeks ago when the worst of the winter hit Minnesota. But now it is warm and sunny, the grass is getting green, the robins are tweeting, and the Minnesota outfielders are shagging flies. With spring, however, comes the urge to be moving. I find these days very distressing and torturing. I am not sure of anything. I have witnessed the disintegration of so many old values—the church, the state, and particularly college—that I don't know where to turn. What values I haven't seen disintegrate fall under my constant iconoclasm, questioning, and critical evaluation—love between the sexes, all forms of social activity, the idea of God ("God is dead"), all defenses for my actions, voluntary poverty as an end à la St. Francis, the "create" theory, etc., athletics, jazz, the scientific method, all these things which I have acquired, not created. . . . I am beginning to learn what "the effects of conscription on personality" mean—all the more reason to write the novel. . . . Perhaps I can find solace in the fact that every man goes through this, that I don't stand alone. But that is bad, too. I must stand alone, be unique, a non-conformist. Enough of this. Of course I didn't go to church. Did you?

May 11, 1944

. . . It is definite now that we aren't going to bed again, but there will be a fast of three days toward the end of June! Getz is now working with Gene and me on standardizing our scores on psychomotor tests. In a sweaty half-hour we run through the whole battery four times—maze, pipe, reaction time, tapping, and dynamometers, working these first few days on using constant methods with the various tests. Tomorrow we start introspection, writing down everything that went through our minds in the half-hour. Next week Getz will try to make us think of just the same things for each test to eliminate the effect of suggestion on performance. As Dr. Keys admitted in a seminar on starvation I heard Tuesday, thinking of strangling Hitler might cause a definite rise in the hand-grip score. Getz will suggest certain words for the different tests and I am supposed to meditate on them while working. If this mild hypnosis has any stabilizing effect on the scores it will be used on subjects in future experiments. Tearing through the tests each day without Jaschka to bawl me out and drive me on like a football coach I feel much more the tool of science, the automaton that Getz wants me to be, without pride, personality, or soul. I can only marvel at what a beautiful machine I am. . . .

May 28, 1944

... Dick Zumwinkel, who left Terry, Mont., C.P.S. camp last fall, incidentally, had his trial in Billings a few days ago and drew a year's sentence probably to be served at McNeil Island, Washington. He waived a jury trial and pleaded his own case before the judge alone, during which, some said, he stood mute. One year is really a very short term. Perhaps the judges are wising up to the fact that their criminology is a little dated. I doubt very much if Dick will accept the new parole plan.

Treadmill reading the past two weeks was Lillian Smith's *Strange Fruit*, really a very good novel, cleverly worked out, flowing along as easily and relentlessly as racial prejudice itself or the Mississippi River. If it is spiced up with sexy paragraphs every now and then so that Boston banned it, the incidents all have deep and convincing roots and are not included to sell the book, though they probably do. Furthermore, they form the thought pattern of ordinary people, as in *Ulysses*, and the Boston censors are included. The picture of racial prejudice and its effects is very moving.

June 4, 1944

... At this point (1:00 a.m.) my writing was interrupted by the entrance of Getz and Michener with whom I had perhaps the best bull session of my life. We started talking about the impressions we had made on each other in our interviews at camp and how those impressions had changed, Ralph from a timid Quaker to a devastating, bold iconoclast and a "good Joe," Getz from a very nervous, scatter-brained professor to an uninhibited, hyperactive "truth seeker," I from one very sure of himself to one not quite so sure. As a psychologist Getz is very anxious to make a good impression on those he interviews so he had us tell him what was wrong with him—his habit of winking, staring, and grimacing as he talked, for instance. I told him to lay off the vulgarity, please. That night I asked what he had been doing with Lauris, and he replied, "Fuckin'," and when I said, "What?" he said, "Screwin', shovin' it up." Even if he was kidding I was disturbed for I look at their love affair as being so pure, and even if Getz does this sort of thing, Lauris, never. Getz admitted he purposely tries to shock me because I am such a puritan, the same technique I always use with you two on matters of non-conformity, etc. Then Getz went into an analysis of why I was a puritan. I had to admit it was because of the way I had been taught, not because I had put it under the light of reason and scientific knowledge. Getz has done this last to the point where he has frequent sexual intercourse with Lauris using contraceptives for the present, and masturbates effectively without any sense of guilt. He would have coitus be as untabooed an animal function as eating a good meal from which he gets about the same pleasure when done with Lauris. He wants no label of "sin" placed on an adult's desire for physical contact and stimulation.

If he were to plot the amount of physical contact among members of this unit since it began, the curve would go up, which is good, kinship coming as much from the intellectual exchange of ideas, à la Hoffman, as from the physical exchange, which I do most with Norm. Although Getz isn't quite sure, he has a hunch homosexuality is not a perversion at all, only the attitude toward it is the perversion. You both will admit that all the hugging we did with you when Norm and I were younger was very pure. Implied in all this is a new attitude toward nakedness, against which I have been unwisely prejudiced, I fear. When Getz and Lauris have children they will all take baths together, and the kids will be allowed to watch them copulate, intercourse being as normal a thing as kissing now is. What is really new in this is its taking sex down from its pedestal of "the greatest experience two people can have," "the greatest display of love two people can show each other," which I have called it, to its rightful place as a normal part of life. I am sure this is right; intercourse while very beautiful is only experience; I am sure I will be disappointed in it because I have come to look at it as something sacred. This is why I say I am not prepared for marriage, why I find another focus like walking out. Getz wants me to do a good job in prison (as if that is where I am going!) and realizing that I may spend long weeks in solitary recommends I read books like Byrd's *Alone* to prepare myself. Also he would have me talk more about it to build ego-defenses without which he doesn't think I'll be strong enough to come through the experience like a man. Of course this is just what I have been doing by putting a paragraph on walking out in every letter I have written for the past six months. . . .

June 11, 1944

By now you two have seen the Crusher graduated from the best prep school in the U.S. [Andover Academy]. It is really such an amazing thing I am tempted to label it "predestined." If it is good that Norm has had Andover, you deserve a lot of credit, Moes. There isn't a mother in ten thousand who had the welfare of her children so much at heart and would have had the vision to put Norm in such a school. Can you think of one mother of all the kids in the dinky Beverly Farms School who had the imagination—nay, the sheer nerve and impudence—to go and ask Mr. Adriance about getting her son into a school reserved for the sons of estate owners, not gardeners? If I yell about your being victims of inertia, you can always throw this up to me. As for you, Crusher, I don't understand where all this drive, loyalty to duty, and maybe even intelligence, came from. For a rickety baby, a pants-wetter, a bawl-baby, and a Mary-contrary, who always had to be coaxed to do anything, you have come out pretty well. Don't spoil it by enlisting in the Navy. . . .

. . . Joe Blair came to me early in the week to say that there would be plenty of clerical work (no guinea-pigging) for me to do here when I was through with furlough the beginning of August—if I was interested. It was a temptation— but no. Michener, who doesn't think I am sure enough of myself to walk-out now, suggested I take a crack at the Fine Arts camp in Waldport, Oregon. Again the problem of having to work eight and a half hours on something besides the Fine Arts, making life unintegrated. . . .

. . . Incidentally, the first public announcement that we C.O.'s are here came into headlines on Invasion Day. It took a speech by Dr. Keys the night before, 2,000 miles away in New York, to reveal it. The article was true to fact, unprejudiced! There has been some reaction—three telephone calls— one from a reporter wanting to know more, two from food concerns hoping to sell the lab their products. In fact, our food comes from the Quartermaster Supply Depot in Chicago. Even we C.O.'s can't escape the Army! . . .

In the laboratory a notice had been posted that a "fine arts program" was being formulated in a camp for fighting forest fires and reforestation on the Oregon coast. Led by the poet William Everson, a few of the men in that camp who were writers, musicians, and artists had formulated the concept of establishing spare time activities in the arts, and attracting men of similar interests from other camps and special projects.

A mimeographed prospectus stated, "Early last summer . . . a movement was begun among West Coast C.P.S. camps to inaugurate a School in Fine Arts. This interest was manifested mostly in Brethren camps, and was serious enough to win the sympathy of administrative officials of the Brethren Service Committee. . . . To this end, we here at Waldport have organized ourselves into a Committee On Fine Arts, and having the proper authorization from the Brethren Service Committee, are issuing this invitation to all serious artists and students of art to attend the inaugural term, beginning February 15, of the first aesthetic movement in Civilian Public Service.

"The Fine Arts School, as we conceive it, is simply to be a grouping together of the practitioners of the various art forms. These include the Literary Arts: fiction, poetry, essays and criticism; the Musical Arts: both composition and performance; the Visual Arts: painting and sculpturing; the Speech Arts: dramatics and readings; and the related fine arts crafts."

In accepting the proposal the Brethren authorities probably regarded artists as trouble-makers and assumed that if they were herded together they would bother each other and no one else. As a clarinettist and aspiring writer Adrian was attracted. He applied for transfer to Camp Angel, as it was called, and for furlough to visit his parents in Connecticut before the trip across the continent. Both requests were granted.

June 19, 1944

My last piece of toast and cup of coffee have been consumed. From now until late Friday afternoon the three of us are to eat nothing and drink only water. If we were going to lie in bed for three and a half days it wouldn't be bad, but a lumberjack's day of work on an empty stomach will be pretty tough judging from today's work done on a full stomach. It was an awful grind of twelve hours testing and treadmill walking ($4^{1}/_2$ hrs. 700 cal/hr) interspersed by three one-hour rest periods. If possible I am going to use the rest periods editing and writing the *Guinea Pig Gazette*, the lab newspaper. By the third day my articles on the lab may sound pretty pessimistic and my view of conscription even blacker. The second and third days I think we do only three hours and two and a half hrs. on the treadmill, but it will add up to a caloric debt of "national" proportions that will have to be paid by body fat reserves. This means loss of weight, and perhaps some sickness while the body converts to the new fat metabolism. . . .

If I am alive I will probably leave a week from today for the East. Joe Blair has mailed in my request for transfer as of July 22 to Waldport, Oregon, but giving no hint I might not show up. Ridiculous to have my trial in a place of which I have never been within 1,000 miles. What trial? You can expect me about Thursday, the 29th. Eat well, because I won't.

June 21, 1944

. . . For a bum who hasn't eaten for forty-eight hours I feel remarkably fine. But I sure could stand a cup of coffee. Only this morning did I really feel punk. When they tilted me up on the postural adjustment table to a standing position everything went black, I broke out in cold sweat and had to fight to keep from fainting. I guess I would have collapsed if Les hadn't noticed my grimacing and put the table down. It was the same way when Angie took a Kymo X-ray and Jaschka tested me on the ataxiameter, two minutes standing still with the eyes closed to measure swaying. I felt just like the first day out of bed—O.K. when moving, stinko when standing still. But by late afternoon when I had put in three hours on the large treadmill and two runs, I suddenly began to feel fine as if I had gotten my second wind. Postural adjustment was just as on eating days, and psychomotors went better than they have for a week. Apparently the marvelous body with which you have endowed me successfully adjusted to the new reserve fat metabolism. My waist is down to my spinal column. The five and a half pounds I lost yesterday to put me at 168, and I suppose as much today, will have to be put on again before I let you see me a week from now. . . .

After a week's reunion with his family Adrian decided to hitchhike to the Pacific Coast although he had been issued a railroad ticket (which he could cash in). He planned a stop in Minneapolis to visit his friends from the laboratory, and another in Trenton, North Dakota, to see his former campmates. He promised to continue to write home several times a week and loaded his pockets with a supply of penny postcards and three-cent stamps. He set out thumbing westward in the summer of 1944.

Carbondale, Pennsylvania
July 18, 1944

Passing through this coal town out of Scranton at 3:30 p.m. Very good hitching so far but I will inquire in Scranton about trains that will get me to Chicago by morning. My last driver was a co-op dairyman answering a call from his brother to come to Waymark because their mother had just died. Meanwhile I munched my bacon sandwich. He wouldn't take any because he had just had lunch. Life must go on!

Scranton
July 18, 1944

Through a number of blunders too disgusting to mention I now have a ticket for Chicago via Buffalo! I will get into the Windy City tomorrow at 1:00. I have just seen *Snow White* again, a very lovely picture especially after Lowell Thomas and the war newsreel. I will have to make up for the money my stupidity has cost me, on the Chicago-Minneapolis leg, but the Streamliner may be too much of a lure.

Buffalo
July 18, 1944

Have just transferred through Buffalo over streets glistening after the water trucks. I passed Big Flats, five lights on posts, a few rows of lighted window panes, and a lonely C.O. making his way from the dorm to the lounge. . . .

Minneapolis
July 20, 1944

Chicago to Minneapolis cost me $10 but I'm glad I yielded to the temptation of taking the Streamliner. . . . It was the most wonderful train ride I have ever had—the speed, the beautiful coach, and the pastoral Wisconsin landscape, so clean in the crisp air and afternoon sunlight. After this I'll be satisfied only with an airplane. Maybe I can fly over the Rockies and the Cascades after my stop at Trenton. . . . Here the University Dentistry School has discovered I have ten cavities in my teeth which will cost $26 to fill. That's a lot of money for one who hopes to fly, but I went to the dentistry school anyway.

5:00 p.m.

Well, the ordeal is over. Conclusions: Suffering has no meaning. Until this afternoon I never really guinea-pigged. I am a pacifist, because I would rather get hurt than hurt. (I actually felt sorry for poor Chris Brown who had to torture me so.) Results: one filling, teeth cleaned. . . .

During the years that Adrian was in the C.P.S. system he often had to resort to dental schools to have his teeth fixed. Few of the men in the camps had health insurance or incomes of any kind, and when they were ill they were assigned to the infirmary in the camp. If necessary a doctor was called in from the nearest town; the seriously ill or injured were taken to local hospitals, and the bills were sent to their parents or next of kin.

Billings
July 24, 1944

. . . The ride through the star-studded Dakota night and the sunny morning on the prairie were magnificent. The Dakota railroad towns are all on the same pattern, two grain elevators and a scattering of houses held together by telephone wires; then there was a long line of poles and cross pieces clear to the horizon with the wires going up and down in waves as we passed them. I reached Trenton in time for dinner. There were amazed greetings. I am the only fellow who has ever come back to the camp to visit after getting out! I was shown all the physical improvements made since I was there. The stage is very functional now. They have a movie projection booth above the beams. Enough room has been left for worship, though organized worship has ceased.

Of course we had a monster jam session and I played my loudest. It may be that this band is the best in North Dakota, but it still stinks. . . . I was dragged out of sleep at quarter to six for meditation, which I slept through, except when one of the Catholics made me repeat some Hail Mary prayers with him. Later I went back to the cafe where I had been hitch-hiking and a soldier came up to ask me where I was going. He had hitch-hiked all the way from an Army camp in Alabama. We both got in with a farmers' tank truck driver who said he would take us all the way to Billings, Montana. Fortunately the truck had a bed over the seat where I snoozed the ninety-seven miles to Custer and the soldier slept there the rest of the way. . . .

Billings
July 25, 1944

. . . A Douglas DC transport, sleek as a fish, big enough for twenty-one passengers, has just roared up the runway and taken off into the rising sun. My plane will leave at 6:35 for a four-hour flight over the mountains, the Rockies, the Cascades, and past Mt. Rainier to Seattle.

. . . Aha! As I expected, priorities have arisen. I can have a seat only as far as Spokane. Well, that's O.K.

. . . Beyond Helena we hit heavy black clouds and soon we were flying into mist. The plane didn't lift over the clouds because of the 6,000 to 8,000 feet altitude regulations. After a while I actually dozed off, only to wake up mad at myself for spending my money sleeping. Slowly occasional patches of green appeared through holes in the clouds, and presently we were flying in bright sun over great fields of cotton, and I could follow the shadow of the plane skimming over the land. Before I knew it the flight was over. . . . A fat Northwest limousine took me into Spokane and I collected the refund for the flight from there to Seattle. The hitch-hiking was dismal. Every driver who gave me a lift was down on C.O.'s. Besides, the day was a scorcher and the eastern Washington desert was not what I expected after the propaganda about the scent of pine forests, snow-capped peaks, and babbling brooks.

In Umatilla I gulped down a quart of milk and waited about an hour for the driver of a two-trailer truck. When he came, he refused me. There were no more trucks so I went to the railroad station and lay down on a bench to wait for the 2:00 a.m. train. I woke up and was stumbling onto a train when the conductor told me, just in time, that it was going to Spokane, not Portland. Then I lay down again and slept, but I did get on the right train and I was in Portland at 7:35 a.m. . . .

I first saw the Pacific Ocean under a blanket of fog, while I was hitch-hiking toward Waldport in the afternoon. Most of the traffic on the coast road consisted of logging trucks, and three in succession gave me a ride. They were carrying amazing logs over six feet in diameter, and the drivers claimed I hadn't yet seen the big ones. I was told that the Pacific is too cold to swim in (58 degrees) and that when it is warm inland there is persistent fog. . . .

C.P.S. No. 56, Waldport, Oregon
July 26, 1944

Liefe Moesje, Dad, en Norm,

The Fine Arts already! Some of us in the Fine Arts dorm where I now have a bunk have been listening to Stravinsky's *Petrouchka* in anticipation of a reading of the action, to be held tomorrow evening. The Arts seem to be a very definite part of the life here, but in the question so often put to me already, "Are you a 'fine arts man'? " I sense a label like a Greek letter at Wesleyan. I am afraid the arts are something separate and unnatural and do not pervade the life of each camper. But in the surroundings there are definite indications of the school's presence. . . .

The style seems to be modern throughout. I saw the very snappy Frank Lloyd Wright music room, a big, solid, sweeping counter in light blue into which the record player and speaker were built. About it there was more of an atmosphere of permanence than I have encountered anywhere else in C.P.S. Over in the Fine Arts rooms I discovered William Everson and another F.A.M. printing a very neat booklet of Bill's poetry, *Waldport Poems*. This booklet and the poems themselves had a more lasting quality than I have seen. They were very excellent expressions of phases of a camp life where the bite of conscription or restriction is felt. So on the whole I am very pleased with what I have seen of the School of Fine Arts.

The camp itself appears superior to Big Flats and Trenton, notably in the latrines being part of the barracks and including flush toilets! There is a guest house with a cozy living-room supervised by gray-haired Mrs. Gregory. The auditorium has a stage just like the one Bob Emeott finished at Trenton. The co-op store is self-service, not having had the sad experience of the Big Flats co-op which was constantly being robbed of merchandise and cash. If supper was representative, the meals are good and I am already starting a fattening-up program. Despite all this, transfer fever is in the air. There were only about eight tables at supper since the rest of the fellows are in side-camps or sitting in fire towers. When I think of this camp as a whole, however, I see what an undramatic answer to my problem this is. After all my unrest, all my burning to be doing, I have come to this. Well, I can either escape in the fine arts or walk-out, but before I have gotten too entangled in the program here.

Some of the fellows I have met have been quite impressive. Everson is not the suave artist I had expected but a gawky, tousled-black-haired dreamer, lover of jazz, especially Pee Wee Russell, and married. Bob Scott is a pianist and has agreed to play some of the pieces Wilbur and I didn't get to. He looks very much like Dave Clark. Vladimir spends full time working for the Fine Arts school, mostly on printing. He used to work for the F.O.R. and spent his evenings listening to . . . Pee Wee, Eddie [Condon], and the boys down at Nick's [a popular hot jazz club in Greenwich Village]. Now he has the most abundant of beards in a place where beards are very abundant. There are some "characters" of course. . . .

I went to prayer meeting last night (it is now after lunch). It was revolting, prayers on your knees, corny hymns, and testimonies from individuals including one innocent who was *sure* God had saved him from getting killed in a dangerous situation with his truck that afternoon. . . .

. . . The *Petrouchka* performance is just over. It was delightful, but had neither the finish, the attendance, nor the coffee of our L'Académie sessions. As far as I can see, this camp, despite its Fine Arts title, is not so arty as Trenton except in its publications and poetry. Certainly there were more painters and musicians at Trenton than I have unearthed here. I am the only instrumentalist (not including piano). But I am not yet disappointed. . . .

The camp grounds with their barracks and paths were shielded from the Coast Road only by shrubs and shaggy growths of salal, a mat-forming evergreen creeper. Across the road was a little cluster of weather-beaten tourist cabins on a low cliff overlooking the long white beach and the ever-changing ocean. Extending northward toward the town of Waldport, the cliff was covered with dense low vegetation that created little tunnels and grottos, in one area surrounding a shallow lagoon.

The cabins nearest the road faced a huge mounted skeleton labeled, on a weathered board, "Tillie the Whale," the bleached remains of a corpse washed up on the beach long ago—an unintentional "found sculpture." Largest and coziest of the cabins was the "Jenny Wren," which had a fireplace as well as a flat-top wood-burning stove as in the other cabins. Because of gas rationing there were no tourists, and the cabins were rented at $16 to $35 a month to the *families and friends of the men in camp. They all faced the ocean with at least one large view window. Mostly two-room cabins, they were of raw bleached wood with peaked roofs, bare floors, and a few pieces of crude furniture. Artistic inhabitants eventually decorated some of them with colored burlap made by bleaching and dying potato sacks from the camp kitchen, and with driftwood and shells from the beach. One particularly ingenious dweller collected the feathers from chicken-plucking at the camp kitchen and made large pillows. There were iridescent mussel shells, and the prized green and turquoise Japanese floats, three- to twenty-four-inch globes, that washed up along the eight miles of beach. They had become detached from fishing nets and drifted all the way across the Pacific to sparkle and shine in cabin windows.*

Of some hundred and eighty men in the camp, ten or twenty at a time were assigned for a week or two to forestry work up in the mountains. They went out in camp trucks and lived in crude bunkhouses. During the spring and winter the project work for the other men was mainly tree planting, and in the summer, fighting forest fires. A few men were stationed in fire towers to report the blazes. A select crew remained in the base camp for maintenance, cooking, laundering, cleaning, and office work for the administration.

Adrian was assigned to sweeping the barracks. He was told that it was preferable to a forty-eight-hour work week planting trees in the rain. On his first day of pushing a broom down the aisles of bunk beds, a fellow sweeper introduced himself as Martin Ponch, the editor of The Compass, *the national magazine of C.P.S.*

July 30, 1944

I would have written you this morning if I hadn't had a hang-over from the five sips of scotch and 7-Up I took at a function of the Fine Arts group last night in a cabin with a fireplace, right on the beach. It was cozy to the point of congestion and smelled like the Goodyear but the talk was highly spiritual, Everson leading on the methods of writing or being creative, why we feel inspired or obsessed, and the relationship between the artist and the mystic. I took the point of view of the straight mechanist; he left room for the freedom of the will and God. The others, including Manche Langley, the camp's "U.S.O." girl, and Barbara James, Clayton's pretty wife, introduced objections, illustrations, and confusion. It broke up about two with Jim Harmon, getting slightly high, reading a criticism by an unschooled pulp writer who couldn't understand why Leonardo da Vinci's men didn't have balls. Everybody thought this was very funny. It was then time to go. As far as I can make out this is as close as the School of Fine Arts gets to school. The rest of it is individual creation and mutual stimulation. Occasionally they work together on publications and on the weekly play readings. . . . As for my own artistic achievement I have been jamming with Everson's records the past two days. He has 150 sides of the best hot jazz, and in lieu of a jazz pianist, or music to play with Bob Scott, I have chosen Satchmo, Bix, Muggsy, Red Allen, and Buck Johnson to stimulate me. I keep still when Johnny Dodds is blowing, and just listen. I like the fellows here pretty well. . . .

I went out on project yesterday with just two others. It was so dusty in the back of the transport the fellows wore bandannas like bandits. One who sat next to me talked very nicely and, I thought, liberally, so when he asked about Guetzgow's girl, since he had known him at Williston, I told all about their being as good as married and having the apartment together. I gave signs of approving of this. When he called it "cohabitation" I began to wonder. Suddenly I noticed the graying hair on his temples sticking from under the pulled-down C.C.C. cap. Oh, Christ, it was Bob Hyslop, the fundamentalist prayer meeting and Bible Study class leader on whom I had been trying to make at least a faint impression of saintliness. It might have been the Lone Ranger confronting me and pulling off his mask, after I had robbed the Nugget Gulch Bank. But having been honest once I had to be consistent, so when he asked what I thought about evangelical religion, since at the Worship Committee meeting the night before he had advocated bringing revivalist preachers into camp on Sundays, I told him straight. It was a good lesson for I felt much better for having been honest both times than if I had put up a false front.

We worked sloping off the ten-foot or over banks along one of the mountain roads to the fire tower back of camp. It was in sight of the thin lines of surf on the beach bounding the great green forest. We could hear the distant hiss of the breakers, but there was no incentive to go swimming for the heavy mist was overhead, and the sunless air was so cold when we stopped working that I had to put on a jacket. When we came back to camp at 5:00, however, the mist had broken for the first time and the dusty dirt campus was yellow and warm in the sun. . . . All the while I was working I was unfortunately thinking—how really ridiculous it was for me to be hacking at this earth when I could be doing so much elsewhere. The three months before jail could be so significant, I could really be productive and I would be saying something. And after all even prison would afford as much opportunity as this. . . .

We had a banquet last night for those who had birthdays in July (they didn't know about mine), followed by a three-man performance of *The Mikado in C.P.S.* [by Kermit Sheets], very clever parodies of Gilbert's words to Sullivan's music. . . .

Manche Langley, as a fervent pacifist, couldn't volunteer for U.S.O. activities, so she moved down from Portland, rented one of the cabins, and "mingled" with the C.O.'s. She became a sort of secretary to the Fine Arts group, enlivening activities with her enthusiasms and outrageous comments. She did all sorts of odd jobs and even learned to run the printing press. Adrian said she was the only one who could feed the press, slip sheet, and smoke a cigarette at the same time.

August 1, 1944

Already this is my last evening at Waldport—for two weeks. About twenty of us have been assigned to the side camp at Mary's Peak, the highest in the Coast Range, 4,097 feet. It will be two weeks of trail and road building and in case of a fire in the area, we will fight it. In anticipation, the Forest Service has supplied me with brand new caulked (spiked) $18 logging boots, beautiful pieces of craftsmanship. The unfortunate part of my assignment to Mary's Peak is that it was done without any consideration of the fact I transferred supposedly for the Fine Arts School, which functions at the base camp here. But along with that, it takes me away from my discovery of this afternoon—the ocean. We had the afternoon off to pack for tomorrow's journey. The bearded Dupre had been ribbing me so much about my not going to the beach, much less swimming, that I finally agreed to go with him. So after sleeping until 1:00 p.m. I dragged him out of the Untide Press room, borrowed a bathing suit, and walked across the highway to the strand. The beach here is clean white sand that blends into mist on both sides, and the surf, even on calm days like today, is as good as on that very best day after the storm at Prides. To my amazement I found the water no colder than York Beach and could have kept on being buffeted by those crashing and hissing waves much after Vladimir called me out to go to supper. Such exhilaration being catapulted on the foaming crests and then dropped behind in the swirling froth! I can still feel it as I write. I tingled all over when I came out, full of health and warmth. Could this be C.P.S.?

Vladimir Dupre was Executive Secretary of the Fine Arts and active with the Untide Press, which was founded in January 1943, by three Waldport men to issue a news sheet, The Untide, *a more informal and critical paper than the official camp organ,* The Tide. *The Press soon became dedicated to producing serious writing and art, but retained the name for some quixotic reason.*

Eventually, at Everson's instigation, a 14.5 x 22-inch Challenge Gordon platen press was acquired for $65 from the neighboring town, where it had originally been used to print the weekly newspaper, The Alsea Times. *For* *twenty years or so it had not been used and the rollers were flattened by the inkplate. Some Goudy Old Style type and new rollers were purchased. After the new rollers were installed the inking was still heavy, for the trucks had been worn down over the years. A letter to the Challenge Company asking the dimensions of the rollers brought the following reply: "We stopped building that press eighty years ago, so you doubtless know more about it than we do." However, new trucks were somehow found, and a number of books of poetry and periodicals,* The Compass, The Illiterati *(a magazine to deflate the "literati"), plays, and programs were produced during the remaining years of Camp Angel at Waldport.*

Mary's Peak
Philomath, Oregon
August 3, 1944

I am writing under a gas lamp because the generator doesn't work, but otherwise this miniature C.C.C. camp in the midst of typically Oregonian forested hills, is very nice, even flush toilets. Just now I have had a wonderful session with Steve Pith, a J.W. from Pittsburgh who plays accordion better than I play clarinet, and knows all the songs. We are already booked for a dinner concert when the base camp has its monthly banquet. But otherwise there are neither intellectuals nor artists here, unless they are keeping their lights under a bushel as much as I am. . . .

During the two weeks we are here we will, among other things, [clear the brush off] twenty miles of telephone wire land. . . . I had a fine lunching place today. Having taken off my boots and left them at the bottom like at a Dutch house because the fire tower doesn't like spikes, I toted my sandwiches up to the top. It was a gray day, completely overcast with mist hanging like moss into the valleys. A break in the velvety hills to the east revealed a broad plain stretching all the way to the foothills of the Cascades but the snow-capped peaks themselves were above the clouds. . . .

August 7, 1944

. . . Our treks along the fifteen miles of telephone line between Alsea and Philomath the past two days have revealed some real Oregon scenery and shown me just how we are located in this camp. We are a few hundred yards east of the pass through which the Corvallis-Waldport road goes over the Coast Range. The Coast and Geodetic Survey has put up a sign in the pass, "Summit Coast Range, El. 1331 ft." The road follows brooks down each side of the range to the rolling forested farm land, twisting and hairpin-turning over the heads of tributary brooks that roar through culverts. Over this tortuous asphalt ribbon the logging trailers grind all day long fairly grunting under two, three, or four fir logs two or three and a half feet thick, and occasionally one really big one four to seven feet in diameter, all thirty-two feet in length so that they will yield two batches of sixteen-foot boards.

When the trucks get over the summit they shift gears and start the joyful plunge into the valley. The brakes on the double back wheels of the trailer steam from the cooling water and leave two-inch tracks of wet on the black pavement. We wave to the drivers as they come lumbering up, and again as they come back, driving fast with the trailer wheels perched up on the back of the truck behind the cab and the beam sticking out over the windshield. The fellows say these trucks last only three months, they are driven so hard, but the drivers who own their trucks clear $40 a day, being paid percentages on the worth of the board feet they haul. It is a frightening industry, this ruthless plundering of the forests and noisy hauling of the fat logs, full of the power, wealth, and immensity of the Northwest.

Our telephone line which connects the Forest Service Ranger Stations in the area, follows the road in general but when it isn't straight enough, or when it twists over a valley, the lines go cross country. We usually walk along the side of the road in our spiked shoes, carrying axes, brush hooks, spurs, and tree saws, and sight down the line every once in a while to see if there are any Christmas trees, shrubs, or maples that threaten to touch the line within the next twenty years. If there are, we have to scramble down banks and into canyons through ferns six feet high, brambles, and veritable fishnets of underbrush. Often we can escape, however, by walking along the fallen rotting trunks of big firs, for most of the land has been logged off and many of the pieces have been too heavy or too far from the spar poles to be taken to the mills. One fellow with whom I hitch-hiked said he had been logging for awhile but when they would cut down fourteen-foot trees [in diameter] and then not use them because they were too heavy, he quit. . . .

It has been interesting to watch the development of, and also cleavage in, the group which came here from Waldport. We have quite a bit of group spirit in the dorm now. Our actions, especially mine, are becoming more spontaneous, less guarded. They are a tolerant bunch and make no complaints about my reading until past midnight under the gas lamp. But there is another dorm, and remarkably enough when we came, the fundamentalists gravitated to it, and we "liberals" moved in here. I hadn't thought about it until last night when everyone in the back of the truck coming home from Corvallis was from our dorm; the evangelists had stayed in town. At meal times it has been the same way. But now we have put the three tables in a row banquet-style and will watch the reaction. Resentment of any attempt at authority has been pronounced. Simply because Bob Hyslop got up and announced what Murray wanted done on project the next day, he is now talked of in the dorms as a usurper who must be squelched. C.O.'s are anarchists because they all want the chair but know they haven't got the stuff to be chairmen.

Going into Corvallis last night was just what I expected. There were three theaters and the best one was playing *The White Cliffs of Dover*, last show beginning around 9:30. We would walk around town until then, looking at the girls and shop windows, meeting on street corners, exchanging a few words, and parting quickly so as not to be conspicuous; we would have a milkshake maybe or a sundae; someone would get some beer; one fellow would phone a girl he once knew who had moved to Corvallis but he wouldn't find her number or she wouldn't be at home; we would watch the soldiers with their dates and want one so badly ourselves; we would pass the U.S.O. and hear the laughter inside; we would go to a beckoning sign that said Dance, catch a glimpse of a lifted trombone in the soft blue and red lights, and move on. Then someone would notice the time and we would go to the movies. All this happened. . . .

August 10, 1944

. . . Already we have finished the Forest Service projects for this side camp, not because the fellows worked hard but because all the telephone lines, trails, and parks we had to clean were already respectable. So tomorrow morning we roll for home after just a week and two days. Really it's been a week's vacation at a resort in the mountains, good eating, clear cool air, tremendous scenery . . . volley ball games each evening, and a pretty congenial, if un-stimulating, group of fellows. But I look forward to the Fine Arts group at Waldport and my discovery of the last day there, the ocean. . . .

Yesterday was the finest I have ever had on project. Carroll McMillen and I started out in the clear blue morning on the east side of the Coast Range in the "Corvallis Watershed, No Trespassing." Immediately we were in thick forest and before we had tramped half a mile we began to encounter big trees, mostly aged Douglas firs. For the rest of the day we were in a cathedral walking on the soft needled floor through arches a hundred or more feet high. . . . Whenever we would come to an especially beautiful grove we would stop and browse around looking up the strong straight trunks into the mossy branches, as if these firs were great leatherbound volumes in some ancient library. . . . I imagine some of the trees we saw were 150 to 200 feet tall and seven to eight feet in diameter. . . . It would have been "Heaven can wait, this is paradise," for you, Dad. . . . The only unfortunate part of the day was that

I smacked a hornet's nest and they all came swarming out, giving me four stings before I had run a mile up the trail, and Carroll three and when he thought they were all gone home and he went to do a plaschje two more in just the worst spot. . . .

I finished Lawrence's *Sons and Lovers* tonight so that it will always be a very definite part of my memory of Mary's Peak. I think it is a very great novel in which every sentence is vital, every incident shrewdly chosen for its symbolism, and the whole a beautiful study of character, love, and home relationships. If it gets passionate after page 300 it is the kind of sexuality Getz told me about, and Lauris said "becomes more beautiful and wonderful each time we make love" . . .; in it I see no sin, but a special means of communication for those who are in love. . . . I do say you must read it. It is so "close to home" you will find it amazingly provocative and enlightening. I want very much to capture the intensity with which Lawrence must have lived, even if it kills me. . . .

My tales of my hitch-hiking exploits and interviews with drivers about my position have met with such keen interest and hearty laughter . . . that I am beginning to write them up. I'm told that my stories have even been relayed to other campers. Written up this way they could make a report on my survey of public opinion of C.O.'s a very spicy affair. Keep yelling at me to finish it. Title: *Wilson's Gallop (across the U.S.) Poll.* . . .

Waldport

August 14, 1944

. . . I came into Elkton Saturday night from Reedsport by Greyhound—my first. It was dark and still in the hamlet, with the sudden meteors flicking by overhead. Dave wasn't there to meet me. But before the bus had departed for Drain and Portland a figure came walking out of the darkness down the road and I knew it was he. It was a mile walk to camp, finally up a very dark and wooded drive. . . . Even in the dark the campus impressed me for its boardwalks between shrubbery and evergreens. Elkton, Dave told me, is a very ideal C.P.S. camp. Everyone is almost too happy there. Our camp government just dissolved, but in Elkton things get done through actual working democracy. The next morning after breakfast we got literary, going over all of Dave's poetry for the past year, not a great volume, but evidence of hours of grinding, which is the way Dave writes. Everson and I had stayed up until 2:00 a.m. Friday night going over the poems Dave had sent in for the proposed C.P.S. anthology. . . . I was still devastating Dave's efforts when someone came in to announce that he had visitors. It was his old girlfriend Martha Hult and family. I had been waiting a long time to meet Martha.

I was rather disappointed—the kind of face you see in a crowd, nice enough, oh yes, but not striking—likewise the rest of the family. She had a certain nun-like quality, a serenity that Dave is very fond of. But I desire intensity, a girl burning with something. . . . The family is the nucleus of a forest cooperative . . . south of Elkton. They are trying to establish a real co-op community with twelve families. Right now they are only lumbering, running their own sawmill, but soon they hope to start agriculture, a school, and community center. I suppose this is very much what I envision. . . .

August 18, 1944
. . . Tuesday at supper Bob Hyslop . . . broke into the regular announcements to say the Ranger had called and wanted the sixteen-man crew for a fire between Mary's Peak and Philomath. This meant me. Now it is Thursday morning and I am completely relaxed. I slept until quarter of eleven and was awakened by Bub Freeman's "Muskrat Ramble," continued now by Bessie Smith shouting some positively filthy words, which you have to hear to complete your education, Crusher. As for the fire, I had fears it might be in the tremendous forest on the Corvallis watershed through which Carroll and I had walked spellbound. How would we cut down trees six feet in diameter in time to keep them all from bursting into flame? But when we came toward the end of our sixty-mile trip and saw the billowing black pile of smoke above the green it appeared rather small and close to the highway before the real forest began. When the truck had lurched to a stop in a pasture we all piled out full of anticipation and lined up haphazardly so that I was no. 16 and given a shovel. When we came to the actual fire it was mostly in the under-brush and fallen tree trunks; only one snag remained upright, bright flame spouting from its jagged top. The men already there—farmers and loggers— had been fighting the fire since 4:00 p.m. so the fire trail was mostly built and the conflagration under control, it being after sundown. All that remained for us was to build a little more trail and make sure the fire wasn't going underneath in roots and buried logs. In the smoky dimness ahead I could hear the "up, up"s of the fellows down the line, telling each other to move ahead with their hoes, axes, and Pulaskis (axe on one head, grub on the other). Along the way black faces, flickering with the flames, told of how the fire began. Somehow a house below the slope had caught on fire. . . .
    Perhaps I had told you that I have agreed to work up the music, a three-piece arrangement, of *My Heart's in the Highlands* for Saroyan's play to be read Saturday, for trumpet, oboe, and organ. I am taking the oboe part and Scott the organ. With the trumpet I have a problem, especially since it carries the melody in this arrangement. Elmer Oleson, the only good trumpet player,

wants to be very convinced of the worth of the play before he takes part in it. "I came to C.P.S. to do certain things and I don't want to get mixed up in any nonsense. I refused to read a part in a Shaw play (*Androcles and the Lion*) because it was ridiculous (it takes Christianity for a ride) and if this Saroyan play is anything like that and most plays nowadays, I don't want anything to do with it." Now I am almost certain he will think *My Heart's in the Highlands* nonsense, which half the New York critics thought too. But I believe this was because of their limitations as it will be because of Elmer's. Personally I think it is a swell play because it pictures so well the frustrated yearning of men in life. . . . I wonder now if I can make the music meaningful enough to cause him to overlook the inanity of the play.

Your letter was again a joy, Norm. When Getz asked how it was I became a C.O. and you not, I said one reason was that you were so well adjusted to American life. Strange you can be so healthy in such a sick place. . . .

August 20, 1944

. . . Now I don't want to be a *college professor* anymore, nor a *minister*. But all the signs point to my being a teacher and creative artist and my heritage turns everything I see and do toward these ends.

After this *Apologia Pro Vita Mea* I want to tell you of my explorations in one area—sex. With Lawrence's *Sons and Lovers*, of which I hope you are in the midst, under my cerebellum, Everson has introduced me to a new school of literature about which even Hoffman hasn't heard, I think. There was a book lying on his bed called *The Journal of Albion Moonlight* by Kenneth Patchen, the big letters of which lured me to look therein. It was fascinating, apparently a further exploration of the world Joyce opened. At first an account of some fantastic journey, it now appears to be a record of all the nightmares and wet-dreams of Mr. Moonlight. I suspect it is really a surrealist interpretation of the relationships of Patchen and certain friends in New York City. It is grotesque, hideous, sickening, full of murder, hate, and the most vulgar sex, the kind you find on a latrine wall. Patchen has written to the Untide Press here about getting a forty-page book published—quite an honor for the press. Dupre said I would have to learn to set type for this, but I said I wouldn't be very interested in setting type if the book were going to be anything as ugly as the *Journal*. Here Everson came to the defense. Lawrence tries to make of sex something beautiful, to deny the ugliness that has caused it to be called sin and go on behind drawn shades for so many years. But Patchen and, before him, Henry Miller have gone deeper, have admitted the vulgarity of sex, and said, "Tough, boys, but this is the way it is and we are going to tell you about it." I think this is the realistic position, the reason why nice people like you who knew don't like to talk about it. . . . Patchen incidentally is a pacifist and makes very violent statements against war every few pages. Much of his writing I think is a reaction to the horror of our time. His literary technique is the only beautiful thing in the book. . . .

I have been going swimming every day of late since I manage my clean-up job with Ponch, the *Compass* editor, to get off at 4:00 p.m. Usually I go to the Untide Press room to get Dupre with whom I have been having the unique experience of discovering his chin structure since he shaved off his abundant whiskers. The days have been sunny and the breakers tremendous. Yesterday they came so fast and furious it was impossible to get set for the big ones, which are wonderful riding if you catch them just as they break. The smaller interference would come and take our legs out from under us. Sometimes, though, we manage to get under them a little before they break so that when they do peel over they fall with a brutal crash on our heads and almost knock us groggy. It is sheer ecstasy when we get them just right and are hurtled along high on the churning roller with the skirt of the last comber four feet below. Arms and legs thrash as if we had never learned to swim and we feel as utterly helpless as if we were going over Niagara in a barrel. All our cares and misgivings are washed away. When we come out and let the wind sing around us and the sand blow fine around our legs we feel like the cleanest, purest beings that ever walked the earth. . . .

August 27, 1944

"I am sitting on pines and needles as I write to you (1) because this is such a beautiful foggy Sunday morning (2) because I have to toodle A. Rubenstein's 'Romance' on my Looney Clair, or as the unschooled around here think, my 'Strange Flute' for mourning worship. I tried to reconstruct from fond memory Bach's Ayer for a G String being unable to find one in camp, but it was no go. My accompianist is David Jackson who worked for the Hedgerow Pa. Theatre before Seductive Service. This is my second public appearance, though the last time, when I played trumpet, oboe, and bass drum (my foot) parts in a partial arrangement of *My Heart's in the Highlands* to liven up a reading of the Saroyan play, Martin Ponch put a screen around Scott and me. But perhaps Martin had a Paunch there."

This is the kind of paragraph Wilbur Held's letters inspire and I include it to convince you I have not gone mystical again. Count 'em boys. Faster than slugs from a machine gun and about as funny. Don't you think I should write scripts or nondescripts for Hop Bope? . . .

Yesterday [Everson] was turning cartwheels and waving a stool over his head in the Untide room because the New Directions Press of Norfolk, Conn.,

had decided to print the *Waldport Poems* in their yearly anthology of
American poets. . . .

August 31, 1944

A stubby, friendly-eyed fellow by the name of Roberts with a brown beard
that makes him look like one of the seven dwarfs has transferred from Cascade
Locks and moved in opposite me. He is doing a lot of talking about walking
out when the fire season ends October 15 and he can get his furlough. "I'm
just selfish enough to want a furlough," he shouts around the place. To me
who has groped through this whole period, his ratiocinations and threats are
very interesting. He is much more pragmatic about it than I. He figures he'll
get a free train ride from Los Angeles to prison and knows that the fellows
at McNeil Island Penitentiary in Puget Sound sprawl on the grass Sunday
afternoons listening to the symphony. He isn't going to do anything revolutionary, bear any cross, do anything to impress the government that he
deserves freedom in the months before the F.B.I. picks him up. Just going
to prison is enough of a testimony against conscription. I find myself now in
the position of wanting to talk him out of departing. . . . But watching Roberts
in camp and on project, where he picks himself a shady spot first thing in the
morning and moves with the shadow the rest of the day, I think he *is* the
man to walk out. Has he given C.P.S. a fair chance? If he were in Minneapolis
wouldn't he forget all about being conscripted? And how about me? . . .

So sure have the foremen been of fire these past two days, I have been
afraid to leave the camp to go swimming. We are expected to be off five minutes after the siren screams. But no calls from the Ranger have come in and
the fire we passed on the way back from the Peak apparently didn't spread.

Glen Evans brought his wife back from Minneapolis Saturday and also the
little pickininny. The two read in tonight's rehearsal of the reading of *High
Tor* for Saturday, she very beautifully because she is a teacher of speech in a
college, while the pudgy chocolate bonbon sprawled on the seat sound asleep.
There is something tragic in this being their family life when it perhaps should
mean most. . . .

Intellectual wit from Cascade Locks, where they are eating peaches like
mad, as we are here: Coffield, quoting, " 'There is nothing more meticulous
than a nun eating a peach.' Can you think of anything more meticulous than
that?" Searles, "A J.W. eating a nun."

September 1, 1944

. . . In my wanderings dragging a broom around the dorms I have discovered
. . . a table spread with gleaming myrtle-wood bowls, platters, and salt

shakers made by one Schliep, whom I have usually seen in that state. But he must work nights for almost everytime I come, there is a shiny new dish. I could stand learning this craft, especially tonight since Wilbur is getting married so soon, and being conventional, deserves a present. . . .

. . . Not only because it touches more people than the sharecropping system in the South is conscription a "social wrong that demands [our] interest and influence," it is far more devastating in its destruction of family life, artistic and religious values, and sanity. This is what I was saying at the lab when I talked of walking out but the boys in their complacency or "smug somnolescence" could no longer see that they were conscripted. . . . And the problem won't be solved one of these days. It gets worse. Even now you, Norm, are being drawn into it without knowing where you are going. . . .

I have been thinking and talking today in my mopping with Marty Ponch, along the lines of breaking down sexual barriers. Is the first step making use of freedom of speech? Kermit Sheets, temporary dietician and chief drama man, was telling at lunch today in the presence of Mrs. James and Mrs. Jadiker, young campers' wives, and Manche Langley, who is staying on as "assistant to the executive secretary of the Fine Arts, Vladimir Dupre," if the fundamentalists get nosey, about a letter from Harry Prochaska at Cascade Locks. . . . "Manche writes that Scott (our highly intellectual and witty pianist) just lays her in the aisles. Is it really as simple as all that?" Everyone roared without the slightest embarrassment—especially at the notion of Scott being the aggressor. Since then Kermit has made it into a very clever cartoon, artistically, of course—a young mother in a hospital bed with her baby in her arms, saying to another woman visitor, "I saw him at the Playhouse last winter. He simply laid me in the aisle." . . .

Myrtle-wood trees are native to Oregon and the wood has especially beautiful grains. Several of the campers became skillful in turning it on the lathe and produced fine platters and bowls. There were, in camp, in addition to the lathe, weaving looms, a potter's wheel and a kiln, and the printing press, all of which were in fairly continuous use in off-project hours. Occasionally the dining room would be the place of an exhibition of arts and crafts made by the campers, including varieties of murderous knives meticulously produced by the Jehovah's Witnesses, who, far from believing in non-violence, were ardent hunting-fishing-shooting men. Their church's position was that since this war was not Armageddon, its members should take no part in it.

The J.W.'s, as they were called, spent much of their free time playing poker in the back of the dormitory and were much more tolerant of the free-thinking Fine Arts men than the "Holy Joes," or fundamentalists, were. During one of the jolly parties in the Jenny Wren cabin, a Holy Joe was found kneeling outside the window praying for the damned souls of the revelers.

September 7, 1944

. . . The idea of jail seems remote, almost as inconceivable as it always has to you. But perhaps this is decadence. I think that whatever misunderstanding there is comes from your unacquaintance with (1) the idea of God (2) my personal idea that his will is revealed in the creative imagination which throws up all sorts of wild schemes which must be materialized 100% (3a) the possibility that the kind of life led by Christ, Socrates, Bill Simpson and other worthies is closer to truth than any other (b) that the martyr besides coming closer to his God performs an invaluable service to humanity far beyond reproduction, great art, industrial progress, etc., (c) that going to jail is a far stronger testimony against conscription and war than C.P.S. (d) that these may be my calling (4) the fact that this life of the labor camp or anything else under Selective Service is less than damnable and to be resisted to the point of death. If Bill's poems did not tell you this last the letter I am enclosing which he wrote to Henry Miller's comment that we "ought to like it in C.P.S. since we are protected" will say it straight. But of course Bill deals with the outward aspects more than the principle, though you can't get away from these either. As for the life of non-compromise being my function it probably isn't. If I were going to walk out I would have done it by now. Of course I still miss an all-consuming purpose to my life. Even as I sit here I wonder. On the fire sweating my guts out I wondered. Eating meals I wonder. Listening to music, going to meetings, everything I do I wonder. Why and whither? I don't care a damn about the Oregon forest or the capitalists who pillage it. All this grub is energy for just the routine. If I could eat this piece of bread to give me strength to write one last poem, love one person a minute more, reveal a truth I would feel I deserved it. But now the food goes into pushing a broom, walking to more meals, sitting through more eatings, and the usual excrement. I am mad at life because it doesn't let me live every moment as if it were my last on earth and I knew it was. What would I be doing in that moment? Certainly not what I am doing now. Or if I would life is just what Shakespeare said it was and I am completely disappointed. You see, I am so much of an idealist, a Nietzsche, I see the possibilities of life from the scattered moments of elation I have had and curse my fate that it isn't all that way. It will be a long time before I can say with the old mother after losing the last of her six sons in *Riders to the Sea*, ". . . and we must be satisfied."

. . . The fire call came in Tuesday afternoon. It was on a forty-five-degree slope, many places steeper, forty miles up the road to Mary's Peak and Corvallis. Loggers had already built a fire trail around the triangle of fifteen burning acres when we came. Fortunately the fire stayed around the ground and didn't crown in the tall firs. We tried to pump water up the hill but the hoses couldn't stand more than enough pressure (150 pounds) to take it only a third of the way up. Everybody was yelling, "Rock, rock!" when I first clambered up the slope dragging hose. I didn't know what they meant until a big boulder clipped me on the hip and knocked me flat whereafter I was more careful. At sundown we left four fellows watching the fire lines and went to sleep in our bags in an orchard. But at 2:00 a.m. shouts came with the roars of falling snags that the fire had broken over the line and was whipping up the hill. It was a terrific climb in the moonlight into an inferno. Practically by sliding down the hill we built another trail, fifty yards over from the old one, and spent the rest of the night watching, and dodging rolling rock. Then breakfast, and digging out the smoke until noon when the eight-man crew from camp came to mop up. They are still gone. The high temperatures you remarked had a lot to do with this fire. But here on the foggy coast it hasn't gone over eighty all summer. More later.

September 13, 1944

If you missed the letters every other day the past week I can give the honest excuse of being too busy. But it has meant my feeling a part of the group at last, which prompted me to say while snacking in the kitchen this evening, "I think Manche fits into *our* group better than any girl I can imagine." Bill immediately said, "I am glad you used that phrase." I now feel well adjusted, happy in everything but the work project, from which I have escaped pretty well, and am never seriously shadowed by the idea of walking out.

Dave Jackson has enlisted my help in the staging of *Aria da Capo* by Edna St. Vincent Millay to be put on next Saturday night. I have to make a curtain puller. My agreement to do the chapel arrangements has challenged my imagination and keeps me busy all day Sunday transforming the lifeless, regimented building into a real place of worship. It astounds me that the churches in undertaking this program and later the fellows ever allowed themselves to live in this miserable architecture. I should think that world reformers like us would have immediately transformed a camp like this into a place of beauty, really liveable and a joy to come back from work to. . . . The Fine Arts group here is thinking vaguely of sticking together after the war. What a community center I visualize perched on the Spaulding cliff. We would earn money from the press and more from crafts—myrtle-wood, etc.

SPECIAL FORM FOR CONSCIENTIOUS OBJECTOR

Order No. __11856__

Local Board No. 10 Essex County	13 009
NOV 27 1942	010
Ho. (STAMP OF LOCAL BOARD) Beverly, Mass.	

Name ____ UBELE _____ ADRIAN _____ WILSON ____
　　　　　　　(First)　　　　　　　　(Middle)　　　　　　　(Last)

Address ____ 646 Hale Street _____
　　　　　　　　(Number and street or R. F. D. route)

____ Beverly _____ Essex _____ Mass. ____
　(City, town, or village)　　　　(County)　　　　(State)

This form must be returned on or before ____ December 4, 1942 ____
　　　　　　　　　　　　　　　　　　　　(Five days after date of mailing or issue)

INSTRUCTIONS

A registrant who claims to be a conscientious objector shall offer information in substantiation of his claim on this special form, which when filed shall become a part of his Questionnaire.

The questions in Series II through V in this form are intended to obtain evidence of the genuineness of the claim made in Series I, and the answers given by the registrant shall be for the information only of the officials duly authorized under the regulations to examine them.

In the case of any registrant who claims to be a conscientious objector, the Local Board shall proceed in the ordinary course to classify him upon all other grounds of deferment, and shall consider and pass upon his claim as a conscientious objector only if, but for such claim, he would have been placed in Class I. The procedure for appeal from a decision of the Local Board on a claim for conscientious objection is provided for in the Selective Service Regulations.

Failure by the registrant to file this special form on or before the date indicated above may be regarded as a waiver by the registrant of his claim as a conscientious objector: *Provided, however,* That the Local Board, in its discretion, and for good cause shown by the registrant, may grant a reasonable extension of time for filing this special form.

Series I.—CLAIM FOR EXEMPTION

INSTRUCTIONS.—The registrant must sign his name to either Statement A or Statement B in this series but not to both of them. The registrant should strike out the statement in this series which he does not sign.

A. I claim the exemption provided by the Selective Training and Service Act of 1940 for conscientious objectors, because I am conscientiously opposed by reason of my religious training and belief to participation in combatant military service or training therefor; but I am willing to participate in noncombatant service or training therefor under the direction of military authorities.

　　　　　　　　　　_____
　　　　　　　　　　　　　(Signature of registrant)

B. I claim the exemption provided by the Selective Training and Service Act of 1940 for conscientious objectors, because I am conscientiously opposed by reason of my religious training and belief to participation in war in any form and to participation in any service which is under the direction of military authorities.

　　　　　　　　__U. Adrian Wilson__
　　　　　　　　　　(Signature of registrant)

Series II.—RELIGIOUS TRAINING AND BELIEFS

INSTRUCTIONS.—Every question in this series must be fully answered. If more space is necessary, attach extra sheets of paper to this page.

1. Describe the nature of your belief which is the basis of your claim made in Series I above.

I believe the purpose of life is growth in body mind and spirit toward Christlike personality. I believe this purpose is best fulfilled by a life which has as its ideals the Ten Commandments and the Sermon on the mount. I believe Christ's teachings mean unwavering pacifism. I believe that there is something of God in each man and that this something can be developed best through the power of love. War or anything which contributes to war denies this credo.

2. Explain how, when, and from whom or from what source you received the training and acquired the belief which is the basis of your claim made in Series I above.

D. S. S. Form 47　　　　　　　　　　　　　　　　　　　　　　16—18144

Adrian's copy of his Selective Service application for C.O. status.

from the looks; perhaps in the visual arts exists our greatest need, and some of our strongest hopes.

But the most important, in a sense, of the "facilities" at Waldport is the Pacific Ocean, a scant two hundred yards from the camp proper, with its superb beach, its ever-changing expanse, and a near-by shoreline of cliffs, rocks, and headlands rivaling anything on the Western Coast.

organization

The organization of the School is still nebulous and tentative. The present Committee is to operate only until the enrollment is sufficiently established to permit a general indication of preference. A School Director, though not necessary, could be of considerable advantage. We are casting about for some man, preferably himself an artist, reputable in his field, who would serve in this capacity.

an aside

Entering men should know that participation in the School does not entitle them to any special considerations not enjoyed by the camp as a whole. Camp government at Waldport is liberal and democratic, with the emphasis in all spheres upon avoiding individual privileges. We feel that the Arts

Program can fit naturally into such a pattern and will act as a stimulant to the camp program, synthesizing its present aesthetic activity, and generally enriching community life. We agree that a School which seeks to divorce itself from the camp, to become too introspective and cliquish, would be regrettable, and would likely prove a failure.

concerning camp

The project at Waldport has been primarily the reforestation, by hoe-planting, of the Blodgett Tract, a waste-land of some 9,000 acres, stripped of its forest by logging operations during the last war and burned by subsequent fires. It is, we feel, of more significance than much of the work offered to CPS men. This project, however, will be completed by March, and it is not definitely known what work will then be offered, but it seems likely that road construction and fire-suppression will figure largely in the program. There has been, so far, no problem in regard to conscience and project work. The Emergency Farm Work provision has not proved an issue due to our removal from concentrated agricultural areas.

As to the general situation, it is only fair to state that the two great disadvantages of Waldport, both as a camp and as a location for a special interest group, are the weather and the remoteness from any cosmopolitan center. The rainfall here is quite heavy, averaging about sixty inches a year, most of which is occasioned in the winter, the summers being cool and quite tolerable. Project work is conducted in the rain,

Excerpt from pamphlet describing the Fine Arts School, written by Bill Everson in February 1944 and mailed to all the C.P.S. units, including

Waldport 1945. Left to right: Adrian Wilson, Clayton James,
Vladimir Dupre, and Bill Everson.

Cover of *The Compass*, the national magazine of C.P.S., Summer and Fall 1944.

Cover of *The Illiterati*, Number 3, Summer 1944, designed by
Kemper Nomland.

WILLIAM EVERSON

Cover of *War Elegies* (November 1944), a collection of poems by
Bill Everson, originally "issued by mimeograph in 1943 as the initial
publication of the Untide Press" (from the colophon).

Adrian and Joyce in front of one of the Tillie-the-Whale cabins on the Coast Road at Waldport.

Title-page spread of *An Astonished Eye Looks Out of the Air*, poems by Kenneth Patchen, designed by Kemper Nomland "from a suggestion of the author" (from the colophon) and published by the Untide Press in 1945.

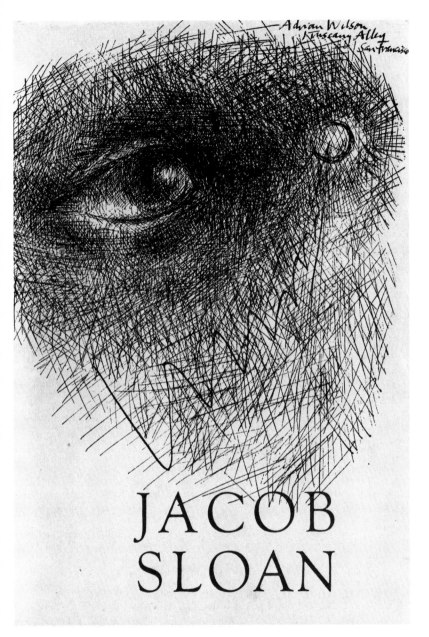

Cover of *Generation of Journey*, a collection of poems by C.O. Jacob Sloan, illustrated by Barbara James and published by the Untide Press in 1945.

THE WALDPORT POEMS

WILLIAM EVERSON

Cover of *The Waldport Poems* by Bill Everson, "the second printed publication of The Untide Press" (from the colophon).

1944

W

ALDPORT POEMS

William Everson

UNTIDE PRESS · WALDPORT, OREGON ILLUSTRATED BY CLAYTON JAMES

Title-page spread of *Waldport Poems*, designed and printed by members of the Fine Arts School.

Vladimir Dupre, Bill Eshelman, and Bill Everson (left to right) at Waldport, 1943. (Photo courtesy of Vladimir Dupre.)

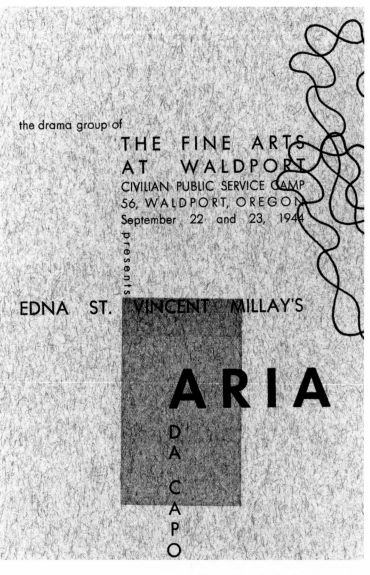

the drama group of

THE FINE ARTS
AT WALDPORT
CIVILIAN PUBLIC SERVICE CAMP
56, WALDPORT, OREGON
September 22 and 23, 1944

presents

EDNA ST. VINCENT MILLAY'S

ARIA
DA
CAPO

Cover of *Aria da Capo* program.

Cover of program for *Ghosts*, designed by Adrian Wilson.

Kermit Sheets, Vladimir Dupre, and Manche Langley (left to right) in
Aria da Capo at Waldport. (Photo courtesy of Kermit Sheets.)

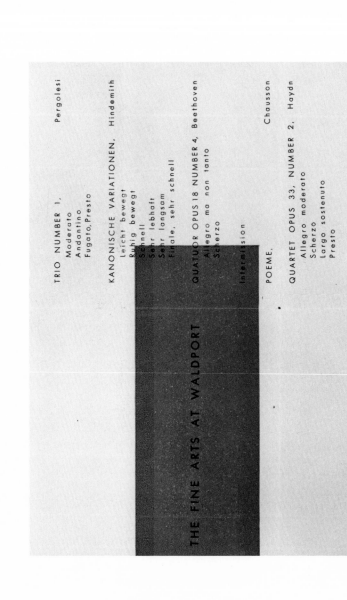

TRIO NUMBER 1,   Pergolesi
    Moderato
    Andantino
    Fugato, Presto

KANONISCHE VARIATIONEN,   Hindemith
    Leicht bewegt
    Ruhig bewegt
    Schnell
    Sehr lebhaft
    Sehr langsam
    Finale, sehr schnell

QUATUOR OPUS 18 NUMBER 4, Beethoven
    Allegro ma non tanto
    Scherzo

    Intermission

POEME,   Chausson

QUARTET OPUS 33, NUMBER 2, Haydn
    Allegro moderato
    Scherzo
    Largo sostenuto
    Presto

THE FINE ARTS AT WALDPORT

Inside page spread of concert program, designed and printed by
Kemper Nomland and Adrian Wilson, March 1945.

JUSTICE

TENNESSEE

presented by
THE FINE ARTS
AT WALDPORT
in cooperation with
other members of
C.P.S. Camp No. 56

January 26, 1945
February 3, 1945
Waldport, Oregon

February 10, 1945
Elkton, Oregon

dramatized and directed by MARTIN PONCH

Cover of program for *Tennessee Justice*, designed and printed by
Bill Everson and Adrian Wilson.

Tom Polk Miller, Hildegard Erle, and Kermit Sheets (left to right) in
The Sea Gull at Cascade Locks. (Photo courtesy of Kermit Sheets.)

But maybe I wouldn't like to live with some of these guys more than I do. Of course the community is fantastic. We all want individual and family life after this experience. We've seen too many people.

When I haven't been working on other people's projects I have been continuing the writing-up of my Oregon trail—eight pages last night on my overnight in Wisconsin. In the offing are two other projects—the anthology of C.P.S. poets to be compiled and published here, on which I expect to do editorial work, and the *Compass*, the C.P.S. magazine, on which Ponch has been having great trouble getting help from our over-worked Fine Arts boys. The Patchen poems—thirty-four of them that will take at least fifty pages— arrived. To me and Bill they were a great disappointment and Bill wanted to send them back even if Patchen did have a fit, but the rest of the Press wants to publish, perhaps for the name. Personally, I think Art, Bob Beloof, and Bill are writing things more worthy of publication. . . .

Of the movements of the Allies I am unaware. It's insane; the arts, the forest, and the ocean here are a direct antithesis. . . . Fred Millett wrote a fine letter ordering ten copies of Bill's poems to distribute and praising them highly. . . .

September 17, 1944

Making the rounds of the slumbering dorms and building fires in the dark last night, as nightwatchman, was a new experience. For the first time in months I was alone, free from premeditating every action for its effect on people. And off and on during the night the rain pattered on the tarpaper roofs tapping out in a code I thought I understood, the end of the fire season. . . .

Roberts left for Cascade Locks yesterday morning. . . . In exchange, this afternoon we got the famous Glen Coffield who wrote the Untide Press's first printed publication of poems—the surrealist *Horned Moon*. For our weekly reading of creative writing tonight . . . Bill read four fine poems by an English anarchist, George Woodcock, and the best of one of three books the prolific Coffield finished in two weeks. I was positively amazed at Coffield's genius. His rhyming particularly is miraculous. He is the first poet I have met who writes systematically. . . . It is strange that for this character C.P.S. has meant a great flowering. I kick myself for not doing likewise.

Monday—Again a rejuvenating letter from you, Crusher. I am glad you met the 4-F soldier, though it is too bad it takes evidence to show you what war is about, lacking the imagination and insight to realize it now. If you are finally sucked into the preposterous mess I hope you will have the guts to say, "no" when you meet the slightest command that goes against the grain.

As you conceive of the armed forces now it is a natural step after Andover, a new experience, an educational opportunity. The idea of killing is not in it. When I hear you say again and again that you hope you won't get into the Marines, I see you shudder for you know that would shatter your dream. And unless you are very lucky any branch of the services will not be what you want. Already you know that. Inwardly you know that the act of killing a man, in which you participate no matter where you are in the Army team, will never settle anything. It is very easy to forget that this is what you are doing when you are studying in v-5 at Wesleyan or cavorting in an airplane. The old argument that is always being thrown at C.O.'s about letting them come over here and rape your grandmother is difficult for you to surmount. O.K. Don't bother with it. Only realize the business of war is rotten. You are not a killer. When they put a bayonet in your hands at Parris Island let it sink in that this isn't football practice anymore. Stand their taunts and long months in the guardhouse. You won't be the only one. This war and all war stinks to high heaven and I don't want a big clean loving guy like you in it. . . .

There are two records I would like you to buy when you get in the big cities. I want them more for their social implications than for their jazz. One is Billie Holiday singing "Strange Fruit" from which the novel is titled, on a Commodore label. The other is Wingy Manone shouting on a Bluebird [disk], "Stop that War (Those Cats are Killin' Each Other)," though it is probably contraband now. Another record you should hear is Lil Johnson, whom I remember you quoting in an Andover letter, singing a tune labeled so as not to offend, "Get 'Em from the Peanut Man." Only don't make the mistake of calling it by its real name, asking the clerk if he has "Hot Nuts" and then blushing and walking out before he can answer as our Jadiker did. . . .

I was running between buildings again tonight which means I was working and happy. I was pasting up Kemper Nomland's snappy layout for *The Compass* from which the printing plates will be photographed [and then printed in Portland]. It is really a splendid issue of a very high-class magazine—plenty of illustrations and solid writing. I'll send a copy. . . .

Nomland was a Los Angeles architect who did much of the typographical design for the Fine Arts publications in a Bauhaus style, and he was co-editor with Kermit Sheets of The Illiterati, *an avant-garde literary magazine issued from the camp. He was tall and slender with a fair complexion and very curly pale blond hair. In camp he was jokingly referred to as "the Albino Zulu." Kemper's resistance to conscription consisted of a "slow down," that is, he reported for project each workday but he worked so slowly that eventually the foreman refused to take him on the truck to the project site. In one case the foreman noticed that a "slow-downer" was digging in the same spot for several hours. His question was answered with the mild statement, "Well, I've been digging here all day."*

The foreman protested, "But you haven't gotten anything done!"

"Well, ya' know, I'm not a very good digger. I can't use a shovel very well—nobody's ever showed me how to use one." And soon there was the foreman showing him how to dig.

Jerry Rubin was known to be a radical and a rebel so he was assigned to do lettering in the sign-shop located far from the other buildings so that his attitude would not infect others. It took him all the first day to inscribe one letter. The second day he produced a second, and so forth, and despite his isolation he had visitors all day long.

September 24, 1944

Just as I was putting a last touch on my draw curtains and David Jackson was giving directions for a quick brush-up on technical matters before curtain time [for *Aria da Capo*] an hour hence, the fire siren sounded. Jackson suddenly was deprived of his light man, Francis Barr, and his record player, me. . . . The red sun playing on wisps of clouds sank fast into the Pacific as our open fire transport rumbled along the finest part of the Coast Road between Yachats and Florence. From cliffs that make the Spaulding terrace seem puny we could see the sea lions bobbing in the breakers that coast into the beaches like long lines of skaters hand in hand. All along this road the dim capes jut into the ocean. As many as ten were visible, each grayer, to Heceta Head with its detached pyramid of rock collared by a lace of foam and chunky lighthouse blinking. When we got to Mapleton the District Ranger told Ed Bowen, foreman, that all was under control, only a hundred burning snags were to be felled in the morning. So we slept scattered all over the side camp in Mapleton. In the early morning the jagged snags looming over fog were a ghostly sight. . . .

The first snag I felled by hand with cellist Downs and Francis Barr was a whopper and wouldn't go the way we wanted it. Warren thought it leaned uphill so that was the way we would fell it. Actually it was an optical illusion. The gray hulk finally went crashing like thunder downhill. On the first count of its growth rings which, incidentally, varied considerably in thickness, I got 467, on the next 454. If I had wanted to count some more I could have arrived at a figure that would have placed its birth in 1492. God, what dynamic things have happened on this continent while the tree I sawed down yesterday morning was quietly growing. . . . This morning we finished mopping up with hose and marine pump sucking from the Siuslaw River in the valley. Forestry pays for eats on fires so we had steak last night and again this noon, eggs, butter, and all varieties of fruit. And we have all day tomorrow to recuperate.

The Beethoven trio which came from the Cundy Bettoney Co. in Boston has been already slated for performance October 21. I always thought the masters might be more melodic and formal than moderns but not half so inventive. Here playing him I find Beethoven with more brilliant ideas in one page than Milhaud and others I have played in a whole score. It's possible we will make a record of this work on Eshelman's recorder, so you may hear us. . . .

The lab [in Minneapolis] has issued a new memo—ten men for a continuation of the thiamine experiment to begin Nov. 1, ending July 15, 1945. It interests me more than the forty-five-man unit beginning the 15th of Nov. I can see you shaking your heads, but you have no conception of the futility of the project here (outside of fire fighting which ends about now). Even doing it for GOD isn't any use anymore. . . .

September 27, 1944

. . . The two violinists, Broadus (Bus) Erle and Bob Harvey have arrived from Big Flats. Any musical reasons for my going back to Minneapolis are eliminated. They are terrific, especially Erle, a radio studio orchestra player who last night played trios by Beethoven and Mozart perfectly at sight. We are all so enthused about their performance we wonder what we have done to be so blessed. We should have some really good chamber music here before the winter is over.

October 3, 1944

. . . Saturday night I am going twenty-five miles down the Coast Road to the town of Florence to join up with a three-piece jam band that plays in the local dance hall, at $10 per man, per night. . . . Our main problem is transportation as we discovered last Saturday when we tried to hitch-hike down. The only driver who stopped in two hours asked us if we came from "in there," indicating the camp, and when we said "Yes," told us to get out. So we went back home. Next Saturday we'll take the 4:45 bus which will get us there three hours too early. The next bus back to camp is at 9:45 a.m. Sunday. Of course, the money is the least of the reasons I'm going down. I want to see "the outside" again, meet some women, buck public opinion and change it, and probably most of all, have some jam sessions. . . .

Tonight Downs, Scott, and I practice again on Beethoven. Harvey and Erle will take over after that. These two have been practicing so much this place is beginning to sound like the Juilliard School. Both fit into the Art School beautifully, Harvey especially. We had a little shindig over at the cabin Saturday night with bald George Reeves, one of the social action boys, who was just released from the government "concentration" camp at Lapine. But Harvey stole the show with his dissertation on "I hate chickens" made up of observations from his experiment in subsistence farming. It was the funniest discourse I have ever heard and kept the cabin rocking for over an hour. Harvey suddenly is one of the most popular guys in the group. Erle is a self-contained, black-curly-haired chain smoker, the product of cities, a tremendous violinist. Every day, especially with my work on *Compass*, I feel more a part of this dynamic group until I am beginning to think that *this* is perhaps the community I envision and wanted to set up. What a stroke of luck! What a transformation!

October 15, 1944

Having been bounced out of the groove of writing to you two or three times a week by the responsibilities of *Compass* and preparation for next week's concert when Warren [Downs], Bob [Scott], and I play the Beethoven trio, I don't feel much like writing tonight. But I will tell you what has happened here to assure you that I at least am alive. You see, George Watkins was killed by a tree he felled on project Thursday afternoon. The ramifications of this incident are so extensive it would take twenty poems to get them across. But I'll never write the poems. Bill Everson, however, has written ten poems about his wife's making him a cuckold. His ideas on love and human nature have been shaken and rearranged as much as mine on life and death. Am I going to go out in the woods and cut the tree in half that struck down George who was my friend? No, and besides the tree is already dead. Is Bill going to murder the guy who is laying his wife every night while he is tossing in his bed in a camp he cannot leave? No, the guy happens to be his best friend. . . .

This violinist Bob Harvey of the chicken story suddenly has established contact with me on a number of grounds. First of all, I discovered he is a cum laude from P.A. [Phillips Andover Academy] about ten years ago. But he hates Andover as much as he does chickens. He was the only one of three guys in his class who didn't get one frat bid in four years. The other two were townies. Why? Because he was good in studies, because he didn't like sports though he looks like a full-back, and he had a caustic wit. . . . He didn't like Dartmouth and got kicked out, whereupon he found he could learn things out of college four times as fast because he needed them. . . . Sunday morning breakfast we talked almost until dinner. When I told him Middletown was home he said he used to go up there a lot to see a guy by the name of Paul

Reynolds. "Christ, my best friend!" I shook his hand. Well, it appears he was married in Middletown and Paul and Anne Lois threw a big party for him. . . . Then the other night after practice when we were snacking in the kitchen as is our custom, Harvey asked, "Say, is your mother a red-head, Dutch lady?" Well, sho 'nuf. Now think hard, Moesje. Where have you met this reddish-blond, big-shouldered, gruff-voiced character. He says he and his wife (the dazzler) took you home to Long Lane from the Reynolds' where you had spent your day off soon after I went to Big Flats. You gave the impression of being a rabid pacifist and made mention of another son besides me. Harvey has given me a haircut, the first in five months, so that everyone thinks I am a new camper. . . .

October 18, 1944

. . . Concerning the *Baal Shem*, which Bus is playing with Bob, we had the most amazing coincidence tonight. I sat at the vegetarian table because the others had liver, and happened to overhear Gertrude Jadiker, Bill's wife, say that a composer by the name of Ernest Bloch came in to the grocery store every day in Newport, twenty miles up the Coast Road, where she works. All the details, long white hair, big nose, French accent, teaching in Berkeley, jibed with Scott's extensive knowledge of the great man. I pressed a campaign for us to immediately write him, sending the program, and inviting him down for this Saturday. The coincidence would be enough to get a rise out of him, and besides there would be the opportunity for him to see a C.O. camp and moreover to hear his own work. But Scott and Erle, who are to do the playing, were rather hesitant, in fact, balky. They pointed out that the great are tired of being pursued, undoubtedly the reason why Bloch lives in a no-place like Newport. He might come if it were the Budapest performing. . . .

October 22, 1944

The concert, in keeping with the program, a performance copy of which I include, was very successful. Bill [Everson] rushed backstage after it was over and wrung all our hands, "Gee, fellows, that was great." And then later when we were taking a leak back in the dorm he speculated that it was perhaps the finest musical affair ever held in C.P.S. He counted seventy-four in the audience that spilled out on the floor at the end of the hall. I had spent most of my time, between serving in the kitchen, [building] the stage. Materials in a camp are, as you can imagine, very limited so that only the utmost ingenuity produces anything presentable. . . . I enlisted the advice of the little Jewish plumber Bill Jadiker in making a semi-circle of pipe, radius $7^{1}/_{4}''$. I learned all about the trade—or as everybody said—all Jadiker knows, cutting threads, and bending three lengths of half-inch pipe between two cement posts of the ice house to fit a semi-circle I traced in the ground. The end result was a stage with a "chamber" atmosphere, walled by the monk's-cloth curtains and ceilinged with dark blue, light blue, and purple flats from the *Aria da Capo* set. A floor lamp set on an over-turned crock for a pedestal, hidden floodlight, and a bed spotlight that shone ten feet to Bob Scott's music, provided illumination. For Scott's sake everything had to be meticulous, formal, and professional. . . . Of course Bus was terrific on *Baal Shem* and even the great Bloch would have been impressed. But we never got up the courage to invite him. If jazz has done nothing else for me, it has stopped my nervousness before public performances. . . . I went out with Bob and Warren and reeled off the Beethoven with more sparkle and accuracy than ever before. . . . A whole mob was backstage immediately after, shaking our hands and slapping us on the back. Two men from the music department of Willamette College in Salem were throwing out, "Splendid performance, great work, amazing!"

For the December 9 concert we hope to do a Haydn trio for violin, cello, and piano, the Hindemith sonata for violin and piano, and the Debussy *Première Rhapsodie* for clarinet which Wilbur and I started work on. . . .

We were in on a new departure in poetry last night, a fusion of the cerebral and the primitive. Coffield chanted a number of poems he has written here. Sometimes they were tunes like those you make up doing work, formless, repetitive, but definitely conveying a mood. Really it is something to be in on these revolutions when they start. . . .

October 24, 1944

. . . We had a revolutionary meeting of the Fine Arts tonight with Ora Huston, Regional Superintendent for the Brethren Service Committee over two problems: (1) Brethren constituency in local churches protesting the drinking of the Fine Arts group, (2) Orville Richmon, Project Superintendent, feeling moved to report to S.S. [Selective Service] that the Fine Arts were attracting individuals who were detrimental to the project. One thing is to be made clear, that we are individuals, individualists in fact, and are only a "group" or "specialized school" while the B.S.C. underwrites the values for which we stand. We are individually responsible for our own actions. The suggestion for solution which we are to ponder until the 9th is dissolution, at least officially. B.S.C. would withdraw the $100 a month, the man on overhead, and probably transfers specifically for the Fine Arts since there will be no group. . . . Of course the Fine Arts wouldn't die itself. The group is strong here and has a big reputation in pacifist and literary circles. It is the most significant thing to happen in any base camp. . . .

[postmarked October 31, 1944]
The rains have come and storm is on the sea. I have the curtains on the
sea-view window [in the Writers' Cabin] thrown wide. On the brink of the
ledge the see-saw where the children played in sunshine is wet and teetering
in the gale. The wild horses running toward the land, white manes blown
back, rear up in fear and plunge. The drummers roll as if the guillotine would
fall, but Madame de Farge continues her knitting—and I my writing. . . .
      Of all the ways of your keeping out of the war, Norm, 4-F [medically unfit]
was the last I thought possible. And after all the persuasion, writing, and
waiting! But of course this is by no means the end. I still want you to see the
evil of war for what it is and the more basic evil of conscription without which
wars could never be fought. I am not happy that you got a 4-F, for you did
not want it, will still feel conspicuous, and will always have the disappointment, and the worry that something *is* wrong with you physically. But I wish
you could see how lucky you are, and will do with your freedom such significant work that you will completely forget about the service. Although
you are very sensitive to the social pressures of the day, I think you will
admit the ultimate validity of this point: that a man is of greatest worth to
his God, country and all that crap when he is doing work of his own choosing,
chosen because it fits in with his talents, abilities, and desires. . . . Otherwise
you would not want to go to war. Is your present life so purposeless that you
want to kill your fellow men to save, spare, or at least have community with
some other fellow men with whom you identify yourself because they live on
this side of the pond? As if there could be any real community, and inter-
influence working to ultimate good among men who had engaged in the
business of killing. . . .
      You have sometimes asked in your letters if you might send magazines,
Fellowship, Life. There is no need. We get them here and I make it a point
to see *Life* or *Time* each week. I think it is very necessary for us in our security
to sense the tragic insanity of the world in order to keep our own direction.
Nowhere is it better revealed than in *Life.* First you get the war, then a magnificent article on the Colorado, then some cheesecake, and finally a chuckle
over the Roosevelt days before the war. What a hodge-podge. My latest
contribution to this papier-machine age comes separately. You once asked,
"Who did that beautiful printing?" Well, I did in this instance, everything
in fact except cutting the stencil and the linoleum block, which Eshelman and
Harvey volunteered. What I have been doing for *Compass* is pasting up
Kemper Nomland's layout. The text has been linotyped in Portland and
printed on long sheets which we cut up and I paste on the pages where
Kemper tells me. Also we paste on photographic prints. Then the photo-

lithographer in Portland photographs the whole page and prints it. . . .

I am getting all hopped up on doing a production of Stravinsky's *A Soldier's Tale* about which I was so enthusiastic in Minneapolis. As I see it now Bus would take the violin part, I clarinet (A and B flat), Warren cello . . . Elmer Oleson trumpet, Paul Foster trombone, Vic McLane bassfiddle, and Harvey the drums. Scott would take Mitropoulos' place as conductor. Dave Jackson or Marty would direct the four actors. We would go on a two-week tour of western C.P.S. units with the play. The vision!

November 3, 1944

It was good to get your letters yesterday afternoon after cleaning ditches in the driving rain along the road that twists into the plundered hills. My year's revolutionary thinking almost came to fruition during the futile morning and miserable afternoon. But in camp your letters, supper, and then the bustle of the arts school kept me too busy to write any proclamations. My idea was briefly this: Having found my community, though I sometimes wonder, I would walk out to it. This would mean my staying here but being carried on the books AWOL as if I had actually departed. Of course living in this community I would contribute to it by working on maintenance, cooking, and woodchopping, not half so many clock-watched hours as I do now but harder and better because it would be of my own volition. Essentially I would be situated with respect to the government as I am now, only I would be doing more work. If I then were arrested and imprisoned it would make clear several things about C.P.S. (1) whether the government wants our work and location or our wills (better, control over us) (2) whether it wants our work or our time. It would be a test case demonstrating whether this government is democratic or fascist. Your position of course is that the government has set up C.P.S. to reflect public opinion that C.O.'s should be subjected to the same controls and to some of the hardships of a soldier. There is really no attempt to command our wills as is necessary in the Army—only a false front that will keep soldiers' families satisfied. In view of the abnormal conditions I should be willing to tolerate this as long as the war continues, perhaps 1948 —nothing sinister on the part of the state about it. But the very basis of the abnormal conditions—the S.S. Act of 1940—is what I stand against. I would recommend that every soldier do something like what I contemplate. I do not think the S.S. Act of 1940 was a reflection of public opinion. There *was* something sinister, forced about it. And you see what it is leading to—the Wadsworth and May bills—permanent peacetime conscription. We have been running a campaign to make it rain in Washington—a WADSWORTH of postcards MAY end conscription—to quote one of my posters. But we are

far too late and way behind other camps like Cascade Locks which is gunning
for 10,000 pieces of mail to Washington. But the Friends are already thinking
in terms of repeal. It is hopeless. . . .

November 10, 1944

. . . Wednesday morning the pressure of doing my clean-up work without
imagination, enthusiasm, or even love became so strong I had to react. In
flashes that once I would have called mystical I realized my dishonesty in
working as I do on assigned jobs and my devotion to the work of the Fine
Arts group, to which my thoughts would always return from flights into the
revolutionary. So I decided to carry out my plan for "walking out to Waldport" and before the group that evening I presented it. I would stay here
in camp devoting myself to the arts, doing such tasks as I would do in a normal
community of this kind, yet be carried on the records as having walked out.
When the authorities would come down from Portland they would find me
here doing my regular work cheerfully and in less time because it would be
under my own initiative. My case in court would show the true nature of this
system. But all this interests me very little compared to the art school. I am
doing this only as a matter of personal honesty, not as a deliberate stand
against the government. I relish this very little but I feel it must be done if I
am to be true. This move comes in the art school's most desperate period.
Tomorrow night the camp votes on whether the school shall continue here
or depart. But the fellows didn't think my action would make much difference.
Anyhow I haven't made the stand yet. Scott made me promise not to "walk
out" until I had informed project superintendent Richmon exactly what I
planned to do. Everything must be above board. Since my decision I have
worked as usual—very pleasant days, in fact, almost too pleasant—but I know
the vise will close again. Don't think I am going to be a desperado, that I am
bitter, that the rain, Dick Mills, the griping, etc. have stimulated this—I
consider it the flower of over a year's thinking. I think it is done with the right
motives, I am being honest. Don't be afraid.

Dave Jackson gave me the responsibility for organizing this week's play
reading—one of Aristophanes' comedies. He suggested *Lysistrata*, but its
whole point was too sexual. So I picked the *Thesmophoriazusai*, which despite
its unpronounceable title is Aristophanes' best. Only when Aristophanes is
best he is bawdiest, and I had to cut all reference to tools. However, I left
breasts, homosexuality, and rape intact. Seven of us had a hilarious reading
rehearsal of it last night, including Manche, and Dupre's newly imported wife,
Ibby, especially reading the cut portions. But despite their enjoyment they
thought I hadn't cut enough, in fact they felt the whole play, even if I cut *all*

"immoral" elements would be risky, especially in this period in the Fine Arts school's life. There will be no play reading tomorrow night. Perhaps we will have a private reading at Dupre's housewarming tomorrow night. . . . Their place is the cozy Jenny Wren cottage just across the path to the beach from our Writers' Cabin, a wonderful place for a high society dame to live in. But already she has bumped into the skeleton of Tillie the Whale in the fog and gotten the house smoked up when the chimney wouldn't draw—the adventures are so inevitable for a city girl coming to the West that I chuckle.

We had a great mass production system Saturday and Sunday running *Compass* covers, five people loading the cardboard liner-uppers I had invented, another passing to Bill, who slipped them into the press at 850 an hour, another pulling them out, one unloading the cards and slip-sheeting (putting used sheets in between each print to prevent off-set) and another handing the cards to loaders. Bruce Reeves took some pictures which I will send when developed. This weekend we plan the same procedure with the brown-ink block. But the cover is hideous, a steal from *Survey Graphic*, and so late that to the printed "Summer 1944" we have to add *Fall*. It is a paradox to have so much fun working on such a cruddy job.

Tonight I cut some linoleum blocks for the cover of Bob Hyslop's book of devotional readings, *Remember Now Thy Creator*. The prints are poor but I am proud of the cutting job, my first since the block of Louis knocking out Schmeling done at the Day School. . . .

November 14, 1944

To relieve any fears you may have about my status I will tell you quickly that I am on furlough. This will last eight days. Then if I feel the same way I do now I will be AWOL or RTW (refused to work) for ten days, and after that, subject to arrest by the U.S. Marshal in Portland. My talks with project super Richmon and interim (until Mills officially resigns) director Brumbaugh revealed two things that warped my great scheme a bit. First, I won't be able to put up a good case in court. My idea of "walking out" and doing exactly the same work I did under assignment was designed for the lab, specifically Getz, and is not applicable here as far as I am concerned. Too much of the work here besides being assigned is of such a nature I am opposed to doing it and while I feel a definite responsibility to do manual work for the maintenance of this community I don't think I owe eight and a half hours of time each day. Furthermore under the present set-up of my living in a camp of conscripted men, my doing necessary work would in most cases mean stealing jobs from fellows who are assigned to them. I might help individuals that way but not add to the total of important work being done for the com-

munity. Or if I did work which was assigned to me I could not be carried
on the records as RTW. Of course, how I am carried on the records is not my
problem anyhow. There might well be a day when I could do work assigned
to me. My problem is to inform the administration what I am planning to do
each day, keep all my movements open, be completely honest. If then they
want to have the authorities pick me up, *they* can call Portland. I am not
trying to go to jail. The second point is that if I stay on here eating meals,
etc., but do not work regularly on project I should pay the Brethren thirty
dollars a month since the constituency which now supports me expects
complete cooperation with the system. Where do I get $30.00 a month? I
don't want to ask the Fine Arts to take it out of their $100 per month allot-
ment as they do for Manche.

November 15, 1944

. . . Ogden [Hannaford]'s visit made me aware of the vast differences between
this camp and Trenton beside the main one, the lights staying on here all
night instead of going out at 10:30. Essentially it rests in personalities. At
Trenton the big men were interested primarily in mystical religion. Here they
are interested in production. . . . The fundamentalist group here must be
always catered to. At Trenton no one took offense at two nudes in Winslow
Ames' traveling art exhibition, while we had to keep those two down in the
Fine Arts office while the rest hung in the dining hall. . . .

[Ogden] did come just in time for the tabulation of the Fine Arts poll. For
a four-year C.P.S. man it was very amusing. The charges against the Fine
Arts group were identical with those against the Communiteers at Trenton
and against every other specialized group he has seen. There was opposition
to certain personalities, special privileges, too many men on overhead, what
looked like group control of politics, etc., etc. Wherever you go in C.P.S. the
pattern is the same, old events with new names. The poll came out well—
forty-six for continuing, thirteen for discontinuing. . . . We haven't ironed
out the difficulties between the group and project. I was told the cause is too
many Bohemian-type men who are useless on project . . . causing some good
project men who protested the Fine Arts spirit to transfer out. In line with
this a very shocking note appeared on the bulletin board yesterday afternoon.

To Whom It May Concern:
This is to indicate that beginning with the third fiscal term of the Fine
Arts Group on Nov. 15, I no longer desire to be considered a member of
the Group; and that I am not available for participation in any program
or activity with which the Fine Arts Group has any official connection.

Robert Scott

Bob, who is Orville's secretary, and therefore considered a "company suck"
has continually urged that we disband, recognizing our precarious position. . . .
His actions and mine are certainly at opposite poles but I hope I understand
him. He has decided to cooperate with the system and is acting consistently.
I, who have decided I cannot cooperate with the system, don't care much
about the group's succeeding in this essentially dishonest set-up. In fact I
still entertain a glimmer of hope that the group will walk out with me and
make its stand. Scott and I disagree but come together in being truthful. Of
course there is the practical matter of his talent being lost to the group. He is
a great pianist and has the best mind of anyone in camp. What are we going
to do for the December 9 concert? . . .

[*November 23, 1944*]
. . . With the extra free time I am drawn more and more into the pseudo-
creative jobs—running the press, *Compass*, and anthology correspondence,
cutting block prints for Bob Hyslop, etc.—instead of writing. I am always
working for someone else instead of using my talent for writing and for other
forms of self-expression. But perhaps the odd-jobs I do with friendship as a
goal are my medium of creativity and I will never go beyond into purer art.
Harvey is the only prolific writer here. He refuses to do anything else—read
in plays, work on the press, come to meetings. Occasionally he plays the
violin or goes over to Clayton James' studio to paint, but mainly he is
burning reams of paper. . . .

Ibby Dupre has dovetailed into our community very nicely, especially in
the play readings with her deep voluptuous voice. The marriage is a storybook
one of the *Claudia* variety. Just now she breezed in with a tale of hitch-hiking
up to Newport and back in seven rides. Vlad frowned but said nothing. She
bought a chair in a junk shop for $2.00 after seeing it upside down. Right-side
up it is the most dilapidated piece of kindling you have ever seen. Vlad is
furious. Their house costs $35/month. Vlad makes $2.50. . . .

November 24, 1944
The work bell is being rung by Robert Scott and the rain is pouring down.
The sun, still far below the eastern horizon, seems to draw the clouds off the
ocean so that they will meet when the sun is ready to peep over. . . .

. . . Conversation last night began with the usual gripes about project,
refuting the kicks against Fine Arts, and Harvey discoursing upon the stupidity of conscripting men on a physical basis when they are so much mind.
I pointed out to him that it appeared to "work," however, but he still fumed.
For a while we drifted into the usual fantasy of what to do after the war. Joe

Gistirak, the new drama (Hedgerow, full time) transfer from Big Flats laid out his plans for a theater in Cairo, but Kemper, Manche, and Ibby insisted upon Mexico [City], alt. 9,000 ft., climate mild, population over a million. The point in question was whether the natives were exploitable. But soon we got back to the pressing point, conscription. Harvey proposed that all government be abolished as of tomorrow morning, that the whole idea of one-man-over-another was ridiculous, that he wanted to be left alone and he was sure everybody else wanted to be left alone, too. There could be voluntary co-operation, but he would never make an agreement that bound him for more than a moment. So we wouldn't have any automobiles and electric irons. The opposition screamed, "But that would be chaos and people would die." "Give me chaos, give me complete anarchy," shouted Harvey, "but by Christ, it would be a hell of a lot better and a hell of a lot fewer people would die than in this [world] where we're organized to kill." And, by Christ, I think he's right.

My new freedom has actually given me freedom to write. I have worked on three poems in as many days with fair results. But now that I know the writing business from typesetting up, people are dragging me into it. All day yesterday I worked on the playreading program for Saturday night. I'll send a copy. It was another "impossible" job for the small press but a completely unorthodox and illegitimate lock-up succeeded very well. . . .

November 27, 1944

The matter of paying the B.S.C. for my sojourn here has been made very simple by the new dance band job begun last Saturday. Vic [McLane], Bus, and I got Eshelman interested in driving us down to Florence using five E-1 tickets meant for Untide Press cleaning gas. Under cover of darkness we funneled it into the tank and headed into the rain down the Coast Road. The second-story Rainbow Ballroom on the Main Street was quite spacious, with a hangar roof, streamers over the lights, and a dais studded with three stands . . . and a glinting set of traps. First we met the drummer in his snappy Coast Guard uniform, then Erda Chestnut, tall, homely country girl, and then Oliver Foss, young sax and clary man, all very congenial and thanking the Lord we had come to save the band. It only took four choruses of "Blue Skies" to show us that our tastes in jazz were similar and that we made a pretty fair Dixieland band. The C.G. drummer was typical; at the end of every torrid number he would yell, "Come on, let's pick the next one up!"; at the bridge of the hot solos he would let out a terrible war whoop, on the medium ones he would talk to a fellow Coast Guard sitting next to him; on the waltzes and slow ones when the lights were turned out he recruited a substitute so that he could dance himself. We gave him the usual stop-chorus solo on "Twelfth Street Rag." He pounded the drum in a frenzy, tried a fancy rim-shot; and in a flash the drum fell off its stand and rolled on the floor. "Jesus Christ," he exploded, "I lost my damn snare" and laid into the next trap in reach of his flaying sticks, the high-hat inanely doffing its top cymbal. It took two sets to bring him back to the stand after the intermission. It's a good thing there was no beer in town. He would never have gotten back.

Bus, being a professional musician, felt lost without the usual [alcoholic] sender. During intermission we had coffee together in a lunchroom. Oliver and Erda explained the situation. The band will alternate between Florence and Reedsport every Saturday night in December, plus New Year's Eve in Reedsport, at $10 a man, gas being supplied by the promoters. So we have a steady job that pays a clear $60 a month, minus beer money for Bus. Esh, who drove us down, cleared $2.50 and got into the dance free (men 75 cents, 50 cents for ladies) because he was with us. It was great to jam again, especially with good musicians and a drum for rhythm. . . .

We have our last transfer, for B.S.C. has clamped down pending the visit of Harold Row, Executive Director. He is Tom Polk Miller, tanned, high cheek-boned, brown-eyed architect, pianist, and poet from Houston, Texas. Already we are very friendly. . . .

Vlad had news this afternoon of the death of his brother, a 1-AO in the medical corps, in the Philippines.

December 4, 1944

After a battle I did get the camp panel [truck] to haul us to Florence, price six cents a mile. The problem then was to find someone with an Oregon driver's license so that in the event we plunged over a cliff into the sea the insurance company would pay off. Most of the fellows with licenses were definitely anti-Terpsichore. But I finally got Jim Albrecht under the condition that he bring Brethren Art Snell along. We left in the pouring rain sprawling all over each other in the back of the panel, Bus, Vic and I and Vlad and Ibby, Manche, Kemper, and Harvey. The dance attendance was very meager and even after the movies were out didn't increase much, besides our gang from camp. At intermission Vic and I went with Oliver and Erda for coffee, while Bus joined the gang in the back of the panel over two cases of beer mysteriously bought in the drug store. . . . [After the dance] while we were getting paid off we were told we would have to take Johnny [Welch, from camp] home. . . . [He] had been working at the mill in Mapleton that week and had come into town that afternoon with the intention of going up to camp in the morning bus. Johnny hadn't touched a drop all week but he had gotten ahold of some in town. Now he had gotten drunk and pulled a knife and was thrown in the jug. The cop said there would be no hearing if we would take him out of town that night. But before we went to the jail there was business of our own to settle.

The drummer, Oliver, and Erda, had had a little discussion and decided that on the basis of the amount of money they could get for the whole band, they would do better with a five-piece band. That would mean $10 a man instead of the $8 we were getting with six. "And they think Adrian is the one we ought to let go," Oliver said. Well, that was O.K. With Oliver playing clarinet, I was superfluous, really. Of course, Vic was going away on furlough, I could play then, and maybe by the time he got back I would be gone. "No," said Oliver, "they'd want it to be a four-piece band, then." We all said, "What's the idea?" "Well, to put it straight, they don't like Adrian's playing." God, that hurt, even more than I realized then, for I could think of nothing else all the way home, and yesterday, and in my sleep and this morning. The manager was anxious to lock up so we adjourned to the sidewalk. But Erle did all the talking to Oliver on the way downstairs. He asked Oliver who it was that didn't like my playing. Well, it was the drummer. Erle told him we ought to find a new drummer instead, and keep me. Vic put it either/or. So we are looking for a new drummer. Of course the guy was getting away with murder as it was. Four dollars for the fellow he paid to stand his watch plus his eight gave him $12. Then too we were paying for the rent of his drum set. But worse than that, he is a very lousy drummer. Nevertheless the plain fact that he didn't think me a good clarinet player was enough to make me reel and gnash my teeth. I reviewed every note I played that night—and there were bad ones—but sometimes I was pretty terrific. I am still reluctant to go again, however, for Oliver never said he liked my playing or wanted to keep me and his first statement implied that Erda agreed with the drummer.

Compass arrived Saturday afternoon, eight tremendous boxes of pages. I quickly slit the cords, gathered one copy, stapled it, and brought it over to Marty in the infirmary. A quick search for errors revealed one, George Reeves' picture in the wrong place. Also the best picture in the magazine— the print shop here—was poorly reproduced. Otherwise things are pretty good. You shall have a copy soon.

I read a novel yesterday by Evelyn Waugh, *A Handful of Dust*, very brilliant in the first half.

Oh, yes. Johnny Welch. We retrieved him from the jail and drove him home. He left on the bus in the morning still tipsy and carrying another knife to cut up Portland.

Bill's adultress has arrived suddenly, glum, and strained, a little cold, but a fine sexual figure.

December 7, 1944

. . . Saturday after Waldo Chase showed me the Japanese method of wood block printing, of which I include a sample done by him. . . . Essentially it involves painting the raised portion of a wood block with watercolor and letting a piece of damp Japanese rice paper rubbed with a "baren" soak the color up. Different blocks—hundreds in some prints—are used for each color. Waldo is in his late thirties, a Seattle "artist" who visits various C.P.S. camps instructing in crafts mainly. The Fine Arts group here made very certain it had nothing to do with sponsoring his visit—since they do not approve of his work. I felt very sorry for him—the way he was snubbed—for he is a very good hearted fellow. . . . He left me with a wood block and lots of paper to go ahead with color printing, but if I do it, it will only be for him, the lonely one.

While I write, the discussion on the Fine Arts is going on between the camp and W. Harold Row. We, the group, had a big pow-wow with Row last night out of which we came triumphant. The only real obstacle is Richmon. We should win tonight, too, except that Manche will probably be deported. As far as we, the group, are concerned, she is wonderful, but pressure from non-Fine-Arts, intimations of immorality, etc. make it uncomfortable for her. . . .

Six letters Monday, including your two. I am not so much sorry for your passing the physical, Norm, as I am for your blind obedience. What will it take to make you realize there is nothing glorious, heroic, or good about what you are doing? I am very penitent for us all this evening.

December 11, 1944

. . . With Vlad gone to San Francisco and Manche moved into the Jenny Wren in his place, she and Ibby held a little exclusive party—Bus, Harvey, Gistirak, Kemper, and I—over rum, records, and philosophy. Bus came to me while I was stamping to an Eddie Condon record, and sat down on the couch beside me. "You like that stuff, don't you?" he said, and then proposed that I go to live in the Village (Greenwich, of course) where I could have lots of it, work with people as deeply dedicated to the values I embrace as the Fine Arts group is, and never be found by the police. Did my philosophy exclude such action? Yes. I want to make my move as pure and direct as possible, completely without regard for consequences, as if the penalty were death. But Bus showed me that my insistence upon this point made me a social actionist, one who is desirous of saying something to promote social welfare, not a simple mystic, and wondered if my philosophy did not demand an expedient method. In short, I was contradicting myself. I haven't thought it all out yet. Perhaps it is high time I had, for Saturday was my first on RTW. . . .

Later when the records had been turned to dancing, the husky Harvey carrying Manche along like a big tie on his neck, and Bus mincing smooth steps . . . with voluptuous Ibby, Gistirak took the couch seat beside me. Earlier he had asked, "Do you have a girl at home?" and I had said "No." Now he proposed to probe into my inner life, pursuant to the early question. "This jail business, you know, I think it would be very bad now, worse than C.P.S." He had delved into my sex life and found what he suspected—repression. His point was that life in society demands certain techniques; while I am proficient in many of them, I fail with women. His amazing "natural perception" had seen it in my actions of the evening. Once I learned those techniques I would find I had a new confidence in myself and could be really creative. It would be too bad in these very important years to put myself in a position where proper development would be impossible. I admitted much of my thinking was fruit of frustration. If I were satisfied with myself on the sex matter, felt I really had something attractive to women, I would not have this will to do revolutionary, heroic things—*ultimately designed to impress and capture a woman.*

Joe wanted to show me that I did have a great virility, very appealing to women if only I would realize it. By this time our earnestness had become magnetic, the shufflings had stopped, and Manche had come to sit with us. Joe put it up to her. Was I desirable sexually? "No," she said. Joe was astounded. "Why?" "Oh, it's his walk. He walks with his toes turned up." Manche was having trouble seeing straight with the rum, but I was sure of her frankness. "But it doesn't matter. He's just like Bill." "But it does matter," insisted Joe. "In fact, at his age the most important thing to a man is if women want to go to bed with him. He doesn't care if he's honest or productive or any of those things." "Well, take it from me," Manche repeated, "it doesn't matter." "But it does matter." And so it went. Of course Joe was right. Manche, twenty-six and a woman, has rationalized sex into unimportance, partly through a natural aversion, partly through unsatisfactory experience. There was a long discourse by Manche on all my wonderful qualities with an implication that they outweighed my failing in the man-woman relationship. But it is there. If I am ever going to be really creative I must learn the techniques, gain a confidence that I have strength which women do desire. Why do I doubt it? For all his insight, Joe wondered.

Bus got a letter Saturday afternoon from Oliver, the sax player in Florence, to this effect, "We have decided to cancel all dances. After the row Saturday night (Johnny Welch pulling the knife) the whole country has it in for you fellows. It would be foolish to try to give a dance. I personally don't have anything against you. I respected your musicianship and enjoyed playing with you. Maybe I can get up to Waldport some time to play records and do some jamming." So that is that. To compensate we (Bus, Harvey, Warren, and I) are working nightly on a Haydn quartet, No. 71. . . . I have to transpose the viola part down a sixth (e.g., up a key, E flat to F) which is hard work but things are going well, and the clarinet fits in nicely on this particular quartet. The main reason is that the notes are predominantly staccato, too short to show that I don't use a vibrato, which would be necessary in legato. We all regret Scott's withdrawal but I am seeing it a little more as his own error. Of course the Debussy will now not be played since no one else could handle the piano part but rehearsals are free from tension and the debt Scott seemed to assume we owed him for condescending to play with us.

If you want to read something funny get a taxidermy catalogue, "13 pairs of glass eyes, one brain spoon" etc. We have one on the bulletin board. Everybody is in stitches.

W. Harold Row's visit ended in good feeling all around, as was intended. A committee of four anti-Fine Arts and four Fine Arts men met to decide conditions for continuance. They are to be posted tomorrow and will say nothing which hasn't been incorporated in our program so far. The referendum was a farce. The committee will canvass the camp for opposition to Manche's remaining, however. . . . Joe Gistirak suggests she go on the road with a strip-tease show billed as "I Broke Up Brethren C.P.S."

Kermit is back from furlough and gave a travelogue of his adventure in the drunken literary circles of New York to our writers' group Sunday night. He reports Joyce Harvey is coming soon—in time to play Regina in Joe's production of *Ghosts* already in rehearsal. . . .

Every day at "mail call" time the eagerest of the men gathered to receive whatever missives or packages were addressed to them. Joe Gistirak had complained at some point that no one wrote to him and he never received mail. Jerry Rubin's wife, Jan, a compassionate soul, thereupon set about clipping out from the magazines every coupon that offered free samples, catalogues, or opportunities, and mailed them in with Joe's name and address on them. He began to receive stacks of third-class mail every day, all kinds, pertinent and impertinent, including the catalogue of studies at a school of taxidermy.

December 14, 1944

Hold everything! I mean don't buy any Christmas cards. Hyslop got me to set up the card on the big press this afternoon. Just before we were through it occurred to me I might as well run some for you. Stowed away in the Fine Arts office I found enough blue-gray cheviot for thirty-five cards and envelopes. So I changed the ink on the press from brown to bright blue and stamped them out. They go in the mail with this letter.

. . . My own status on the records has been RTW. Crumpton awakened me yesterday morning . . . to show a letter to W. Harold Row he wanted to get out in the mail. It told how I had "returned from furlough" and "refused to work under a system which made slaves of men" and a lot of other misconceptions. Crumpton does his best to protect his position, make everything look as if it were running smoothly, it makes me furious. He has been studying the S.S. bible and discovered various rules about AWOL and RTW. It seems that RTW may get me a transfer to government camp rather than jail—at least at first. Then I would be AWOL from Mancos [Colorado], Lapine [Oregon], or Germfask [Michigan], and be processed in the courts of [one of] those districts. All of this would take much longer than a straight AWOL in which the marshals would come and pick me up. Crumpton is giving me a break by carrying me AWOL. . . .

. . . A rumor has it that a tidal wave is approaching the Oregon coast. Manche thinks it is the Japs with eggbeaters. Can't you see them—millions of them—slant eyed with big glasses and buck teeth squatting on the ocean edge whirring their bright eggbeaters like mad?

December 26, 1944

. . . Christmas Eve we had an exclusive orgy in one of the cabins—Manche, Bus, Harvey, Joe, Kemper, Kermit, his friend Josie from Portland, and I. About eleven, strains of "Hark, the Herald Angels Sing" drifted in, the carollers who were finished with the worship service at camp. Everybody hid his glass of booze so that we could acknowledge the singing of the Holy Joes. . . . I did go to a Christmas carol sing in the guest house (Kimmel Hall) Friday evening, but it soon deteriorated, once having reached the limits of Minear's accordion repertoire. Before the evening was over, he was playing the Notre Dame Victory March, while the rest were doing parlor tricks with chairs. Fine Arts, you may be sure, was not well represented. . . . The spruce that hangs upside down from the ceiling of the Fine Arts office, undecorated, is symbolic enough. Manche was listening to the proceedings from her bed in one of the cubbyholes down the hall. . . . She hears some remarkable things from that unroofed room. The other morning she was eavesdropping on [one of the Brethren wives and a beautiful Christadelphian], who, although she is a schoolteacher, Manche classes as "the dumbest female in the world."

They were talking about going to movies, that it was really wrong and
worldly. Said [the teacher], notorious for cornering people and hammering
into them the tenets of the Christadelphian faith, with her brilliant black eyes
and fluent tongue, "Of course, I don't know what you believe, but our church
believes in the second coming of Christ, and Art and I don't go to the movies
much because it wouldn't be very nice if we should be sitting there when
he came down to earth, don't you think?"

While Manche is a very good influence here I am beginning to see that she
isn't completely good; in fact I am beginning to think it was time she left
this depraved camp society. Camp life has broken down most of her restraints.
Instead of maintaining a reserve before the bawdy conversation that goes on
here she has fallen into it. She used to protest when someone yelled a long
drawn out, "Shiiiit," but now she says it. In Oregon, it takes a liquor license
to get booze. Of course Manche has one. To quote Everson: "Yes, and she
uses it indiscriminately. . . . And then look how we're on the spot. After you
practically have to get on your knees to keep her here she gets everyone
likkered up including herself. My God, we've got to do something. Say
Harvey and Erle serve Christmas dinner drunk, Christ, that will be the end."

Fortunately, the booze was completely exhausted by yesterday noon, and
the violinists were playing in tune again, which they certainly weren't when
we practiced Haydn Friday night. The meal went quietly. Of course, it has
been amazing to me that Manche has made no attachments, sexual, marital, or
otherwise. I remarked this to Bill Saturday. "Oh, but don't think she hasn't,"
he said, looking over his glasses. . . . Gosh, I'm dumb, naive, innocent, in
spite of Henry Miller. Don't I have eyes? What did I expect in a set-up like
this? Somehow I can't condemn it, call it immorality, "living in sin." This
is life and it's about time I learned that what the blues singers shout is pretty
accurate. It goes for the Fine Arts as much as it does for the New Orleans
bawdy houses. And I am no Christ, this Christmas time. . . .

Marty is in hot water again, this time bad. There isn't a thing he can do
with *Compass* but it goes haywire. He calls the magazine jinxed, but it is
Martin Ponch. This time he decided to send out all West Coast subscriptions
from this office—which I mainly did—instead of from the central subscription
circulation point at Ames, Iowa. Instead of 800 copies he sent 480 express
to Sehnert in Ames with a letter of explanation, "Send these to East Coast
subscribers only." But the letter came late. . . . Result: 300 subscribers have
gotten two copies. . . . Something has to be done because *Compass* is in the
red, the printer demands pay, for which Marty is personally responsible, and
a lot of subscribers haven't gotten copies. . . .

. . . Plans for the Art and Literary issue, on which I am doing most of the work, go on. Marty is busy with his *Tennessee Justice* adapted from the court-room drama in an old *Fellowship*. I am doing the set. Gistirak is having difficulties with the women for *Ghosts*. Ibby is too busy with work and Manche is unsuitable. He is counting at least on Joyce Harvey who is coming west next week by plane—my influence, and of course the $50 Bob got for one of his paintings. Bob needs her badly; he is such a powerhouse and yet so weak. A pretty low character I guess and yet tremendously sensitive. She is a gem, it is reported. . . .

Bill has formally separated from his wife. They talked it over when she came. It was no go. . . . Bill has outgrown her.

January 1, 1945

. . . Wednesday night I gave my "lecture" on the technical aspects of [Everson's] *The Residual Years*. The evening measured up to the Christmas night class, really getting into the guts of the work, much better than any Wesleyan classes. The technique of having one student prepare the lecture occurred to me in Middletown as being far more educational than what we were getting. The professor could be a guide and check, the function Bill serves here, but the initiative would come from the student. . . .

Joyce has been telegraphing Bob all the way across the continent. Her airplane trip has been a repeat of mine twice already. Yesterday she wired from Minneapolis where she was grounded, "Flying tonight. Don't try to meet." But Harvey was already pacing the airport in Portland and has stayed over another day. She should have come in this morning, but I'll bet she's stranded in Spokane. . . . At any rate I feel somewhat responsible for all the trouble she has had in flying across.

I walked all yesterday afternoon with Gistirak down the beach to the rocky paws of the headland that sleeps over Yachats like a watchdog. The steady rain bit into our faces like iodine. The wind swirled the loose sand in great cloud fields over the hard sand that the tide had planed and tamped, and roared in our ears louder even than the crashing surf.

New Year's Eve here was quiet. All the booze was gone by Saturday night. Welch was on the rampage then, threatening to murder Harvey and Erle, who were the forces of evil, with the famous knife. Even puking into the print-shop stove didn't slow him up. . .

Adrian's chagrin at having urged Bob Harvey to insist that I fly across the continent was wasted. At both Chicago and Minneapolis my places on flights were taken by priority personnel. So I traveled by train to Portland after a miserable lonely New Year's Eve in the Minneapolis Y.W.C.A. During the

journey I talked to no one. The train was jampacked with soldiers. There was
an occasional woman on the way to an embarcation point to say farewell, or
returning from a heart-rending parting.

Kermit's accounts of "Camp Angel" at Waldport had been lively and
included a description of Manche Langley. I took the bus from Portland to the
camp and immediately recognized her on board. I was delighted to meet someone
with whom I could talk, at last, and we found each other very agreeable.

Bob had rented one of the "Tillie the Whale" cabins above the beach and when
we arrived, on January 3, 1945, I was eager to settle in. But first Bob took
me to the Fine Arts office, to show me off I guess, and there I met several artists
and poets, among them Adrian Wilson.

January 14, 1945
. . . The storm broke this afternoon so I took a mile run up the beach toward
Waldport, reversible clasped tight around me by the heavy wind at my back.
(I am getting a little flabby around the gut so I try to run whenever I get
the ambition.) I turned back where Big Creek spreads out over the beach.
No salmon were splashing up the fresh water. I hadn't walked a hundred
yards through the sand and driftwood when I spied the glass fishnet buoy I
am sending. . . . They are said to float all the way from Japan in the current
and be cast up in storms. If you turn them under a light you can see the
moonlight shimmering on the Pacific. . . .

My projects the past week have been mainly carpentry and printing—the
stage set for *Tennessee Justice* and the fir-tex display board for the new "art
gallery" in the press-craft room, and some jobs with Bill Shank on the monster
[press]. Kermit Sheets has been helping me on the play design with so much
enthusiasm and so many ideas I am beginning to think the socialization of
art, particularly the theater, is possible. Of course, *Tennessee Justice* is a dis-
couragingly bad play, but the transformation of the church into court and
vice-versa may save it.

The art gallery will open with an exhibition of photographs from *Popular
Photography* magazine. The trunk with the large-size mounted prints stands
behind me, locked with a combination padlock for which no one knows the
right numbers. After that will come local talent, Harvey, James, Nomland,
and an exhibition from the Museum of Modern Art. Isabel [Mount, a friend
of Tom Polk Miller who was renting one of the cabins] and Joyce, with her
art gallery experience, have done most of the design for the room. I have seen
a lot of Joyce since she came. She lives up to all the rave notices.

A week ago I spent the day with Gistirak and Harvey making models for
the stage set for *Ghosts*. I built a model of the stage here 1″ x 1′ out of ply-

wood. All our forms are in cardboard. Placed in the stage they give a good picture of what Harvey has in mind. Of course, Joyce had as many ideas as any of us. Every time I see her she looks stronger and more beautiful. They have the smallest cabin in the row facing the sea. The cobwebs are being swept out, the bulbs being covered with paper, and the woodwork decorated with abstract doodads. Bob has five of his paintings up. They must be good. I got the point of every one with considerable force. Maybe abstract painting isn't so obscure after all.

But Isabel has done a miraculous job transforming the cabin next door. . . . She has painted all the floors blue with yellow and red paint dribbles for decoration. It began as an accident. The curtains are dyed burlap, likewise the pillow covers. An ordinary bench was sawed off and painted to make a shorter bench and a coffee table. She had open house last Sunday afternoon.

Doc and Mrs. Workman who run a secondhand junk shop in Waldport came out to tell why they are pointed at as Russian Communists in Waldport. Real characters. Her asides to his stories were tremendous. Seven years ago they came down from Portland after years of orthopedic practice and radical activities, with a moving van loaded with secondhand goods, headed for no place in particular. They stopped for coffee in Waldport, saw a vacant store, rented it, and moved in. During the dim-out years he was hauled into court for lighting a fire after dark. But he out-smarted them and after that his junk business increased tenfold. Things had been tough before. When he imported radical speakers, particularly on Technocracy, his house was bombed. But when his hecklers were revealed in their lies on the witness stand, the town, even the morons, turned to his side. He vows he will never leave Waldport now. . . .

All of this was very pertinent because one of the chief reactionaries was [the] editor of the weekly Lincoln County news, who had flayed us C.O.'s for going to Capp's roadhouse two miles down the road and *jitterbugging*. Why should we be allowed to jitterbug when boys are out there dying—? But Doc Workman and wife still like us. I actually sold him a subscription to *Compass*. He is really an amazing man—radical, foot doctor, secondhand junk dealer, and to top it off designer of the tombs of Rudolph Valentino, F. W. Woolworth, and thousands of others all over the country. It got so fantastic some of us were beginning to wonder if all this wasn't imagination. . . .

Did I say the storm broke? The night was terrific, thunder and lightning, wind ramming against the flimsy sides of the dorms and roaring in the chimneys, and the rain gusting on the roof. The boys still went on project— twenty minutes late.

Norm's final induction, of course, had its effect on me. Already his first letter from [Camp] Devens stated conditions and attitudes which I could no longer tolerate. I suppose I should devote my letters to pointing these things out to him in hope of some revolution. But if Norm has any awareness and moral fiber he will have a tough enough time without my drizzle. . . .

To everyone's amazement the Portland newspaper, The Oregonian, *published a defense of the C.O. jitterbuggers, among whom the Jadikers were perhaps the liveliest. The supporter stated that individual freedoms were what the war was being fought to protect, an unusually liberal attitude for those times.*

January 21, 1945
. . . Things look brighter on the penal front. Three Lapine and Cascade Locks walk-outs were given sentences of only four months apiece by Judge Fee in Portland, who usually hands out three to five years; the judge is irked by a system that sends him so many C.O. cases. Of course the "cat and mouse" [Selective Service] policy will get the fellows when they are released. . . .

January 28, 1945
As you can see, *Tennessee Justice* hasn't died yet. The persevering Ponch is doing a repeat next Saturday night, and hoping to take all twenty participants, plus material for a set, to Elkton the weekend of the 10th. Friday night's performance went without a slip, including the intricate lighting which I operated from a booth at the back of the auditorium. Learning to run the four switches and three [salt water-jug] dimmers was like learning to play a new instrument. One sequence had to be practiced over and over before I could move my hands fast enough from saltwater jug to saltwater jug to make the lights flash punctually on the stage. The whole week was integrated (no time even for a shower until Friday evening), everything directed toward the set and lighting. The Barbary Coast [the huntin'-fishin'-shootin' men] thought it was the best thing ever done here, the Holy Joes said, "Maybe the Fine Arts has got some good in it after all," but the Fine Arts thought it stunk. . . .

The program layout and typography were done by me, another big compromise, but perhaps better in the end for its simplicity. The best idea I could think up to follow in my *Compass*-request-for-material tradition was a gavel made of two pieces of printed paper . . . but no one liked the idea, too tricky and souvenirish. They suggested I give each person a wad of paper all folded up, or better get a homing pigeon to fly into each person's lap, bearing Marty's notes. Stymied, I hit upon a conservative two-color paper folder and cover with *Tennessee Justice* stamped through the blue to reveal the gray. But Eshelman and Kemper were clamoring for the press so Bill and I stayed up through the night to do the conservative job enclosed. In its clean simplicity it is more effective I think than many more complicated jobs. . . .

Joe and I had dinner with the Harveys last night in their snug little cabin facing the heavy surf. The weather has been crystal for a week now after the storm but the swells of the breakers are still immense and in yesterday's wind blew back long manes of foam as high as the horizon, just before they crashed over. After sunset the moon was brilliant, making the long moving lines of wash luminous. Harvey would go out for a while and come back raving about all the power and energy.

Conversation followed the usual channels. One of Bob's favorite themes is the actual material poverty of this great abundant America. Here we sit at the humblest of meals and are grateful because for once we don't have to eat like serfs in a castle scullery. Here in wartime America thousands of people have to live in medieval squalor while millions are being blown up overseas. Why, Joyce couldn't get one measly little transport to fly a few thousand miles, when you read in the papers of a hundred bombers lost in a night. [Harvey] was up in a hotel in Portland, sleeping in a crowded serviceman's dormitory [when she arrived]. His bunkmate was a Canadian airman. Said the Canadian, "Do the people in America really live on this level? It's fantastic." Bob doesn't even talk about the spiritual failure of democracy. Look at the material failure! The stupidity of it all.

For relief we usually get into sexuality, homosexuality, bisexuality, incest, and Henry Miller. Henry Miller is then compared with Joyce, Proust, Lawrence, Patchen. For laughs someone tells a few of Henry's dirty stories. Oh, you would be shocked! And Joyce is such a *nice* girl. Then we compare the merits of the art media, drama, novel, poetry, painting, music, movies, radio, and television. Eventually we get to mysticism and Clayton James.

But last night we had something else to talk about. Joyce posed the usual question, "What have you heard from the law?" This time I had something to tell. Friday in the shower Art Snell, Orville's secretary told me, in his I-hate-to-tell-you-this-but way, that he had typed a letter that afternoon to the Forestry Supervisor, Furst, in Portland, saying that my work on project and the fire crew had been excellent but that one day I had failed to report for work, so in the interests of camp morale, something should be done about my presence here immediately. My first, and present, reaction—although I have rationalized his psychology as best I could—was "Where does he get that idea?" In actuality my presence here, particularly my work on *Tennessee Justice* and other projects, has been very good for camp morale. There has been no slow-down of work in the woods. I am sorry to see Orville work like a cog in the wheel of the great machine, completely oblivious of the personal angle. But Orville is doing more than work as a cog in the wheel. Camp morale is not his concern; it is the director's. He is definitely overstepping his bounds in demanding action on my case. This is what gripes the other fellows. [The permanent Sick Quarters "invalid"], who knows everything that could possibly breed a scandal, made his nightly round through the files last night and discovered the letter. Now the whole camp knows. Jerry Rubin is demanding an investigation. . . . Everson says it is time to kick back. The rest go around muttering, "Jesus Christ, that's low!" I, of course, remain impartial, not wanting to cause anyone any trouble. But I suppose a little revolution—say a work strike or mass walk-out would be interesting. There are some things I still have to decide. Should I talk to Orville? Should I leave camp and play fugitive with the F.B.I.? This week should be interesting. . . .

February 4, 1945

So that I won't unnerve Norm by commenting to him on his letter, I will let off steam by writing you first. This throwing of live pineapples makes Norm's going suddenly real and purposeful where before he was merely conscripted. Despite my new anti-conscription stand I could tolerate his doing soil conservation work in an Army uniform, but now he is being drilled for active fighting, with which I can have no truck whatsoever. The idea is so fantastic it is insane. My soul cries out like a revivalist, "Save him, save him!" . . .

. . . The talk at Harveys' last night began on abstract painting—does a Harvey painting suggest, or does it exist as a new created form? . . . After the crowd left, Harvey, Joyce, and I got going on schooners, while Joe got Warren into a corner for the heart-to-heart about life he makes it a point to have with everyone of any promise. By schooners I mean Bud Hawkins' wonderful idea for post-war. Hawkins, who transferred here from Gatlinburg for the Fine Arts, but mainly the ocean, has $10,000 to sink into a schooner. Already he is building boats on project time for Forestry. He is experienced enough to build a boat big enough to call his home and make his family world-citizens. Think of it, when a man leaves port he no longer owes allegiance to any government. As long as he stays out of ports he cannot be molested. What would this mean for a family or a group of families? The children would have a completely new perspective on the world. Instead of patriotism, they would love the world. . . .

Rent the boat for a month's cruise during summer (Bud has done it) and you would make $2,000, enough for years of food, the main part of it coming directly from the sea. Or if you have a freight hold, take a cargo—there are always cargoes—and make enough for another few years. There could be free interchange of wives. This appeals to me when I look at Joyce. . . . [Children] would grow up in the best climates; cruising to the warm latitudes in winter, the Aleutians in summer, but always close to nature, the sun, the storms, the water.

And have you considered the creative possibilities. Say a string quartet, which can't make a living anyhow—were to try it—Bus, Bob, Warren, and my wife (who plays viola), with me as guest soloist practicing every night all summer and then docking at coast cities for one night concerts, or for a month in New York while the boat was in dry-dock for repairs. . . . Bob, Joyce, and I are sold on it. And here we have a fellow with the skill and finances to work it for us. Of course, Bud is interested in building boats six months of the year anyhow, so the rest of us could use it while he was a landlubber. So you see, the schooner is the salvation of the world, the Noah's Ark for the preservation of culture and humanity. How about it? As for me, first a wife. . . .

February 11, 1945

. . . When the rain stops in earnest, Captain Hawkins and I hope to make a triangle tour, hitch-hiking, first down the Coast Road looking for schooners, then over to Yosemite from San Francisco and back up #99. But maybe his Maine coast "peapod" for which he is steaming the oak ribs this afternoon will be done by then and we can sail down. I have watched Hawkins at his work this week. He is doing his best to stretch out the boat-building for Forestry but he is just too efficient. The big spruce rowboat built for a Girl Scout Camp ("work of national importance") was caulked yesterday afternoon and now is ready for painting. But he has another twelve-footer to go, for which he can manufacture all sorts of "problems" that will keep him off road maintenance for another month or two. The work is beautiful, somewhat reminiscent of the wooden shoe factory I distinctly remember from Holländsche, because of the clean white wood, but with the additional attraction of perfectly fitted pieces. As Hawkins says, of all the things you can build, a boat takes on the most life, is closest to human.

. . . I have moved into [another] cubbyhole which has twice too many shelves for my meager material possessions, two desks, and two thick cabinets for insulation against the Barbary Coast. Si Miller . . . across the aisle has equipped me with a light so that I now read in bed, namely Thomas Mann's *The Magic Mountain*, and do all my writing on the taller and very solid $3/_9$ " plywood desk. A little materialism can work wonders. But the quarters still have a monastic bareness which is counter-acted only by two chunky plaster-of-paris nude torsos. . . . Shank's going, however, heralds the disintegration

of the Fine Arts at Waldport. Bus, Warren, Dave Jackson, and Vlad have applied for transfer. Manche has more or less resigned. . . . Nomland is going through the formality of being personally refused on project by Orville when he reports at work call each morning, part of good "slow-down" technique. He and I can't last. The rest of the group will be split by side camps and wives across the road. Is there something wrong with the original idea?
—that artists by being together would stimulate each other to greater creativity? . . .

February 21, 1945

. . . After Sunday dinner we left for Eugene [to put on *Tennessee Justice*] arriving at the Methodist Church around 5 p.m. . . . Afterwards the Wesley Foundation, mostly girls who had been at Elkton, which sponsored the play, had an amazing conglomeration of activities in the rooms downstairs. First there were games such as tug and Shoo Fly designed to get us acquainted but more to make us sweat. When we were all out of breath, we sang negro spirituals which were supposed to set the mood for a worship service. This was the most sentimental, un-profound pap, hymns that never ended—all about the trials and tribulations of life, platitudes from the dame who played the piano, and then sentence prayers around the circle progressing from prayers for tolerance to negroes to prayers for tolerance to poor C.O.'s like us. It was sickening.

Of course there had to be eats afterward, and everybody put on his best Christian Endeavor smile while guzzling cocoa and dainty sandwiches. I stayed with the Etters, F.O.R. people in Eugene that night in their new raw-wood-interior home. They keep a lovely room with double decker bunk ready for carpet baggers like me. It averages a C.O. a night. . . . A Japanese-American traveling through the West to relocate high school graduates in colleges, occupied the bunk below me. We talked for a long time before we went to sleep—about his teaching experiences in the relocation centers, about his coming to the West Coast to do this relocation work even before Japs were allowed back in the area . . . and C.P.S. compared to Tule Lake [one of the relocation camps], etc.—but everything led to "living in the light of the eternal," which I have rejected for the time being. As Joe was saying in our usual frustration fest with Hawkins after supper, "It is so stupid, these pure Christian Endeavor girls visiting camps, and F.O.R. people providing nice beds for you to sleep in when all you want is somebody to sleep with."

February 25, 1945

What a wonderful afternoon it has been! We sprawled in the warm bright sun on the lawn in front of Harvey's cabin that overlooks the blue sea, listening to Ravel, Debussy, Bartok, and Gershwin on Crumpton's vic and reading now and then. "If this is conscription give me more of it," said Manche, who isn't conscripted. I went scrimmaging in the cold surf after five, and then took the usual mile run up the beach, from which my legs are tight and my body glowing.

But it isn't by the grace of the American Legion that we could have an afternoon like this. No, to them we were being sinners, traitors. We weren't properly sharing in the misery of the world. [An American Legion] post was established in Waldport recently, apparently for the sole purpose of keeping us confined to camp. They sent a questionnaire to Colonel Kosch of Selective Service asking:

1. How much are these men paid and what for?
2. Are women permitted to take their meals regularly in the camp mess hall?
3. Are women permitted to roam promiscuously over the camp grounds?
4. Are men permitted to live with their women off the camp grounds?

Of course Colonel Kosch answered "No" to the last three questions, because that's what it says in the [Selective Service] Bible. But you know it happens. The Legion is sponsoring dances at Cap's roadhouse every two weeks now. The Post Commander hinted that there would be bloodshed if any C.O. appeared at the first affair last night. To alleviate the frustration of not being able to go, we held a dance of our own in the mess hall. I had hoped it would be something like the Trenton shindigs . . . but Vic didn't come back from Portland in time to fill out the band and only five wives and Manche showed up. Without a band to play in I was left with the obligation of dancing myself, which I had always escaped at Trenton. Odd jobs such as building a fire, covering the lights with colored paper, spreading the floor with soap chips to make it slippery, and choosing and changing records quickly ran out or were performed by others . . . who were in the same predicament of not wanting to dance but having no honorable excuse for making a getaway. Joyce, voluptuous in scarlet, sensed it and said, "Aren't you going to dance?" offering herself. What else could I do? So I danced for the rest of the evening —with her, Manche, Ibby, Jan Rubin, De Coursey's wife, though not the tiny Hildegarde Erle, not enjoying it much from an aesthetic point of view since I am still very rough (on toes), but nevertheless relieved that I was at least "dancing," and that if I were making a bad impression there would be plenty of opportunity for redeeming myself with these women. Most of them thought I was pretty smooth, anyway. Dancing, from my prejudiced point of view, still looks very ridiculous, the position of holding each other, the meaningless shuffle. If this is "life" it falls far short of what I hope for it.

But I'll be damned if I can break the pattern, think of anything so much better, even the schooner. . . .

March 4, 1945

. . . Hawkins' peapod is upside down now for the planking on the bottom. I helped him set the nails on the sides Thursday afternoon, and also lent support in fitting the breast hooks. . . . I have seen this boat grow step by step so that I think I could build one myself, with a little technical assistance. . . . In the three weeks before Cap'n hopes to have it vaulting the surf (it used to be three months), planking, caulking, first with cotton, then paint, and finally putty, installing of two sets of oarlocks and seats in the bows, and a final painting will have to be done. The fellows suggest I sail off to some island in it and wait until Hawkins' schooner comes along to pick me up—only every island in the ocean I know of has some military significance.

I read a swell novel, *The Innocent Voyage* by Richard Hughes, about the amorality of children and the casuality of life as brought out in the experiences of five children kidnapped on a pirate schooner. It is a wonderful pre-view of what our children will do in the schooner home. They will climb the ratlines, swing from the yard-arms, get stabbed by marlin spikes, play pirates, commit murder without any qualms of conscience, and forget about ever having known or loved us when they leave the boat. . . . Now I am steeped in Gogol's *Chichikov's Journeys; or Home Life in Old Russia*, one of the best Russian novels, a hilarious and cutting description of the serf system. Of course Mann's *Magic Mountain* is finished, as big an accomplishment (713 pages) for me to have read as for him to have written. The parallel of the T.B. sanitarium and C.P.S. is quite remarkable. . . .

March 9, 1945

If you don't believe a word of the story I tell in this letter I won't blame you. The events of the past two days are so fantastic I might be living in a completely different world from yours, the one I used to know; life is a dream, such a violent, incredible dream that the novel I will write about it, once I wake up and find myself on the planet where I really belong, will turn that planet upside-down. . . . Thursday, waiting for grace at lunch in the dining hall, there was mumbling about someone being hurt, George Moyland being hurt on project. The doctor from Waldport had gone up. Otherwise no one knew anything. . . . Roger Sheets, who was cooking the evening meal recruited me to make the apple pies, twelve of them. The rumors began floating back to me as I mixed lard and flour and water and salt in the bakery —first that George had been taken to the hospital in Toledo unconscious, that a branch, a big one, had broken off the snag he was felling and hit him in the head, then, that the base of his skull was fractured, then that the doctor gave him one chance in a hundred to live. I started praying for that one chance, "Come on, George, you gotta live," meanwhile dumping sliced apples into the crusts I had fitted into the tins. But Roger called out from the kitchen in his musical North Carolina accent, "Adrian, did you hear that? George is daid." He had died at 2:30, without regaining consciousness. . . .

Tonight there was a meeting of the radicals over at Dupre's. Rubin and Ponch were going to make sure this death did not go by like George Watkins' death. First there would be action on a local level . . . and then there would be action on a national level. Both these men died because (1) they were unfit for the hazardous work, which even experienced woodsmen would refuse to do; (2) they were doing work which was *not* of national importance, ergo, insufficient precautions were taken. Jerry saw it as a wonderful chance to dramatize the evils of C.P.S.—no insurance, insignificant work—But first on the local level. Before anyone went out to fell any more snags we would demand (1) insurance, which would mean that a man would be physically qualified to fell snags, no old, clumsy fellows like the Georges, if the company would insure him; (2) that he be a volunteer; (3) that he receive proper training; (4) that he wear a steel helmet—otherwise, "strike." Marty's individual action was to do only as much percentage of maintenance work as there was work of national importance on project, i.e., fire-fighting, in other words something like my old scheme and about as shaky, probably a technical RTW. He is going SQ [sick quarters, or infirmary] tomorrow to think it over. The discussion fell apart when it came to the national level—writing releases for *Time* and the newspapers. Any other time in history, perhaps, but not concurrent with Iwo Jima. . . .

. . . Tonight Joe and I ate fried eggs. Three nights ago George and I ate fried eggs. He liked fried eggs better than I do. Now he is dead. Why? . . .

March 19, 1945

With George dead, Muriel [his widow] still around, Marty in heat, my clarinet falling apart, my teeth needing fillings, and a promise to Don Roberts that I would come up for the weekend unkept, . . . I agreed to accompany Si [Miller] to Portland on Sunday. It was high time I got away from it all. Close to 2:00 a.m. we were hunting for Wasco Street in the wet N.E. section of town where two free beds were promised by the International House, when a car pulled up alongside us. The snarling cops wanted to know where we were going so late and where we had come from. Si said we were C.O.'s from Waldport C.P.S. camp. "Where's your uniforms?" they said, shining a flashlight in our faces. "We don't wear uniforms," Si said. "How come?" It occurred to me that they thought we were commissioned officers, so I explained our real identity. "Aren't you supposed to stay closer to camp than this?" the bozo at the wheel asked. "We're on dental leave," we said. "Where's your papers?" asked the other, getting out of the car. "Papers?" said Si, "we don't need papers." I thought he was trying to protect me, for I was AWOL. We would take the rap together. Afterwards I found out Si didn't have any papers either. The ignorant cops actually believed Si's statement. But the bulges under Si's coat and my black clarinet case looked suspicious to them so the big cop had Si produce the newspaper he had underneath, had me open the clarinet case, and felt us both all over for gats, tommy guns, or for homosexual reasons. The stupes didn't have any idea where 17th and Wasco was and pulled away in their snappy Ford leaving us to slosh in the rain for another hour until we found the place. These are the guardians of residential peace, the army of unalterable law.

Ideally I hoped to earn enough there to get myself a new Buffet clarinet, and my teeth repaired. . . . We spent the afternoon getting appointments from the [dental college] students—mine for 10 the next morning, Si's for two weeks hence—and then separating on our own business. I went to every printer in town for a few days' work, but something like the daily menu business would take me that long to learn. If I could stay longer, break in, they would hire me at $1.25 an hour, but not for just a few days. Sorry. At the dealer of Buffet clarinets—the best French make—I found he had none in stock. He suggested I hold on to my own, not even surrendering it to any of the butchers who advertise as repairmen, until he got a supply, then come up and try them out. I took this as good advice and met Si at the "Y" from where we proceeded to the Hungerfords' for a pot luck supper and F.O.R. meeting. What luck! The meal was sumptuous and all for free. But we had to pay the price finally in the F.O.R. meeting. All exits were blocked by fat old women and we sat and suffered while a young dynamic priest laid his soul on the floor . . . a young, oh so fine, so true, reverend—whose super-healthy brats rolled on the carpet through it all—waxed metaphysical, from Einstein to Thomas Kelly—and Mr. Hungerford lifted the bushel off his light with a speech on goodness. Then there was the final indignity of holding hands— Si, the atheist Jew, and I holding hands!—singing of a closing hymn. We made our escape as quickly as possible but not without being cornered a few times by the fat old women. . . .

Talking with the fugitives at St. Vincent's Hospital across the river was very refreshing. Si stimulated the rabid anarchist, John Hartman, a parolee from McNeil to his brightest and loudest conversation. . . . [He] spoke very vividly of the life on McNeil, the strata in prison society, the beautiful location on Puget Sound, and, in another vein, how fellows going into their third year would suddenly and quietly crack, their spirits would die. We talked so long it became foolish to go to the International House, so we slept on mattresses on the floor of Hartman's room.

It took the Junior who worked on me at the dental college four hours to put in a temporary filling. . . . I met Don in the thick-carpeted, panelled music room of the public library for a playing of one of his discoveries—Hindemith's *Eine Kleine Kammermusik* for wind octet. We were very noble in escorting a blind violinist to the public toilet and his bus, going on ourselves to Wiley's shop. Wiley runs a window washing and tree surgery service that depends on transient C.O.'s for labor. Wiley either pays a dollar an hour or splits the price of a job half and half, in which case a fellow makes as much or more. Wiley had a job for us, an hour and three quarters of cleaning up prunings in a yard, for which we earned $1.75—enough for a good feed in a classy restaurant downtown afterwards. At eight a.m. the next day I could work for his tree man Lundquist—at a dollar an hour which I did—ten and a half hours felling and bucking two big, hard cherry trees in a muddy yard. . . .

March 26, 1945

One of those airmail stamps deserved to come back to you before this, but you know how it is. I have been knocking together the platforms . . . for Joe's *Ghosts* and designing and executing a typical Wilson program for the concert, now scheduled for Thursday. My programs, "monuments to our papier-machine age" have come to be a standard gag around here—and this one with all the folds, three press runs, and three slits is definitely in the tradition. Some day, they say, I'll reach the ultimate, a piece of paper folded so many times it becomes a wad or a spitball.

Then too there are the sessions of *the* game, usually at the Erles' cabin, lots of laughter and screaming, while little Robin sleeps through it all. One member of a five- or six-man team acts out in pantomime the words or syllables of a title—book, song, or otherwise supplied by the other team—for his teammates, their job being to guess the title in as short a time as possible. It is a difficult exercise in speechless communication, wonderful training for foreign relief and reconstruction, I suppose. The actors are usually the best— Joe, Kermit, and Hildegarde—in getting across the often fantastic titles. My knowledge of jazz and literature helps on the supply (and guessing) end— "Our Exagmination Round his Factification for Incamination of Works in Progress," "It Must be Jelly 'cause Jam don't Shake Like That," "Wham Re Bop Boom Bam," and "I Wish I Could Shimmy Like my Sister Kate," being sticklers good for over five minutes, but I am a lousy actor. . . .

We had another dance Saturday night, orange wrappers around the bare light bulbs, corn meal on the floor that made it, despite Ray Johnson's good intentions, more like sandpaper than polished with the wax which bears his name, and three victrolas, the last of which proved satisfactory. Thanks to Joyce I enjoyed this affair—after midnight when only a few were left and I could have every other dance with her. She has a strong, solid body that is ecstasy, almost, to press to mine, and when it moves together in perfect rhythm with mine it makes a sort of union. She caught on to my steps quickly, so that by 2:30 we were dancing the slow ones without a hitch or stepped-on toe. I think she is perfectly aware that it is the confidence smooth dancing gives a person which I need most of all and she consciously suffered at first under my hoofs, then danced way past bedtime to give it to me. There was really something to get up for Sunday morning—breakfast at the Harveys'. It was like being a bit in love with Joyce, controlled of course, and going to pay court. The sun was bright, the surf heavy, and in me a satisfaction in my virility that gave the day a new meaning. I am very grateful to Joyce and admiring that she could give me life without compromising her love for Bob a bit. . . .

Bill handed me the typescript for his *A Chronicle of Division* tonight. They are poems of his going to C.P.S. (*The Waldport Poems*), of his wife's adultery, of their few meetings, and their final separation—experiences of deep suffering, almost too personal and intense for publication, which he hopes New Directions will do, having accepted the first section. The meditations on the reasons for the adultery and the nature of love are too abstract, too much in the head and out of this world for my taste, but I suppose this is exactly what happened to Bill and happens to every man when he is struck by events so unforeseen and incomprehensible. . . .

. . . The *Oregonian* (Portland) changed the whole walk-out perspective last week by a statement from Judge McCullough to the effect that all C.O. cases in the Portland court would hereafter be handled directly by the probation officer, men going to hospitals *with pay* for the duration and no prison sentence. But there won't be any mass walk-out until it is confirmed. Could I accept this conscription? When do I hit the bottom?

March 31, 1945

. . . Our own concert Thursday evening went very nicely, Wesley being in good voice and the audience receptive. *Night Piece* [by Lauris Steere Guetzgow] . . . we did twice in succession, because, to quote my little introduction, "the atonality, the difficulty of the harmony and of the structure, make it impossible to apprehend on the first hearing." [It] was "very interesting" to all who had listened to music beyond *Ave Maria*. . . . There was a sort of reception for the artists afterward in Kimmel Hall. Some of the wives poured and served up civilized cookies such as I haven't had for months. ([Your] sand cookies are out of this world, therefore excluded.) Rubin showed his kodachrome slides of *Aria da Capo* and San Francisco, and Bruce [Reeves] threw a magnificent and revealing panorama of Mexico, where he had laid sewer pipe in an A.F.S.C. work camp, on the tacked-up bedsheet. Crumpton recorded six sonnets [read] by Dave Jackson on his six-way machine. They played back very accurately but of course disappointingly to Dave, who was unaware of the tin edge of his voice. . . .

Paul Foster was in camp last night, out on bond from the Portland jail with trial pending April 5th. He gave a vivid picture of county jails from Oklahoma City to Baker, Oregon, a picture of bed bugs and cockroaches, dope fiends smuggling it in and going on benders, jailers in league with the supposedly outlawed "kangaroo court" of which one prisoner is the judge, the other is the jury, which decides on a basis of how much money you pay, whether you have to mop the cell block and whether you can eat off the grocery wagon, the jailer making a nickel or dime extra on each purchase. Of course the $1.25 a day you are allotted for food goes mainly into the jailer's pocket, making it necessary to buy off his grocery wagon if you want to live. It is amazing how quickly men develop a pattern to take care of essentials. [He found] traveling with the U.S. Marshal up to Portland was very pleasant, however, good jails to sleep in, $1.10 a meal, and stops at all the scenic points in Colorado and Utah. Paul had lost about twenty-five pounds but was very cheerful, though too obsessed with his experiences. . . .

April 13, 1945

When you read this you will understand why I haven't written. To you in Middletown who know us both . . . it will seem utterly fantastic, inconceivable, as it often does to us. But to Joyce and me our discovering each other seems also wonderful, beautiful, and good. When we danced together, as I described in a last letter, something awakened in Joyce as it did in me, something which had been dead in her relationship with Bob for a long time. I knew something was happening between us, and for each day I had a new theory of what it was. First, she was in league with Joe to give me what I most needed if I were to weather prison—a confidence in my virility, a joie de vivre. On the second day when we had so much physical contact on the beach, it was "the natural affinity one healthy animal has for another." When we worked so hard together in the woodshop hanging the collapsible platforms for *Ghosts*, I was "substituting for Bob," who was too busy with his novel to have much companionship with his wife. I had been all along, dancing, on the beach, camp functions, movies, poetry.

Monday night when it took an hour of subtle speechless persuasion to get her out of Ibby's house where we had been having a record orgy, and home by 4:00 a.m. I was sure she was either sick of Bob, the boor, or trying to make him jealous by staying out all night with me. Tuesday, seeing the first *in toto* rehearsal of *Ghosts* there was still a chance that she was acting the part of Mrs. Alving, who wasn't "treated right" by her husband either, in life as well as on the stage, one of the requirements Joe makes of his actors. But that was out.

That afternoon on the way to Sea Lion Caves, a great room hewed by the sea in the cliff, eighteen miles south, where hundreds of sleek glossy lions slobber over the rocks between fishing trips, she assured me she wasn't playing Mrs. Alving at all. Yesterday afternoon holding her in my arms on the soft moss bed . . . in Morris Graves' . . . big lean-to studio in the under-growth just off the beach, I told her all these theories and found every one was wrong. Something had simply awakened in her, and believing in the validity of the emotions she had followed the impulse. How honest should we be with Bob and society? To hell with society. But to Bob it would matter. Despite all his belief in individual freedom, we are sure he has a strong feeling of possessiveness about Joyce. He is proud that she is such a gracious hostess, boasts that she writes, is flattered when we sleek college boys pay her so much attention. It might crumble his foundations, destroy his tremendous energy and creativity if he knew what was going on. Joyce is very concerned about keeping him writing and painting and sober. She doesn't want to take the responsibility for destroying his art, even for something as big as our love. . . .You can understand why I was amused when your letter came saying, "Someday the right girl will come along." If you want to get the dramatic quality of our experience read some of Jeffers' poetry (*Tamar*, *Roan Stallion*, etc.). The element of nature is all-powerful in it, the sea, the great rocky headlands, the wind-flattened trees, the driving rain, and brute clouds. . . .

Morris Graves was a mystical Northwest painter who had been drafted into the army despite his pacifism. He was a non-cooperator and after a year in the guardhouse was discharged as a psychological oddity. He found kindred spirits in the Fine Arts group and spent some time in and near the camp. He built a romantic Japanese-style lean-to over the lagoon near the beach and lived there. During this time an exhibition of his paintings was hung in the new Fine Arts gallery, where some were sold for $10 to $25. In 1956, eleven years later,

Adrian was commissioned to design, for the University of California Press, the catalogue of the large Morris Graves Retrospective Exhibition which was shown in eight museums throughout the country. The prices of the paintings were in four and five figures.

April 19, 1945

The insignia above [*Compass* letterhead], designed and executed by me these past three days, is almost universal as I explain to anyone who enters the print shop. First there is C O for conscientious objector; then there is M P, the editor's initials; then two words describing the editor, or, if not him, the Selective Service system with an extra S for emphasis. Of course C.P.S. has always been in the word Compass; the other meanings, which pretty well cover the scope of this life, are brought out by the special layout. I can't put my hand to the press without revolutionizing the industry. The individual pieces of type were placed like Stonehenge in a small plywood box and plaster of paris poured round to a depth of $3/4''$, so that the heads of the type still protruded. The casting lasted through 3,000 impressions and begins to appear indestructible. In fact I am beginning to wonder how I am going to rescue the type.

But don't think this has been my absorption. It is only a way of getting through the hours when I can't be with Joyce. . . . We have found a magical new place in which to make love, the forest of wind-flattened pines on the bank just right of the path to the beach, so thick there is no undergrowth, always the roar of the surf, sunlight through the chinks in the green tent, occasional windows looking on the shimmering water, and a springy floor of pine needles a foot thick. Besides, the boards under Graves' moss bed were beginning to cave in. By Saturday Bob was saying how glad he was to see Joyce so happy, for she is bubbling over, as I am, with the constant discovery.

April 24, 1945

. . . Of course I knew all the facts about Joyce's "past" that you gave. She has made a point these past weeks of giving me a very complete background, all except for her first marriage, which she preferred not to discuss on the particularly happy night when I asked her about it. . . . I have been as aware of the "instability" as you have, but less able to explain it. It has been inconceivable—and I constantly say this to Joyce—that a tremendous figure like Bob could lose the dominant position in her life. . . .

April 27, 1945

. . . The impermanence of human relationships is too obvious. We are all really alone. Look at your friends, how they have come and gone. Why then must *marriage* be till death us do part? It should continue only while the "love" lasts and while it is dedicated to some end—a home, say. Joyce has no regrets. Her marriages to Gordon and to Bob were not mistakes, but relationships which grew, matured, and died. I recognize that the same thing will happen between us; children might keep us together, give us a new sort of happiness, but not the happiness we have now. There is no such thing as "lasting happiness." The happiness changes. . . .

May 12, 1945
4:00 a.m.

I am hardly in condition after a frustrating night of trying to make the press ready for a long *Compass* run, to write a letter which would dispel all your fears, misconceptions, and "ghosts." And as it happens, I am pretty well ridden with them, myself, almost willing to admit I am in a mess, but not quite. The situation can't be as complex as we are making it, nor as scandalous as you are making it. . . .

May 13, 1945

I have just reread your letter, Moes, and was even more impressed than when I said "magnificent." Such an attempt at understanding! Such love and genuine concern, your real self, pouring through each sentence. How I wish I could reward you with clear, specific answers to every doubt, emancipation like this experience has been for me. But, despite all my flair for literature— I admit I am guilty of doing most of my experimenting with it on you—I probably am less able to convey my point of view than you are in a letter like this last. And then, I have always had as one of my major vices a powerful desire to shock you who are so puritan. . . .

Art [Hoffman] may be right about e. e. cummings' *Enormous Room* being a more accurate picture of C.P.S. than *The Magic Mountain*, but my own situation here, along with Si, Nomland, Marty, and the Merry Wives of Waldport, Mann has caught. Of course, the whole picture has changed again with the discovery Joyce and I made. It is more weird yet more magical than ever. I have an idea you missed most of *Ghosts*; I practically know it by heart from running the lights through so many full rehearsals. It's worth reading again. Joyce is tremendous as Mrs. Alving, now has aspirations to the theater. There is the nucleus here for a fine post-war co-op theater à la Hedgerow. . . . [This period] has been a very gradual but definite emancipation, a breaking of patterns, a dispelling of Ghosts, and finally through Joyce a complete change of my concepts of sex from a hocus-pocus of pink garters, booze, and burlesque houses (all "idea," all "in the head") to a totally new experience that is completely physical, stimulus and response, hence, pure. . . .

Meanwhile the Art and Literary issue of *Compass* is shaping up into something of a souvenir edition of me and my friends (Hoffman, Beloof, Everson, Lauris, Marty, Coffield, etc.). Morris Graves . . . has submitted eight photos of his paintings which we will make into a folio. Wilfred Lang, the Portland artist . . . has designed a snappy cover. I am doing the layout—conservative but solid—and much of the printing, 3,000 copies, on the press. Enclosed is a *Ghosts* program by yours truly, kept in check by Nomland of all people. The motif is Bob's, painted as the twelve-foot window in the set. Performances Wed., Thurs., and Sat., a week late because Kermit's brother was killed in a mill accident in Redding, California.

About the middle of April Hawkins' peapod was finished and he launched it into the rolling waves on the Pacific shore in front of an excited and admiring crowd on the beach. The day of the opening performance of Ghosts *Hawkins let Adrian and me take the peapod into the ocean again. It was frightening, handling it with a couple of paddles in the heaving waters, and suddenly with the onslaught of a towering wave the boat capsized and Adrian and I found ourselves struggling to swim to shore through the breakers, the boat and oars floating away from us. Somehow we managed to reach the beach and lie there exhausted while several of the campers hovered over us with blankets. The boat and oars were retrieved and we recovered, but Joe Gistirak, the director of the play, was furious at us for taking such a chance on the day of the opening when we should have spent all our time in preparation for it. Despite our dangerous adventure, the performance went well and the audience was impressed, even the Holy Joes who had never seen a live theater performance in their lives. One of them came up to me afterwards and expressed amazement that I could transform my usual self into the elderly impassioned Mrs. Alving, and experience such intense emotion on the stage every night.*

May 21, 1945
. . . At dress rehearsal of *Ghosts* that night I had a premonition something would happen: life was too good. But Tuesday morning, already tipped toward the afternoon, I cached the blanket and explored the Graves property for more love-nests. First I found a weathered wooden post marking the spot where one S. A. Jacobson had been interred on November 17, 1898. I had forgotten all about death. Then I crawled through a hole in the wind-flattened mat of pines and came into the most exquisite grotto, a completely enclosed room with a needled floor, like a bed with a canopy. A dead gull marked the entrance. By that sign we would know it in the afternoon.

But when I saw Joyce at lunch things were grim. . . . Bob announced that

he was going up to Portland Thursday for work for ten days until he had
enough money to travel on and then decide whether to go east or stay on.
A telegram came from Addie [the wife of Joyce's imprisoned C.O. brother]
saying that two Harvey paintings had brought $300 at the Jane Street
Gallery. . . . I made an all-night press run (Thursday morning), heard Bob
leave for Portland, went to sleep in the grotto at 9:00 a.m. and was caressed
awake there by my love around noon, as suggested in a note to her delivered by
the naive Kemper. Thursday night was the last performance of the play. The
Dupres had a big party for the cast afterwards, much good insight into the
play, lots of fun, and delicious Italian spaghetti and garlic bread by Kemper.
Perhaps you associate booze with my present debauch. Let it be known that
I still can't down more than half a glass of port or sherry, and the smell of
whiskey—of which there has been little now that Manche and her Oregon
liquor license are in San Francisco—still nauseates me as it did when we kids
sniffed at the bottles the college boys left after weekends in Northampton.
I didn't want Joyce to be lonely that night. It wasn't until Saturday, however,
the third night of our marriage, that I realized emotionally what it means to
have a wife. If Bob thinks he has lost this I can understand why it hurts. . . .

Bob had called Friday from Portland to ask if the money ($300) had come.
He wasn't working and wanted to get out of the miserable city and go east
without even coming back to camp. The money came Saturday. . . . Joyce
hitch-hiked up to Portland with the Dupres Sunday. Just before she left, Bob
called, wanted the money quick. They would save discussion until she
got there. . . .

In the meantime I am killing time in such profitable undertakings as
dropping a whole case, caps and lower case, of Bodoni italic which will take
me at least a day of blinding labor to "unpi," and finding forty-six unprinted
pages when I just cleaned the press. But that is what happens when all you
think about is making love. . . .

May 22, 1945

Joyce is back and life is ecstatic again. I had two letters from her in the
anxiously awaited 1:30 mail today, the first, mailed Monday morning, about
the bus trip to Portland and finding Bob in Lang's sordid studio, drunk, and
with a wench, the second, mailed Monday evening, about Bob's going to
San Francisco with Joe Gistirak . . . and her coming back today to stay until
June 1. . . . They made me cry with anguish at what had passed through
those brown eyes and fine ears, and laugh with joy at her coming back, her
tentative decision in my favor. Even before I got out of the shower in the
dorm she had arrived and we had a glorious reunion in the cabin. All my fears

about her cooling off, her making a decision to break with me vanished in the realization that she had stayed "true," that she was stable. So we are in deeper than ever. . . .

June 8, 1945

Cessna [the new director] came into the infirmary where I am finishing off six days of curing a sore throat and swollen glands in my neck, the effects of an inflamed tonsil stump, and said a very strange thing. I was writing in bed as I am now. He asked, "Are you writing to your parents?" "No, not at the moment." "Well, you'd better write to them once in a while." I hope my silence hasn't disturbed you more than any immediate reactions to your telegram to Cessna, and to your last letter, would have done. After this wait and after a few days respite from the other batterings we have been getting—the Reynolds and Bob—I can write quite coolly.

The infirmary has been a little hard on Joyce and me, but fortunately I have been the only SQ until today and have managed to get away in the afternoons for "extended showers." Joyce has brought wild irises and luxuriant pink rhododendrons, and her own blooming, to transform this from a "bed of pain," as it is called by Kermit, to a beautiful rest. . . .

The only place where I can see our relationship has been destructive is in the way it has affected other people. We have certainly failed to make Middletown understand, and Bob's philosophical sanction has changed since he has reached N.Y. to complete condemnation. . . .

Joyce and I are going to San Francisco, and I hope Yosemite, as soon as I am well, planning nothing beyond then, living as much in the present as possible. Perhaps outside of this weird social pattern we will be able to see things more clearly. Write to me General Delivery, San Francisco, as I once did to you from Trenton. . . .

June 23, 1945

Even though this will have to be short to get it in the mail, I want to get some word to you before you think I have eloped and jumped the country. Joyce is now at the farm in Prattsville with Bob. Not that this is the end. But, as I said in my last letter, we had to do something about Bob's condemnation and rejection before we could go on. The last word I had from Joyce was from Chicago—very low and tired.

. . . We started out for San Francisco a week ago Monday down the Coast Road—spectacular between here and Florence and again below Port Orford—and made Crescent City, California, by nightfall, seeing our first redwoods going into the town. In the morning we had a marvelous ride through the redwoods in the back of a big truck so that we could walk around just as if we were having a leisurely stroll through the forest. Our *rides* in the afternoon in the redwoods below Eureka were short, and pretty far between, so that we could walk around in the beautiful groves while waiting for cars. The California sun that has burned up all the hills south of the redwoods was blazing, but under the big trees it was cool and shady, almost nicer to wait than to ride. Just before Garberville we got a ride with a little man who was stopping for the night near Laytonville, going on to Oakland in the morning. We decided to stay with him, spent the night in cabins high over the Eel River, went on in the morning into the brown Santa Rosa valley. Our little man was immaculate, very sporty, took great delight in making us happy. So that we could have a good view of the Bay Area he took us into San Francisco by the Golden Gate Bridge, past the old exposition buildings, the wharves, over the Oakland Bay Bridge and drove us all over Oakland and Berkeley until we located a very fine auto court—kitchen and everything— for $2 per night, an excellent center of operations. Instead of the bridge we used the Southern Pacific ferries for getting over to Frisco, so much cooler and romantic. Of course we saw Chinatown, some crummy nightclubs, fine views of the city from the parks. I stopped in at the General Delivery window Thursday but no mail from you. I should have left my address. Joyce left Friday morning on a slow train. I wanted to hitch-hike with her to Denver, have her fly from there, but she thought it would be even harder parting. For our days on the road and in San Francisco showed us new lights. Joyce is more marvelous than I ever dreamed. It was a very beautiful trip, almost ethereal, so easy, magnificent, full of love. . . .

July 1, 1945

. . . Your letter Saturday was overwhelming. I thought San Francisco with Joyce might have been the last straw for you, like an elopement, but instead you recognize it as the great experience that it was. . . . I am leaving for the East Saturday, would have left today if it hadn't been for *Compass*, hitch-hiking if I can't get the Streamliner out of Portland, perhaps flying if I get tired of hitch-hiking. At the farm in Prattsville Bob finally came to recognize the fact of Joyce's and my "one-ness," felt that we should be together, logically in Sedgwick, Maine, because of Bud Hawkins' viewpoint and hos-pitality—house, money, thirty-four-foot sloop and other boats, and went to New York, not without hurt, to paint the mural for a downtown restaurant. So Joyce and I will be together in Sedgwick for awhile or until I am picked up. . . . [From San Francisco] I chose the inland route 99 because I wanted to make Waldport in two days and because it would take me through new country and past Mt. Shasta. I struggled along the hot first day on the leavings of the Army and the Navy who stood ahead of me in as many as four clumps, and even when they were behind me got picked up first. My last ride, 150 miles into Redding was with a young Union Oil Company salesman whose radiator was clogged so that we had to stop to put in water every mile until a garage man fixed it. My patience with it got me first a milkshake, then root-beer, at suppertime a big veal cutlet dinner, and finally when I told him I was a C.O. the information that he was a J.W., had spent nineteen days in the Fresno County jail in '41 when he said he was a C.O. and was given a 4-F for flat feet he didn't have. I spent the night in a gloomy hotel over the Main Street of Redding and set out the next morning with a very dull sailor, just off the boat in San Diego. Even with him for a front, thumbing was very bad. Going around Mt. Shasta, completely snow-capped against a blue sky, I had my first flat in all the thousands of miles of hitch-hiking. . . . Then as the sun was setting over the long low Coast Range a panel truck driven by a sailor and his wife picked me up. He wondered if it wasn't tough for civilians to get rides and why I was still a civilian. I told him I kept a civilian status even though I was drafted as a conscientious objector.

"And for what reason are you a consci- conch- conchie- objector?" he asked, intentionally stumbling over the words.

"Mostly personal and philosophical reasons."

"What's this philo- philos- philosophical stuff?"

"The way I think life, and particularly my own life, should be lived."

"You know this war isn't being fought on those principles," he said hotly.

"Yes, I am sure of it."

Suddenly he turned off the road into a lumber mill yard.

"What are you doing?" his wife asked.

"I'm going to beat this bastard up."

He got out of the car.

"Get out."

"If you don't get back in here I'm going home this minute," his wife blurted.

"Well, the bastard—"

"It's just the way you feel about it yourself, there's lots of them," she defended.

"Well, I've put in my time over there and this yellow . . ."

"You know very well you joined up because we weren't getting along," she snapped.

He went around the car to open the back door. His wife said to me, "He's just—you know."

He threw open the door. "Get out!" I grabbed my satchel and coat, mumbling something about wishing I could make him understand.

"I ought to run over you, you son of a bitch," he said and jumped in the truck and roared out of the yard and strangely enough back to Medford; I wondered if to get his buddies or the police, or maybe in such a rage that he didn't know where he was going. I went out to the road and started thumbing again. About the fourth car was the sailor coming back. He swerved in to hit me, didn't even come close, and roared north.

The experience had affected me more than I thought. I could well have used Joyce's beautiful shoulder. And with my hunger, the night coming on, and no cars, things looked very black. But then a jolly "war widow," very much in love with her husband overseas, picked me up, going all the way to Salem. I was careful about revealing my status and we hummed along laughing and singing. . . . Two milk trucks and some other rides got me . . . finally [to] camp. After the parched air coming off the brown California hills, the Oregon air, and particularly that on the coast, is glorious. I haven't stopped noticing it. . . .

Cessna, a 230-pound Neanderthal, whose bull manner always gets in the way of his good intentions, is not the man to help me with the affairs of my heart, I am afraid. Of course I told him everything, but he was utterly helpless and incompetent, really concerned only about how it might cause talk among the Holy Joes. You would have done better to ask Everson who is just as old and ten times as mature and perceptive, and has been in this same experience on the end where it hurts. I have talked a lot with him and with Bus and with the Dupres. Those who have seen our relationship think it very wonderful and are glad that it is going on. But you must see for yourself.

With the train trip described in the next letter Adrian began a new chapter of his life. When he "walked out" of Waldport, he left Civilian Public Service behind, and was free to go wherever he would until the F.B.I. would apprehend him and he would be tried and sentenced. Just before he left Waldport Adrian received a deeply disturbing letter from his parents. They were horrified by his illegally deserting camp, by his love for me, and by our plans to go on the cruise together on Hawkins' boat. Adrian's closeness to his family, faced with his new obsession, created a torment in his mind. He wrote them during the train trip across the country.

Cheyenne, Wyoming
July 9, 1945

. . . I am having one of my disorientation experiences, "mental migraines," as I used to call them. I am living in the world of my night dreams. Who am I, what am I doing in Cheyenne, Wyoming, halfway to Chicago, writing a letter like this? Philosophically I am beginning to feel that until I have solved the problem of "who am I," "why am I I," nothing is worth worrying about, going along in the traditional patterns may be all wrong or all right; I know nothing. I am not so disoriented that I can't tell time, however. The train leaves at 9:45. It is 9:30.

Trans Nebraska
North Platte

This train trip is some grind. . . . I have a little cubbyhole right at the end of this old fashioned car, where the door slams in my face day and night, and I can tell just how many times a day each passenger goes to the john. The soldiers and sailors are doing their best to get drunk. I am sick of the word "chow." In front of me is a sailor who has been making hay with a very cute girl from Iowa, married but just the same— . . . A soldier who got on in Boise has sulfa compound on his back where new skin has been grafted over a gasoline burn suffered in an airplane crash. He has the Distinguished Service Cross. A stewed soldier just got on in North Platte. The sailors call him colonel. But all are terrified of the M.P.'s.

Lasalle Station
Chicago

After Omaha, the train was packed and the sailors got drunker and drunker. The youngest of them had been boisterous all day. With the lights in the car out and the unconditioned air dense with smoke from the cigars they were giving away, he started yelling for a shipyard worker whom they called "Fat" who had been in on the revelry. His buddies tried to restrain him. So he put his hand through the window. "Christ, look at that son of a bitch bleed!" They led him into the next car. Blood spattered over the floor and luggage as he went. This morning he was wearing a sling.

A fellow who was getting out at Council Bluffs just after this incident told me he had left a seat vacant in the next car. I snatched it, glad to get out of my sweltering madhouse, but the air conditioning was so good I shivered all night. Of course I have waited in line for an hour to get into the diner only to discover that they only serve military personnel at lunch, or that they are taking off the diner at Pocatello, or that it closed at eight, or that they have served 240 which is all they counted on. Prices are down—you can't pay more than 75 cents—but so is the service. I seem to recall fingerbowls on the Lackawanna two years ago. Henry Miller's title for his new book about America occurs to me: *The Air-Conditioned Nightmare*. Fortunately I have talked to nobody. A railroad car would be a very bad place to get a reaction like my Medford, Oregon, sailor's.

My train pulls out of here at 1:30. I plan to meet Joyce in Albany at the ungodly hour of 5:06 a.m. and go on directly to Sedgwick. I think I should discover how things go with us after a month apart and in a different social set-up before I talk to you. I hope you can believe that none of the virtues you saw in me before I left home have been destroyed by this experience. I think rather that my loyalty, love for people, awareness, honesty, etc., are intensified by loving Joyce. Objective evidence? Perhaps that I stayed a week longer in Oregon to finish *Compass*, and a "gathering" the fellows had for me Friday night, attended by all the Waldport worthies, even Brother Scott.

I have not been burnt. I am far more ready to go to prison knowing that there is at least one desirable woman in the world and that sex is a wonderful reality, not the myth instilled by society's propaganda that I was beginning to think it. . . . As far as I know the new address is c/o H. S. Hawkins, Sedgwick, Maine.

At Large

Hawkins' House, Sedgwick, Maine
July 19, 1945

Liefe Moesje en Dad,

. . . If you have a road map of Maine and New England I will tell you about
the week and a half since I wrote from Chicago. But first you must know
that I wore the shirts, pants, and socks that arrived the day before I left
Waldport through the whole trip, and the box of brownies saved my life the
first night when the diner for which I had starved all day was closed. The
Paul Revere out of Chicago was fast, and the stories the tough sailors just off
the *New Mexico* and other island invasion battle-wagons were comparing
were very gripping. I slept little with the anticipation of meeting Joyce. But
she wasn't in Albany when I got off at 6:35 a.m. The bus terminal told me
she couldn't arrive before 12:30 from Prattsville. At 10:00, however, two
nuns and behind them the searching eyes. We bought bus tickets to West
Lebanon, N.Y., knowing only that it would be in the Berkshires. The driver
recommended a row of cabins on a hilltop overlooking the lovely Lebanon
valley. Our little house had a Swedish fireplace; the clean wind was rushing
through the woods behind it; the clouds were making shadow patches on the
green valley floor. I loved New England, the East, that day as never before—
and Joyce. We hitch-hiked the next day to Concord, Mass., planning to connect
with Manche and Glen Coffield, the poet, who had been at the farm in
Prattsville and were going up to Bud's too. After the West, houses which
took time to design, build, and maintain are very heartening. And the elms,
which I thought would seem puny after the redwoods and firs, were very
impressive. We stayed at a tourist home opposite Emerson's house, read a
particular Emerson essay in the town library, and had delicious mulled cider
with dinners at Wright's Tavern (1760) and the Old Mill Dam (1689).
Manche and Glen were in town the whole time, but they didn't get our
message and we didn't get theirs until they had gone to Boston. . . .

Friday we hitched up the Newburyport Turnpike. . . . At a corner in Portland Manche and Glen jumped out of a car we were thumbing. The same thing might have happened in Portland, Oregon, a month before! In the morning, in Rockland, we decided to take the ferry to North Haven Island at the mouth of Penobscot Bay on the chance that we could get a boat over to Stonington, or that Bud could get us in one of his boats, thereby saving seventy-five miles of hitching around the Bay and getting boat rides. When we got to North Haven, however, the fog started to roll in, we figured Bud might not have gotten our telegram, and it would cost at least $10 for us to stay on the island overnight until we could get the regular boat in the morning. So we hired a motor launch for $12 and were ferried across to Stonington.

. . . After the wind blew itself out Sunday we started on a cruise in Bud's sloop hoping to get to Eastport and back in a week. But the wind was dead; we got only to Stonington Monday. Glen left us there to get a job before going back to his salt-deficiency experiment in Ann Arbor. Well, there is hardly room for four anyhow. Bud and Manche occupy the fore cabin in which the john sits like a throne [between their two bunks] and Joyce and I the main cabin with the motor, the cook stove, and the sink.

Cruising the first four days was mainly sitting in the hot sun under the limp jib, listening to the swells hissing on the ledges or the granite bases of the faery isles, ducking the swinging of the boom, and eating. We spent the second night becalmed in fog near Isle au Haut, rolling on the heavy swells. I felt like the Ancient Mariner.

On Wednesday there was still no wind. We limped into Frenchboro on Long Island in a cold fog, searching for milk and eggs. Of course the engine wouldn't go Thursday but somehow we got to Northeast Harbor which apparently, since the war, has taken over Bar Harbor's position as a resort town. Our sloop, with its black hull, sleek lines, varnished cabin, and brass polished by us, is always the snappiest boat in even these wealthy harbors. Yachting gives one special privileges too. When we came into Southwest Harbor a [skipper] invited us on board his new John Alden sloop and opened a bilge of icy Schlitz. Yum yum. But we were still far from Eastport, so Bud decided to turn back and start the next cruise that much sooner. Of course a wonderful breeze came up out of Northeast Harbor that whipped us into Eggemoggin Reach by early afternoon. Bud let me handle the tiller after we got out of the fog and into blue white-capped water. Such exhilaration! The boat heels over at forty-five degrees, the wind howls in the rigging, and spray dashes over the bow. Give me more of this.

So we are going south, leaving tomorrow or Monday, touching at

Gloucester, Marblehead, Boston, through the Cape Cod Canal to Martha's
Vineyard and perhaps to Westport, Connecticut, where Bud will pick up
some people who want to come up to Maine. I will come up to Middletown
from there.

But Bud wants me to come and dig some clams for supper. Joyce and I
are very happy. But more from the sloop.

July 27, 1945

Northwest wind at last. We have been roaring south all night and this
bright morning. Hope to make Marblehead by tonight passing York Beach
and Boon Island light. Will show Joyce the Spaulding estate, etc. What a life!

*There is no letter from Adrian describing the cruise, but we set out the following
week in a strong wind with the hope of sailing around the ocean side of Cape
Cod after a stop in Provincetown for supplies. We left there on a bright blue
afternoon with a spanking wind filling the sails. Suddenly Bud called out,
"A whale! There she blows!" and a hundred yards away we saw the jet spout
against the sky. A few minutes later a huge shiny black hump rose above the
water and spouted again, much closer. We were stiff with fear when its gleaming
back glided directly under us lifting the bow up, and then the leviathan
slithered down again. It could easily have overturned the sloop as a playful
gambit, and we were much too far from the coast to swim ashore. But the
monster's next spout was farther away, and soon we saw it no more. Shades of
Moby Dick!*

*Bud soon realized that the waters of the ocean outside of Cape Cod were
much too rough for us to handle the sloop, and our captain decided to turn back.
That night he gave in to the need for rest and turned the tiller over to Adrian
with instructions to keep the bowsprit lined up with the North Star. While
Bud was below Adrian and I exulted in the starry sky and the strong wind that
filled the sails, and watched the occasional light of another ship across the
dark water. Suddenly the lights of a big motorcruiser seemed to be almost on top
of us. Bud, awakened instinctively, was instantly on deck, grabbed the tiller,
swung the sloop about, and missed a collision by a few yards.*

*The next day we blithe fugitives were in for another scare. We anchored the
sloop in the harbor of Scituate near the wall of an old brick building on which
was painted in huge letters "HORE INNERS." The initial letter of each
word had been in another color which had completely faded away. On the way
toward town to buy supplies, we stopped to stare into the window of the "Shore
Dinners" restaurant. A policeman strolled up behind us and put his hands on
Adrian's and Bud's shoulders. They were immediately petrified. This was*

*surely the moment when they would be arrested for being AWOL from camp.
After staring at the menu in the window for a few seconds the officer smiled and
shook his head. "Will you look at that spelling! And this guy has a son at
Boston University!" and he walked away. Little did he know that two
dangerous criminals were simultaneously within his very grasp.*

*There are no more letters from Adrian to his parents for many weeks. Manche
left us in Scituate to join Bob Harvey at the Prattsville farm. Adrian and I
hitchhiked to Middletown, where Adrian stayed at home for a time, and I
visited the Reynolds, whom I had known even before meeting Adrian. But we
took long walks together, talking of the horrors of the bombings of Hiroshima
and Nagasaki, and, of course, discussing what we should do with our futures.*

*On August 14 came V-J Day. The war was over. Like millions of other
young people, we had been uprooted and we felt ambivalent. Should we try to
return to the lives the war had interrupted—Adrian to college, I to some
business or teaching job? Could we somehow gather our Waldport theater
enthusiasts somewhere to work in drama? That became our ultimate hope, and,
to prepare for that, I applied for entrance as a student to the Hedgerow Theater
near Philadelphia, where several of the workers in our production of* Ghosts
*had been trained. Joe Gistirak, like Adrian a walk-out from Waldport, had
returned there already. When I was accepted, I moved into the communal
living quarters at Hedgerow in Rose Valley, Pennsylvania, where I was assigned
to share a remodelled chicken coop with an older woman who had been a
dedicated member of the community for years.*

*Adrian, after a brief job as a cook in a resort hotel in Old Lyme, Connecticut,
came to see me, but found himself feeling like a fifth wheel in the enclosed theater
absorption of the Hedgerow people, including mine and Joe's. Adrian tells in
the following letters how he came to settle at Pendle Hill, the Quaker graduate
study center, which was only a few miles from Rose Valley.*

Pendle Hill, Wallingford, Pennsylvania
October 5, 1945

I walked with my coat and bag away from the Hedgerow theater this
morning, not sure whether nightfall would find me in Middletown or New
Mexico. Joyce had to cook in the kitchen all day, Joe Gistirak assisting. . . .
I would be "in the way." I had to leave. These people had their responsibilities. I wasn't Josh White or Sean O'Casey. I might be the "biggest"
person in the world, but I was nobody. So I walked toward the Moylan-Rose
Valley railroad station. Joyce had suggested I look around Swarthmore, talk to
somebody, anybody, but the answer I got at the University of Pennsylvania
yesterday—three times as many applications as admissions, no consideration

until March, go back to Wesleyan—discouraged me. . . . Where then?

Nancy Foster [the dietician at Trenton] had been on the train going out to Moylan last night. She had gotten off at Wallingford, was staying at Pendle Hill while working at the A.F.S.C. and waiting for a passport to Finland. Well, why not go to Pendle Hill, tell Howard Brinton you are lost—But I had missed the train to Wallingford by a few minutes, so I walked to Wallingford and the two miles beyond to Pendle Hill, very sad inside, keeping to the conventional roads instead of striding across meadows, only the faintest hope— From the sign it looked like an estate—greenhouse, solid stone buildings, a man—who proved to be Japanese—running a power mower.

Then around a corner came two ladies. The elder one said, "Are thee coming to stay with us?" I wasn't sure. "Are we expecting thee?" "No. I would like to see Howard Brinton." "Are thee from C.P.S.?" "Walked out of Waldport, the Fine Arts camp." "Do the authorities know where thee are? If thee are staying I would prefer that they did, so that there will be no searches." "I'm willing to tell them." "Have thee any testimony against sleeping porches?" "Certainly not." "We'll install thee then in the 'portico.' I am Anna Brinton. Howard will be back from his class at Swarthmore soon." Howard came soon. . . . [He] remembered the name, not the face, from the talk we had at Big Flats. The talk on a bench in the back yard the Brintons occupy as directors was warm, wonderfully impersonal—I mean no probing, my maturity and good intentions in coming here were taken completely for granted. He could understand perfectly my skepticism about getting into the juvenile, standard educational patterns, and thought this might be an ideal place to find direction. I could help Edith Hall . . . in the kitchen for my tuition and maintenance, and even earn a salary if I wanted. I almost talked him into getting a printing press to do the Pendle Hill pamphlets—he had thought of it often, wanted to do something with his hands, but lack of space and the desire for non-involvement prevented him. Maybe now, if I will stay—

This acceptance in a place whose ideals, physical layout, and proximity to Philly are better than anything I dreamed, is so amazing after floating and accomplishing nothing the last few days, that I am still dumfounded. Here I, a bum, a tramp, am suddenly having tea with Clarence Pickett, meeting all sorts of profs and Quaker worthies. . . . I talked to Dave McClelland about Holland. They need a man to work in the Dutch Friends' Center at Amsterdam. What qualifications do I have??? How's my Dutch? And I wonder myself, am I stable enough to hold down a job for *two* years, the requirement? When would a personal revolution send me to the moon or Timbuktu? And this man must be solid in his religious conviction. . . . I am the only volunteer so far with a smattering of Dutch. And here at Pendle Hill where a number are training for China, etc., foreign service is in the air, I am developing enthusiasm. So things look rosy tonight and you can send on the box of stationery I left home, because I will be writing from here for awhile.

October 10, 1945

Your letter this morning, the first piece of mail I have received here, gives my life a little more continuity. Of course I am glad you are so happy with this solution. But you realize, as I am beginning to, that this place is worth only as much as I put into it. The discipline is not going to come from Howard Brinton or Teresina Rowell or William Sollman. I am completely free to do as I choose. Their thinking and way of life, however, are very much in the air, and I must be on guard against the part of it that is, as the Heretics used to say, "transcendental bullshit." I mean the hazy, unscientific thinking in metaphors and pretty pictures . . . and the vagueness about educating the "whole man," instead of just the intellect, as the universities do. But I like the direction and my function here can be making what is now so vague explicit. . . .

I am very wary and a little tired of the happy Christian smiles which flash on like stoplights hereabouts, realizing all the time that I am probably the chief offender. So I haven't made any companions. . . . No one, except Anna Brinton in her own Friendly way, has demonstrated any wit or good humor. But she was really magnificent Monday night in her preface to the Business Meeting, a speech full of homey and personal touches that did much to draw the group into community. I think she has a fine mind and a remarkable openness and warmth.

The acceptance here is still amazing. At Hedgerow it is all challenge, complete devotion to the theater, exclusiveness. Joyce is very disturbed. She and Joe gave a reading of *Ghosts* for Jasper Deeter, the director, and some of the others there. "It will take a long time . . . ," which is probably what they say to all newcomers. But here, by their faith in and hope for you, they stimulate you to work as hard as you can. It is a wholly different approach. . . .

I now have a testimony against sleeping porches. A head cold has plagued me since the first day here. Cold feet at night don't help. . . .

October 14, 1945

A cold library with a fire dying in the hearth. Here I do my writing, this week *The Merrie Wives of Waldport*, a fine play to be writing at Pendle Hill, and some reading in the meager collection of "literature." Quaker weights and wits stack 99% of the shelves. But everything is available between

Swarthmore, Haverford, and the big Philly Public Library. . . .
This weekend we had the International Garment Workers Union conven-
tion in, twenty tough factory women mingling their city accents with the
quiet Friendly speech. The only point at which I met them was a folk dance,
called by another ex-Trentonite . . . last night in the dining hall, squares,
reels, mazurkas, schottisches. The girls weren't very bright, but it was fun,
at least winding. Some remarked how strange it was to be together—the same
gang—in this peaceful place after the frenzied city. But of course they went
back today. . . .

October [*21,*] *1945*
I guess I am the chief hero here this weekend, having made everyone
happy with my apple pies and parker house rolls. Anna Brinton said I should
work twenty-one hours a week, spread over Thursday, Saturday, and Sunday
to earn my keep; a scholarship would take care of the rest of it, since when
people work more than twenty-one hours plays don't get written. It was
about as quick and efficient as that. What a woman! Completely free of all
the academic red tape— The reason I am still being complimented for my
pies is that it was Edith's day off and I innocently got at the sugar can. The
Board of Managers was in for its annual meeting last night and kept getting
up for refills on the rolls. Oh, it's great to be a success and have a standing
in the community!
     The letter from [Marty] at Waldport which you forwarded held good news.
Cessna went up to Portland the 12th to put nails in the coffins of all offenders
on the Waldport books—Marty's, Bob's, Joe's, mine, etc., but somehow the
Grand Jury didn't indict me or Si Miller, "insufficient evidence," or something. Now compared to me all these guys, especially Marty, are innocent
babes. I don't get it. They figure I now have until next spring. Seems to me
they were saying just that a year ago.
     I am glad you read "Self-Reliance," but don't understand your saying
that Thoreau, who lived in a shack in the woods, who said as long as one man
is unjustly imprisoned he should be imprisoned too, who went to jail for
refusing to pay taxes, had his feet more on the ground than Emerson. I should
think to you Emerson, who did none of these things, would seem a much
solider citizen. Continue your reading with Christopher Morley's *Thunder
on the Left*. I went over to Hedgerow last night to see Jean Black's dramati-
zation of the novel. It was the most engrossing thing I have ever seen on
stage, partly because of the provocative idea, a child's birthday party wish
that he won't grow up because grown-ups are so unhappy coming true, at
least in a dream of the same group twenty years later; partly because of

personal identification; partly because of the skillful writing; and partly
because of the Hedgerow acting and production. It humbled me almost to the
point of dejection. I might just as well quit trying to write now. Where did
this man Morley who wrote a poem called "Smells" get it?

My clarinet finally came back from the repairman in New York and after
one hour's playing everything is wrong with it that was wrong when I left it
there. Well, I'm not going back to the rubber band era after shelling out $20.
I am sending the horn back with a stern note. Meanwhile weeks go by when
I could be playing Haydn trios and Bartok. Disgoosting. . . .

October 25, 1945

The sandcookies came yesterday and will no doubt be eaten tomorrow at
tea with relish. (Easy on the onions, Joe.) They are hardly necessary as tokens
of Wilson good will, however, since my baking of last week and this week's
chocolate eclairs (yes, the authentic), gingerbread, "simeon" buns, patty
shells, and braided soft rolls have taxed the stomach approach almost to its
limit. If Friends wouldn't devour my wares so fast I could keep you supplied
with day-old pastry and under-sell the First National. But the stuff I put
out is so good the corps of urchins who hang outside the kitchen door and
have appointed themselves official tasters eat it raw. The ingenuity that made
me revolutionize the industry every time I put my hand to the press at
Waldport is standing me in good stead. The eclair shells rose beautifully,
hollow in the center, the cornstarch pudding filling was nice and gooey, but
how to get the second in the first? No pastry tubes, no injector bags . . . so I
cleaned out a tire pump, filled it with pudding instead of air, punctured the
shells with the sharp stem over which the hose had fit, and squirted in the goo.
This method was so efficient (only twelve eclairs per pump full) I had to
make three times as much pudding as the recipe called for. . . .

. . . I admire [Anna Brinton's] easy, unharassed administration. I admire
her speech and her own practice of Quakerism. It seems to me she hasn't
adopted Quakerism or Quaker talk; she has *created* her own individual brand
of it. Her "theeing" and "thouing," like her delightful turns of phrase and
homey touches, is not done in conformity; it is done as a "gag," almost, a
trifle which makes life a ceremony, an art. I think she sees through Quakerism. . . .

I was looking at the alcove of our modern dining room as a stage last night.
It struck me that maybe I have to take a new approach to playwriting: Instead
of reworking experience, picking dramatic elements, adding imaginative
elements, and giving them form, I have to sit in front of my stage and ask
myself, "What can I see happen there, how can I transform this bare stage to

awaken people, what can I say from there to the people out here?" I have
to learn to work with the material of the theater, a stage, scenery, actors. What
I am doing now is writing plays for publication, not production. . . .

November 4, 1945

This fourth full week at Pendle Hill has taken on more the aspect of a
routine, one which I would like to continue—writing leisurely on the terrace
in the autumn sun the first three days, cooking Thursday, Edith Hall's day
off, odd jobbing at seventy-five cents an hour Friday, being a hero again
Saturday and Sunday with my cooking and baking. . . .

Joyce has been sick this week and is up at the farm for the weekend,
recuperating. All along, the wall of silence which the Hedgerow company
throws up to newcomers has been very disheartening, just the opposite of the
openness here at Pendle Hill. When at Mahlon Naill's (George in *Thunder*)
drunken farewell party the silence was revealed to be deliberate, and Mahlon,
who had been the only one to befriend Joyce, condemned for it and their
conversation which had been on a high intellectual level dubbed "chit-chat,"
Joyce was badly shaken. The atmosphere had some psychosomatic effect on
her cold and put her in bed for several days. Looks like Joyce should find
another place to live and a job, and work at Hedgerow part-time and go into
the school at night to get Jasper Deeter's teaching.

The clarinet is back and really fixed, so that it plays like pre-C.P.S. One
of the girls here, who is studying at Swarthmore . . . and plays the cello, and
I got together with John Rue on a Mendelssohn trio last night. John was
comparable to Scott, reading the difficult score almost perfectly at sight. . . .

November 13, 1945

By the time your last letter came your suggestion for Joyce was already
acted upon—not exactly as you stated it, but approximately. Through a
connection here at Pendle Hill . . . we have gotten Joyce a job at the private,
progressive Rose Valley School, just up the road from the Hedgerow theater.
. . . Both the principal and the teacher of the oldest group, ten or so eleven,
twelve, and thirteen year olds, were sick and the school in the market for a
substitute. That night we had an interview with the Spillers, he a University
of Pennsylvania English prof . . . , she teacher of the first graders, both among
the group of parents which founded the school for their children sixteen
years ago. The openness and faith was just like I found at Pendle Hill.
Between her teaching experience . . . and her obvious qualifications Joyce
was immediately "in" at $25 a week over withholding tax until December 16.
Then they would see again for the term beginning January 2. Between the

teachers they figured they could dig up a place for Joyce to live. Afterwards we went to the Turners' modern house, designed by a student of Frank Lloyd Wright, for cocoa. . . .

Joyce is finding it exhilarating to be in an atmosphere where she is appreciated after the nightmare of Hedgerow. Classes in the evening with Jasper Deeter still continue but despite Joe Gistirak's admiration and *The Provincetown* dubbing him "ecstatic and irascible," Joyce doesn't think he has much to offer.

. . . A long letter from Marty, with samples of his printing now that he has put his hand to the monster, and a sheaf of comments on *Compass*, all enthusiastic but one. This one was from a Mennonite privy-building camp. "I am returning my copy. . . . There runs a tinct [sic] of vulgarity in that the countryside outhouse type of art picturing naked women casts a shadow on the whole magazine. . . ."

Si Miller, though unindicted was arrested in Frisco, now out on bail. What's the matter with me? They know where I am. . . .

December 2, 1945

Two vivid letters from Norm, written the 11th and the 15th of November, brightened last week. John Rue helped me locate Fukuoka on a *National Geographic* map, and Kusuo Shirota joined us to point out his home, Kumamoto, not a hundred miles away. So I suggested to Kusuo, who has heard only once from his parents during the four years he has been in this country, all of which were spent interned at Tule Lake, that he let me send a letter to his folks via Norm. It was positively artistic the way he dashed off the Japanese characters. John, who is studying the language, assured me they were not the process for the atomic bomb. Perhaps this will give Kusuo a better opinion of Americans. "My people live on farm. The Japanese farmer is good. He is different from the Japanese city-dweller. The people who live in cities are like the Americans." Kusuo has a sister in Japan who graduated from an American high school. Norm's first date! Norm's writing about the geisha girls, the street scenes, and teaching the kids English was particularly wonderful. I still miss any questioning of his function there, any search for the values in Japanese culture, however, at an age when this sort of consciousness should be awakening, or at least was in me. . . .

What does Pendle Hill propose? The last after-dinner session of the course in "The Education of Man" presented Cora Balle Hunter in a talk about the psychology of education. . . . Then everybody threw in his own theory. Concretely it meant Quaker work camps, labor unions, welfare agencies, and co-ops. When it became unbearable I said, "I should like to put in a plug for the Arts, which it seems we have completely forgotten. To my mind the arts give a social criticism and an implied way of life which is the answer to many of our problems." When Anna Brinton interpreted this to mean it was a good idea to keep people amused, I said, "I don't deny that function of the arts, but I should hope their function would go far beyond that. Art, particularly its creation, gives life dedication and meaning." For the next three days people kept coming to me saying they agreed with me one hundred percent. . . .

I think it is high time I put my ideas into practice. I think in January I shall go to California to start a community theater and buy some land, out of which food, buildings, everything can grow. I am forgetting about the atomic bomb.

January 14, 1946

. . . I have hooked up with a very attractive, level-headed, and, I imagine, talented woman, Mrs. Seyril Rubin, who has been directing dramatics at Swarthmore College and is anxious to start a cooperative repertory theater on the West Coast. We are in the process of writing a prospectus about how it will be organized, like a co-op grocery, pay actors, technicians and playwrights a decent living salary, and provide the best in classical, experimental, and children's plays. . . . The site is undecided, but either Seattle or San Francisco. The Rubins are definitely going west in March, he being a dentist, recently discharged from the Army, who wants to study some special branch at the U. of Washington or the U. of California. I may go out before them, as scout and herald. Anna Brinton thinks, too, that this is a wonderful idea. . . .

January 24, 1946

. . . Another meeting with Seyril Rubin about the theater, on Tuesday night. She and Dr. Rubin are going west in early February now, establishing headquarters in Portland from which they will investigate Seattle and San Francisco. I wonder if I shouldn't go out simultaneously, hitch-hiking by a southern route. We planned the prospectus and tonight I went over to Swarthmore with Beloof, to see about using the press for printing it, which I think I'll do tomorrow. The instructor there is Walter Kahoe, who works for Lippincotts and has his own press in his basement, on which he does fine small editions. He was impressed by the Untide Press books which I showed him, though I think his tastes are conservative.

At the same time the theater plans go on, I have sent for an application for foreign service with the A.F.S.C. I don't see that working on the theater idea should exclude foreign service, provided I get an appointment and a release from the court, unless the theater proves to be just what I want.

January 27, 1946

. . . No sooner had I signified my intention of going west in a week or two, when I was informed that a Mr. . . . was driving to the Coast beginning Monday, and could take me as far as Chicago, where he is picking up another passenger. This seemed to me too good to pass up, especially with the hope that I will take his fancy and get him to drive me all the way to San Francisco. So tomorrow at 9:00 a.m. he is picking me up here and away we go. I understand he is a literary gentleman of some accomplishment, is mentioned in Gertrude Stein's last book, has spent a number of years abroad, so I expect that riding with him will be interesting. In San Francisco I plan to investigate the possibilities for beginning the co-op theater by talking to theater people in town, at the colleges, to co-op people, and some people at Mills College to whom Anna Brinton is giving me letters of introduction. Meanwhile the Rubins will be investigating the Northwest, Portland and Seattle. . . .

Of course, Adrian and I were sad about his imminent departure, but we assumed that he would do the scouting and I would join him as soon as he had assessed the situation in San Francisco. He later recounted the experiences of this trip to me—a section that he couldn't possibly share with his parents. He rode with the "literary gentleman" to a small town en route to Chicago where they stopped for the night. They had dinner in the greasy spoon restaurant of the hotel, and the driver suggested they go right to bed and make an early start in the morning. As they undressed he began homosexual overtures which Adrian vigorously resisted, so that he finally gave up, and they got some sleep. Conversation was not as literary as Adrian had hoped. The next morning there was grim silence. At an intersection on the outskirts of Chicago, the driver abruptly said, "Get out here!" and as Adrian climbed out, he threw after him a book, yelling "Read that and maybe you'll learn something about life!" The book landed in a dirty snowbank and on picking it up Adrian found that it was a well-thumbed copy of Psychopathia Sexualis *by Krafft-Ebing.*

Adrian carried it in his satchel, hitchhiking all the way to San Francisco. From time to time he read snatches of it with incredulity, and he wondered what would happen if he were apprehended by the F.B.I. with such "pornography" in his possession. When he arrived at his destination, he went into Holmes Bookstore on Third Street and sold the volume for fifty cents, with which, in a Chinese restaurant, he paid for his first meal in San Francisco.

Ames, Iowa
January 30, 1946

A discharged soldier and I skidded into Ames about three this morning, too late to call the C.P.S. unit or to get a hotel room, but the lobby of the

Sheldon-Munn being preferable to a manger, I snoozed there. This lobby being also the bus depot made sleeping a little difficult. Everytime a bus would come in, the negro bell-hop would make his rounds of the sprawlers on the couches. He would tell me that the bus was going to Minneapolis or Des Moines, or east or west, but when I mumbled that I wasn't interested, he always looked disappointed. About five, he started vacuum cleaning the rugs, which meant furniture moving. Sleeping is permitted here, but not encouraged. All the while, it was pouring outside and the bus drivers were speculating on what the roads would be like if the temperature dropped as forecast. I wondered if I hadn't better head south right away, and forget about the C.P.S. unit. The prospect of a shower, a meal, and a bed, plus seeing merry Frank Ripley, etc., plus the rain, lured me into a telephone booth. Frank sent Bob McCoy, formerly at Big Flats, in to town to take me four miles out to this miniature model C.P.S. camp, back of the Iowa State College campus. Frank was in the kitchen just as at Trenton. . . .

Casa Grande Hotel
Elk City, Oklahoma
February 2, 1946

This is a town 120 miles west of Oklahoma City, boasting two [movie] theaters, sidewalks with ramps in the curbs for perambulators, and fat men like Ed Hutchinson, and a radio station with its transmitter right above our rooms, which Ed is putting on his expense account. He works for a Kansas City oil company, is on his way to Wellington in the Texas panhandle, to take gravity meter readings on some land where they suspect black gold. He picked me up outside of Oklahoma City on Route 66, which the *Grapes of Wrath* people took to California; he will take me on to Shamrock, Texas, tomorrow. I hope I can make Carlsbad or at least Roswell, N.M., by tomorrow night. . . .

I got to the boarding house run by Bob Beloof's folks in Wichita, early yesterday afternoon. When I called Juliette Reeve, the Daniel Defoe scholar of Pendle Hill, teaching at Friends University, she bid me come to the President's reception that evening. But instead of Juliette meeting me, there was a very lovely blond girl, in evening gown, daughter of a physics professor, a junior, who was just as bright and responsive. After the receiving line, "the subtle punch in tiny sips," to quote Beloof . . . , there was a Brunhilde singing two sentimental songs, a wisp playing a Chopin ballade much too difficult for her, an amusing play about an old-ladies' home, and the Alma Mater. All the formality and phoney tradition was a little surprising after Pendle Hill. I had forgotten that Alma Maters existed. Then all the young people, including me, went downtown to the Twentieth Century Club for a dance, since Friends doesn't allow dancing on the premises. . . . This morning, to the open road. How my worlds shift!

I can understand Bob Beloof better. His mother and father are revolutionaries, socialists, overjoyed that I had walked-out and told the government to go to hell; at the same time they are capitalists, making a very good living off their apartment houses, putting on big feeds, and listening to the radio and reading their newspapers in the evening. . . .

Carlsbad, New Mexico
February 4, 1946

It's true that this is where the sun goes in winter. I have rented one of the cabins in an auto court on the highway through the town, having come in too late to make the daily exploration of the Caverns. The street is full of sunlight and Mexicans, the sky an ethereal blue, and the clouds fat and luminous. Otherwise, however, the country is the last that you would expect to hold a national park—just miles of baked rubble with a little thorny vegetation poking up between. But the signs have been extolling the fifty cent lunch 750 feet underground. Tomorrow I will see. . . .

I got up before dawn this morning anxious to be on my way to Carlsbad. The hitching was very good though Carlsbad was much farther than I had thought. I am discovering that New Mexico is the fourth largest state in area. Fifty miles northwest of Roswell I sighted the first of the mountains, their tops in cloud balls, 100 miles west. They looked twenty miles away. Now, in Carlsbad, I walk in shortsleeves down the main street, hiding my ten-cent-store pencils from the legless monstrosity on the sidewalk waving his hatfull of pencils at me.

February 6, 1946

This is a laugh. Coming north out of Carlsbad at dusk last night, just when I was beginning to think I'd have to stay over in town another night, an Air Corps flyer picked me up. "Where you going?" "Roswell, Albuquerque and west." "I'm staying over in Roswell tonight, fooling around there tomorrow and then going to L.A. Does that suit you?" I pondered it awhile. It would mean missing the Grand Canyon, but one trouble with Carlsbad had been that I had no one's hand to press at the breathtaking places. Maybe I should postpone the Canyon. So I said O.K. I would go with him to L.A. He said we could stay at the Army Air Base that night for fifty cents. I was on the verge of registering my conscientious objection to this, but he said I would be his guest, and I figured it would be a fine insight into Army life.

So we got out his flying map marked Roswell, located the Air Base just as if we were ten thousand feet up, and came in on the beam. We got a room at the B.O.Q. (Billetting Officers' Quarters), showered, shaved . . . and then we went into town to find the Busy Bee Cafe. One of his buddies, now discharged, had been set up by his father in the restaurant business. We would get a free steak. . . . If we drive straight through we should be in L.A. tomorrow.

Frankly, Carlsbad, as an experience, was a great disappointment to me. Maybe I don't like guided tours where you are restricted to a line of doddering humanity on paved sidewalks, assailed in front by stupid similes, "Oh, it's just like a Christmas tree," and behind by complaints of being tired. I missed completely a sense of freedom and exploration. . . . Also, lack of personnel prevented taking the walk-out route, so that I had to wait an hour for an elevator. There is something devilish about going into the hole, all these people winding into the bowels of the earth, like the souls of the damned going to Hell. Maybe I don't like the idea of being one of them.

Of course, the caverns are out of this world. Some of the structures are so delicately drawn by gravity they made me gasp. And then there are yawning mouths of other caverns, ceilings completely covered with icicles, groups of crystals as fine as frost work, formations like draperies, that transmit an orange light. But for grandeur it wasn't much more impressive than the Swarthmore fieldhouse. Certainly the domes enlarge the perspective of low-ceilinged apartments and bungalows. I still prefer the dome of the blue western sky, with clouds that are pure luminous white. One thing you realize, however, is that you have to be there a long time. Walk ten feet and everything is as different as though you had shaken a kaleidoscope. Perhaps, too, it takes a long time to sense the force of gravity, everything pointing downward, obedient. I thought of Dali's paintings where the watch, everything, droops to gravity. Some of Carlsbad is Dali crystallized. Then there are rocks, flat, smooth, suspended from nowhere, with a water-worn hole off-center, that is very abstract. This time of year the three million bats have migrated south where the insects are still flying, so we had no bat flight out of the cavern mouth at sunset. . . .

Friends Center
San Francisco
February 8, 1946

Only two days ago I was writing like this in the Busy Bee Cafe in Roswell, N.M., and already I have had a Chinese dinner (fried shrimp) as Anna Brinton recommended, and a good night's sleep in the basement of this place. The flyer kept driving all through the night, Phoenix at 1:30 a.m., the

California line at 4:00, the wall of the San Jacintos at dawn, Pomona, his home, at 8:30 a.m. California must look like heaven to the Okies after the miles of brown desert and the dead mountains. We drove through endless green orange groves, the fruit a bright orange or yellow, the smudge hanging over them against the frosty morning. The fruit stands were proclaiming the new crop of dates, the lawns were green, the palms were waving in the winds.

I was tempted to investigate the Pasadena Playhouse when I passed through, but I knew our idea was different. It took California, of course, to have the best mountain scenery of the trip. The country coming north on 99 out of L.A. is very rugged and precipitous and there is a 4,000 foot coast down into the great valley at the end. The Air Corps was very good to me again; a captain going to Sacramento, averaging about 60 (m.p.h.), so that I was in Oakland at 8:00 p.m. and San Francisco an hour and a half later.

Your letter . . . was here at the Friends Center when I arrived. It occurred to me you might be a little startled at my sudden departure. Your letter this morning, however, showed not too much alarm. Also, this morning, was word from Kermit about the theater, suggesting that I get in touch with Bob McLain in S.F. as a business manager, etc. Things are moving! Thank God I have something like this. The other C.P.S. men moping around here are actually sick. There are twelve of them, just bailed out after being in jail for five days. They refused to obey an order at Minersville camp: to take down some blankets they were using as partitions. For this they will stand trial and probably get two years. The tragedy is they love it, feel like heroes, righteous martyrs.

In the fall of 1945 Kermit Sheets had begun sharing the thoughts of the various C.P.S. people who had been involved in producing plays in the camps and wanted to start a theater. By this time they were scattered all across the country, and Kermit copied the impassioned and visionary letters and distributed them, together with his own ideas, from one to another. Before the Waldport camp closed, a production of Shaw's Candida *was staged with Kermit and Ibby Dupre. A number of Fine Arts men were transferred to Cascade Locks, where David Jackson directed a production of Chekhov's* The Sea Gull *in which Kermit played Trigorin and Hildegarde Erle played Arcadina.*

With Adrian in San Francisco, scouting, several of the correspondents were considering gathering there to start a theater group.

1853 Webster Street, San Francisco
February 12, 1946
Through friends, of course, the McLains, Bob and Naomi, I have a very

nice temporary room on the third floor of a typically San Francisco dwelling
two blocks from the Friends Center. Their apartment is down the hall so
that we share brunches. Bob is the fellow that Kermit suggested as business
manager for the co-op theater, but he isn't really a theater man, and has
gotten going again running the anti-conscription campaign, so he has declined
the position. Nevertheless he is very helpful. Other than the brunches, I am
observing a strictly Chinese diet. Around the corner are three Chinese restaurants, but Kum Far Low, where I ate last night, was the most enjoyable,
possibly because I thought I was getting so much for fifty cents, a big bowl
of rice, tasty chop suey, and unlimited quantities of tea. There is a quality
about the food, the dishes, the privacy (a cubicle for each party), and the
service, that makes me want to make a ceremony out of every bite. Don't let
the three Chinese restaurants mislead you, however. This is the negro section
of town, if anything, negro night clubs, cafes, record shops. And then again it
is just cosmopolitan, Filipino restaurants and a Spanish movie. . . .

I haven't had to start work yet —the Pendle Hill $12.00 being good for
twenty-four Chinese meals, I figure, so I have been writing here in the room,
reading Katherine Mansfield, and doing a little spasmodic investigating.

Mr. Arthur B. Gleditsch, who runs the Theater Arts Colony, a combination
theater school and playhouse, was not very encouraging. You have to have a
place to play, and there just isn't any. Fire ordinances prevent his using his
building more than three nights a week. There are six groups in town contemplating essentially the same thing. Do we realize how much money it
takes just for lighting equipment? It's taken him seven years to get as far
as he has, and only now is he breaking into a full-time production schedule.
It still takes the school to support it.

So we have been thinking of other possibilities—a theater across the Golden
Gate Bridge, buying an old liberty ship or landing barge from the Navy
(swords into plowshares, you know). My own preference is [the Cliff House]
cafe where I had lunch Friday. The location is perfect for my *Merry Wives
of Waldport*, in which the surf roars throughout. Fine views too. It was obvious
this cafe wasn't making any money. I should think renting the site wouldn't
cost so much then. But probably the fire ordinances would stump us. . . .

There are moments of loneliness here, moments when I think I should be
out of the city, working on the land, moments when I wish the F.B.I. would
make up its mind, but I haven't had any regrets that I came west and not a
bit of homesickness for Pendle Hill.

February 18, 1946

Thanks to Marty Ponch, this time, I am now a pressman in a print shop
off Broadway in Oakland, Cal. Marty wrote suggesting I look up Ralph Odom,

one of the C.O. ministers . . . who had started the West-O-Craft Studio of
Fine Printing. When I came to the shop, above a shooting gallery on 12th
Street, Ralph and his brother-in-law, just out of the Navy where he saved up
the money to start this business, were moving in three new platen presses,
acquired from the third partner in the enterprise. . . . Ralph, young enough
to have taken a 4-D to go to seminary, instead of a 4-E, was very accommo-
dating; put me right to work after I told him of all my experience at Waldport.
Of course, he didn't know the monster there lumbered along at 800 impressions an hour, instead of 2,000. My days since have been a matter of trying
to keep up with these commercial machines. . . . And it is only my pride that
makes me keep on. I am going to master this craft, be something but mediocre.
And in the end it will be very useful, as it has been, for the theater, *Compass*,
and perhaps some books of poetry that no one else will publish, like Art's
which he mentioned in the letter to me today. So you can think of me every
morning riding the trolley up and down hills to the East Bay terminal, then
the A train across the Bay Bridge, and off at the Broadway stop in downtown
Oakland. It is very grubby, this competitive world, the dingy printshop, but
a means, I hope. . . .

March 3, 1946

Yesterday was a lucky day: (1) I learned that Seyril, husband, and five-
year-old son were arriving the 19th, (2) I found a place where I could get
lunch for fifty cents, (3) I found a wonderful little theater for us. . . . The
situation is this: the side of a hill, of course, at the crossing of the Washington
Street and Hyde Street cable cars, fourteen blocks up from Market, a stucco
building not too different from the apartment houses around it, with a faded
sign "Ferrier's French Theater of Art." The entrance to the basement theater
being blocked off, I rang the door to the house above, was ushered in by
Mrs. Ferrier, elderly but still businesslike. "Dees ees dee bes' leetle teatre in
de world. You want to buy?" I told her, not right away, we might like to rent
first. "But you have money later, yes?" Her husband, the director-founder,
who was older, and spoke less English, managed to convey that they had been
here twenty-five years, wanted to retire and turn this wonderful theater
which they had developed over to new blood.

A few flips of the switchboard downstairs and there was revealed before
me the snuggest little theater ever, 152 cushioned seats, stage twenty-five
feet wide by forty feet deep, intricate lighting system with two dimmers,
pulley arrangements to change shutters, a fine p.a. system which he built
himself, some cleverly hinged flats, so that he could make twelve scene
changes in *Peleas and Melisande* without once pulling the curtains, lots of

furniture, drapes, pictures of old productions lying around. He began complaining how he had been working like a dog building some of this scenery, even a clavichord, for an opera, "but for three days they don't rehearse, and they don't understand." Behind the stage, cubbyhole dressing rooms, and a shop with a stove on which he mixes colors, and outside a wonderful little studio where he did his scheming for the French plays, in the good old days before the war.

Upstairs again, Mrs. Ferrier told me the rest of the house came with the theater, living room, dining room, kitchen, five bedrooms on the second floor, a single big one on the third. Would I like to see? Yes, very nice, and baths between each room with "l'eau courante" which she turned on for me, as if we were still in France and it were such a novelty. The possibilities of this building for communal living for those who want it, of course, appeared tremendous. And how much for this wonderful place? I would have to see their agent about that. . . . For renting just the theater it would be $35 per performance. The fire ordinances would permit four performances a week.

So I went down to their agent on Sutter Street, Chester C. Terrill. "They want $25,000 for the place. . . . Banks are reluctant to give loans on a one-purpose property." The dream was fading. . . . "You could make a nice roof-garden where the theater sticks out behind the rest of the house. . . ." Roof-garden . . . restaurant . . . work for ourselves if we are going to have to work on the side . . . serve only supper, like the Golden Spike [a great $1 crab cioppino dinner] . . . A two-purpose building on which the banks would pay a loan . . . or five hundred shares in the co-op at $50 each . . . at least we'll eat. Such wonderful reveries! You must read Harold Clurman's *The Fervent Years*, the saga of the Group Theater that lasted from '31 to '41. . . .

. . . Marty is out on bail in Portland and at the Locks. Kermit should be down here soon, since *The Sea Gull* is over.

7410 S.E. Division Street, Portland, Oregon
March 19, 1946

. . . The F.B.I. marched into the printshop on Monday, March 4, and took me away, right in the middle of a press run. I spent the next eleven days on a tour of five jails [handcuffed to another prisoner] on the trip up to Portland with the cigar-smoking U.S. marshals. Of course the buildings weren't nearly as depressing as the people in them, both the prisoners and the indifferent guards. I talked with a lot of soldiers—one who roomed with me contracted elephantiasis in New Guinea. Paddock, with whom I traveled to Portland, had been in the Army eleven years, on the Death March of Bataan, escaped out of Manchuria, was shot up in New Guinea, patched up and sent on a

War Bond tour through the States where he naturally got drunk and got mixed up in the robbery of an interstate express, for which he has spent the last ten months in guardhouses waiting for the decision to try him on a federal charge.

These men here are killers. I was surprised they didn't try to kill me—not that they gave a rap about my being a C.O., or disliked me personally—but just because killing is a habit with them. . . . What joy when I finally did get out.

This last was probably the happiest weekend of my life, a big reunion with the Waldport gang . . . and a reunion with another, completely unexpected, that of course, ranked with nothing I have ever experienced. I won't describe it, unless you really want me to. I'll just say that we are very much in love and that we want to go on together. She will probably be in Seattle until June, working at the "Y" and seeing Bob on visiting days. By June I should know what the government intends to do in my case, though that is certainly questionable. Joe Gistirak, who was picked up in October and came out here in December, hasn't heard a word. We all met in his room Friday night, Kermit, Marty, Tom Polk Miller, Bill Eshelman, and even Manche. Joe was in extra good form, free of Hedgerow's oppression, full of gags and wisdom—that radiated to the rest of us. The next night, after plank steaks in The Broiler, we went en masse to hear Baccalone and the Commedia del Arte players go through excerpts from four Italian woperas, very ridiculous. More merriment afterwards in Joe's room. Sunday afternoon we were all at the performance of three modern violin sonatas at the amazing Portland Art Museum. Afterward, a big Chinese smorgasbord. . . . When Manche left, we six men adjourned to Joe's again to talk theater. You can gather how steamed up we were by this; we started talking not about organization, location, salaries, but about what play to do first. It came to a choice between Shaw's *Doctor's Dilemma* and Ibsen's *Hedda Gabler*, with a week's wait when we can find other plays before we decide. I am to write to Seyril Rubin, who is arriving in San Francisco today, that we are starting a production unit here . . . and ask her if she wants to come up and play with us. Of course it is terribly nebulous, Kermit leaving for San Francisco yesterday, Tom for Houston on Thursday; Marty's, Joe's, and my states being uncertain, and not one competent woman available now. But we have the enthusiasm.

I am living with Marty now in a wonderful modern bungalow that he has converted into the *Compass* office. . . . We hope to get everything to the linotyper Thursday, and get me a job with the printer. The Art and Literature issue has been a financial success, $80 in the black and still five hundred copies to sell. . . .

A few weeks after Adrian's departure from Pendle Hill I received word that Bob Harvey was in the McNeil Island Federal Prison. In an emotional turmoil I left the Hedgerow Theater and the teaching job in Rose Valley and traveled to Seattle because Bob was allowed visits of only wife and blood relatives. I was deeply moved by the privation and loneliness that he was having to endure. In my confused state I broke off correspondence with Adrian, found a job in Seattle, and made the trips to the prison to comfort Bob. Our meetings every two weeks talking through the chainlink fence of the visiting room were miserable. Our marriage had finished long before, and he and Manche Langley were expecting a baby in the summer.

About the middle of March Kermit wrote me that some of our friends from the Fine Arts were going to have a reunion one weekend in Portland, and wanted me to come. So I took a few days off from my job at the Seattle Y.W.C.A. and bought a ticket for Portland. It was my first air flight and a most dramatic one, sailing down the coast over the gorgeous peaks of Mt. Hood, Mt. Helena, and Mt. Shasta, all topped with snow in the gleaming sunlight. I was met in Portland joyfully by warm friends from the Waldport days. In the evening there was a party in Joe Gistirak's room during which Kermit hesitantly took me aside to tell me that, while he didn't know what my feelings were now for Adrian Wilson, he thought I should know that, at that moment, Adrian was in the Portland City jail. I was stunned, and totally shaken by the emotions that swept through me, but I knew I had to see him.

The next morning I was in touch with the A.C.L.U. office to try to arrange for bail to release him. Then during visiting hours I went to the jail. There he stood, on the other side of the chainlink dividing fence and we looked through it at each other and wept. Later in the day he was released and we were reunited amidst a celebration with our Waldport friends.

Adrian described to me later some aspects of the trip to Portland that he didn't share with his parents. The two marshals started talking about pornographic books, which, apparently, they both collected. After a few minutes Adrian's fellow prisoner spoke up and said that he had some examples of good pornography in his satchel in the back trunk. The marshals wanted to see them at the next rest stop. There they took off the handcuffs and allowed him to unpack his treasures and display them on the trunk hood. The marshals expressed amazement and approbation and slapped him on the back. "You're a great fellow," they said. "You don't need to wear these things anymore" and put away the handcuffs. Then they all went into the restaurant and shared a jolly lunch during which the officers recounted tales of their raids of bookshops, and particularly juicy finds. They would drive a leisurely distance each day, put Adrian and his "mate" in the local jail for the night and go off to pursue their jollies in the local bordellos.

May 15, 1946

Here is a newspaper tearing to match your clipping about the tulips, liberation symbolism and all. It appeared in Monday's *Oregonian* [regarding upcoming case dismissals] and besides me, includes Marty, and Joe Gistirak. But it is all such a sham, so corrupt, I hardly get any feeling of liberation. Today Judge Fee sentenced a walk-out from the Lapine camp, a J.W. who had not been transferred once, to three years. *Three years.* For a minute you think the judge has become enlightened, sympathetic, liberal, and the next you see he is blind to everything but the most trivial legalities, as if his glasses were fitted with microscopic lenses. So I hardly feel honest about accepting this dismissal. But the thing to do is to get out of the whole rotten structure, forget about it, and think of building, nature, writing. And that is what we are going to do.

Waldo Chase has some land at Union, on the Olympic Peninsula, that can serve as the hopping off place for a new way of life, either a community on that land itself, or homesteading, isolation, in the miles of wilderness, far from roads. Lang calls it "the big country," a miraculous combination of snow-capped mountains and sea water, with infinite opportunities for building log houses, living simply and self-subsistently, and doing creative work—plus surviving the next atomic war. Clayton and Barbara James are already up there with Waldo, taking trips up the rivers in Waldo's Indian dugout canoe, and working in the garden they have put in. Betty [Wilfred Lang's wife] went up today with Sonia and Teenie [their two little girls]. This weekend I plan to go up with Lang in his ancient Buick, with trailer behind, looking like something straight off Route 66. I suppose I'll have to come back to Portland, though, for another week at least. *Compass* will be finished printing Monday or so, but there are still odds and ends, like publicity, to do.

Since beginning this letter I have been up to the Peninsula. It is all that Lang said. Coming around the corner into Union, after leaving 101, we saw the first of the mountain-water combination, the great Olympics rising up, two miles across the Hood Canal, jagged and snow-capped, with the sun behind them. . . .

Waldo's home-made house is a very elaborate, Japanese lodge, a strange concoction of straight poles, rammed earth, plywood, woodblocks that he has carved, glazed chicken netting, canvas, shakes (hand-split shingles), and the window from the old Mecca saloon in Seattle. Everybody was working in the garden when we came, transplanting tomatoes from the hot bed (or cold frame, what's the difference?). We had a big vegetarian supper in the portico, civilized enough to have coffee in the Silex on the outdoor fireplace, but distinctly otherly. Clayton, who is living with Barbara in the teepee, was raving about the feeling of going up to the mountains: how you lose all the dogmas, find a new pristine self. There is lots of land here, high-priced, but you don't have to buy it, you just go "squat."

We talked of home industries. Waldo is a good loom builder. With us doing the sand-papering, etc., he could turn out a dozen in a week. J. K. Gill's in Portland would buy them up at $65 each. And we had music, lots of quartets and cello suites, more than I have heard in two months. A rich, rounded life is opening out, I know. I am planning to go up there for good this Friday. Write care of Waldo Chase, Union, Washington. . . .

When the C.O. walk-out cases came up before Judge Fee in Portland, one of the A.C.L.U. lawyers discovered a clause in the government ruling on C.O.'s stating that they could not be transferred from the jurisdiction of one state to another. Probably the judge was happy to find a good excuse for dismissing the cases of men who had been so transferred, and Adrian's, Marty's, and Joe Gistirak's cases were to be dismissed on those grounds.

In the meantime, Waldo Chase installed Adrian and me in one of his shake-roofed A-frame shelters, and we gardened and cooked with the rest of the group. At Union there was the Robin Hood Lodge, and after we had lived a week or two at Waldo's, we moved into a derelict log cabin nearby, which the kindly owner of the Lodge lent to us. The total furnishings were three sets of double-bed bunks attached by their posts to the ceiling and the floor. Each one had a primitive straw-filled mattress. We could have played "musical beds" each night but we settled on the one with the best mattress. Besides the sleeping accommodations for twelve, there was a rudimentary brick construction at one wall, with a flue through the window, which served as a cooking-heating stove. There was no sink or running water and the privy was a few yards away. In the clearing nearby was the village water tower which had an overflow drip, and we held a bucket beneath it to catch our water supply. When the wind was strong it was a merry dance to keep the bucket in line with the thin shifting stream from above.

Along the shore there was a fantastic compound of tourist cottages owned by Orre Nobles, each one a unique combination of Chinoiserie, Gothic carving, Art Nouveau, and carpenter's baroque. Orre was an art teacher in a Seattle high school and had made many trips to China. He took a fancy to us and let us slice the bark off the cedar trees on his property, with which we wove cedar bark table mats to sell at the Robin Hood Lodge. His cottages faced a broad beach which was covered during the summer months with Olympia oysters, and he gave us permission to collect as many as we could carry in our bucket every day. We developed some dozen recipes for preparing oysters and they were our major sustenance that summer.

June 29, 1946

Judge Fee intoned "The indictment is dismissed, the man is released, and his bail is exonerated" on Wednesday, a minute after he had sentenced a Catholic fellow whom he didn't believe to be "sincere," to two years, for walking out of the Lapine camp. Marty came after me, and so, as he reminisced later, ended the chain reaction that began with that day, on clean-up crew, when the catatonia set in so much that I couldn't push the broom any more. Marty called me here on Monday, from Portland, saying that the cases were being dismissed this week and that Lessard, the lawyer's, men were coming up the next day. . . . I went to court with Lessard and his men, three walk-outs from Elkton. A word to Twining, the Assistant D.A., from Lessard before the judge came in, got a fourth C.O. dismissal squeezed in.

The first regular case was over some shipments of adulterated eggs from here to Philadelphia. "How do you adulterate an egg?" asked the judge. "Er, uh, they were too old, your honor," said the D.A. Then some bald-headed men in their jail clothes, towed in by the marshal, who had been caught selling liquor to Indians. Then Twining mumbled something about permission from the Attorney General to dismiss, while Lessard and the first C.O. stood by. Judge Fee said his piece and the C.O. walked out. Then the second, the third, and fourth. I was sure I didn't need a lawyer for this, so I saw Twining afterward. He said he could get me dismissed the next day at ten, without representation, though it would have been nicer to have a lawyer. As Swetland once said, when you go to court without a lawyer, you're bucking the strongest union in the world. So even if the Catholic fellow hadn't been sentenced before I was dismissed, there wouldn't have been an ounce of victory in it. . . .

. . . Monday is my twenty-third birthday. I'll have to read Milton's sonnet or write one.

September 1, 1946

September first, and just as the rain stopped on July first, it has begun again. The Pacific Northwest summer is over. We are better off than we were two months ago, though, a blaze in the corner fireplace à la Frank Lloyd Wright. It was converted from a pottery kiln to a stove, and we have a marvelous Aladdin kerosene lamp to augment the little daylight that creeps in through the woods. I think it must have been our rubbing of the lamp that brought Kermit Sheets to talk San Francisco theater plans, as well as orders for $45 worth of cedar bark mats yesterday. The cedar bark money is all going into a cache for the San Francisco trip. Yes, it looks like what we want—a sense of community, theater work, the stimulation of nearby colleges, and sunshine. There will be more of all these down there, than here, so we are going. The approach to theater will be different from what I thought in Frisco in February. Instead of looking for high-priced places in which to perform, Kermit proposes developing a repertory of four plays in a year's time— rehearsing in someone's front room, perhaps the front room of a farmhouse where some of us could live cooperatively, like at Hedgerow. We want to make sure we have a good balance between "theater" and a way of life, and that we take some of the advantages of this life here with us. One thing might be cedar-bark weaving, the mats to be sold through gift shops in S.F., but the problem will be, as it already has become here, to get the bark. We have exhausted Orre's 200 x 600 foot plot.

. . . We took a marvelous canoe trip with the Jameses, and were closer to nature than we have been all summer, hearing the archaic cry of the blue heron, digging clams, picking berries and apples, watching the great mountains. I'll send mats, but send no money, pliz.

San Francisco

c/o *Sheets, 1853 Webster Street, San Francisco, California*
[c. October 3, 1946]

Liefe Moesje, Dad, en Norm,

There it is. Nothing to do about it but gnash teeth. No boats were docking in Seattle because of the maritime union strike. Two boats of troops were due Sunday in Frisco, which was not affected by the strike. . . . Of course Norm would arrive in Frisco. But he arrived in Seattle, the telegram said. Gee, whizzikers, if only we had laid over a day we might have gotten your ship-to-shore wire (though Waldo has forwarded your letter, written on the boat, but not the wire?) I could surely have been on the dock and we could have had fine talks at the Fort even if they wouldn't let you come to Union. I suppose you took the Great Northern route east. Did you remark Trenton, North Dakota, and Williston?

We had another magnificent hitch-hike down the coast and through the redwoods, though it is amazing we are still alive considering some of the degenerates we rode with. We stayed overnight in a shake shelter that Clayton James built at Waldport after he walked out, quite primitive after the masterpiece at Union. From there, though, you can hear the breakers booming. We didn't half appreciate last year that open, vast, deserted beach. It is so vast that another figure looks tiny at ten feet away, as if through a telescope held backward.

California at this season is a wonderful combination of soft golden hills nubbed with oak, a great contrast to the poles and intense green of Washington. But we are thoroughly swallowed by this city now. The Ferrier French Theater of Art is still for sale, at $25,000, and the group, about ten, is all for buying it, both as a theater and a living place. It is such a marvelous monument to creative theater that we already feel loyal to it. And why pour our separate rents into landlords' pockets when they could pay for this?

We tried to make a break from the city yesterday, and went to Marin

County, Mill Valley, the beaches, drowned in fog, Muir Woods. But this Theater of Art set-up is too perfect and we are back. There are readings of plays every night this week, Pirandello, Shaw, Ibsen, James Joyce's *Exiles.* One will be chosen to begin rehearsals next week. Kermit is directing. I may act, but I hope my concentration will be on design and writing. I am thinking of going back to school, either the Schafer School of Design, a Bauhaus offshoot, or the U. of Cal. Architecture Department. I may have to wait until the beginning of the year, however. This will be a time, then, to earn a little tuition money at some not-too-dumb job, and to get settled in that dream theater. It is really amazing to see all those hopes of last February in San Francisco materializing; a whole room full of people come expressly to do theater work, willing to spend every night in rehearsal and to mortgage their next years toward a working place. . . .

At Union we had heard that Naomi Binford Kirschner had a part-time job teaching in a cooperative nursery school in San Francisco. I wrote to her and on her suggestion sent the most persuasive letter I could formulate to the director of the school to apply for a teaching position. Much to our amazement and delight, at the end of my first interview I was hired as the teacher of a group of four-year-olds in the mornings. A few days later I landed an afternoon job with the A.F.S.C. helping to expedite relief goods to Japan.

There was absolutely no housing available at the end of the war—four years without residential construction. For a while we slept on the Kirschner's kitchen floor and hunted feverishly for an apartment.

Waldo had mistakenly sent all our earthly belongings in the coffin-shaped box by American Express instead of common freight, and our funds, saved from weaving cedar-bark mats, were completely wiped out by the cost of that shipment. Fortunately I had the two part-time jobs and we were not destitute.

162 Beacon Street
[c. October 10, 1946]

It's good at last not to have to pore over the Apt. for Rent ads in the *Examiner* and scan the house windows for un-curtained ones as you go by on the cable car. We finally have an apartment high above the city—the best view toward the Bay Bridge that I have seen in fact, isolated though it is, in the geographical center of the city, and completely surrounded by eucalyptus, broom, etc. Nearby on the bare brown hill that commands an equally fine view of the Bay Area is a lot I can buy for $400, $100 down.

How I came upon all this was something of a miracle. I went chasing one of the *Examiner* ads yesterday morning again. Of course it was already taken when I got there. But the area was so magnificent, so different from the hot, tawdry, downtown district that I had been scouring, that I couldn't leave. So I stayed on the hill, breathing the good air blowing over the brown hills, wandering like a mountain goat where the paved streets ended. The people up there had goats, cows, chickens, rabbits. It was unbelievable. I finally talked to a woman about houses and land. I must have looked just like her son in the Merchant Marine, because from then on I was the recipient of such overwhelming hospitality and openness, I thought I was coming to Anna Brinton's again. It was an entirely new San Francisco, or the old one discovered. The woman led me all over the brown hills, to the neighbors, to her aunt, to a Mrs. Roark who wouldn't rent her apartment, simply because she didn't need to. Then Auntie (Mrs. Ben Ezra) would put us up. But as we were moving in, Mrs. Roark relented. We could move into her apartment after all. . . .

We have decided on Pirandello's *The Pleasure of Honesty* to begin rehearsals, pretty intellectual, but intellect that is converted into emotion. Kermit and I are having fun collaborating on "Four Four-Minute Plays for Four People" to be read between rubbers of Bridge. The things are basically worthless, but the disciplines are good, and preparatory to larger works, I hope.

October 20, 1946

. . . I have taken a job with the only music printer in town, the Pacific Music Press, mostly to unfold the riddle of how music is so perfectly drawn in the printed sheets. We used to ponder this like the mystery of life, at Waldport. Did they use type? Impossible, too many combinations. Did they draw it big and then reduce it by photography? Yeah, but what did they do before photography? Even the Erles didn't know. But now, despite the fact that I have spent the first two days wrapping 9,000 copies of Spike Jones Song Folio No. 1, I know. They use dies that look like leather punches to punch the notes, clef signs, etc., into a soft metal plate. The score is then transferred to paper and from the paper to a zinc plate. The zinc plate is etched and the printing done from it. . . .

October 30, 1946

. . . Last week the great plans for the Ferrier place fell through. Kermit finally went to see the Fire Inspector in the City Hall and got the Building Code. The gist of the section on theaters is (1) all theaters must be Class A buildings, i.e. built of structural steel and reinforced concrete; (2) buildings which are not Class A, which means the Ferrier's, can be used for theatrical performances only three nights a week and only *thirty* nights a year. The

Ferriers hadn't told us this. . . . The law may be very arbitrary, the making of capricious government, but there it is, far too formidable to risk $25,000 on. The 1906 earthquake is still in the air, and justifiably, the way the city has been rebuilt. Oh, but it was such a wonderful dream. Pity the Ferriers with their white elephant.

We thought the Los Angeles architects, Kemper Nomland and Tom Polk Miller, who flew up for the weekend, might cheer us up with a quick scheme for building an equally good theater for the same money, but that wasn't so easy. . . . We looked over the lot I can buy for $500. The slope and the lack of materials on it is discouraging but the view and the utilities are all there. . . .

November 19, 1946

The rains have finally come, whipping in over the brown hills. The old lady's wood hasn't had time to swell yet, so that assorted pans, bowls, and jars are tinkling all about with what gets in. It is really quite exciting, this sudden violence after the weeks of mildness. Suddenly the ground is giving off odors that transport me back east. In another month the hills should be green! . . .

We are using the Friends' Center auditorium and stage for rehearsals now, having ousted the last remaining C.P.S. men who were sleeping there. Studios and lofts we could call our own have been impossible at $25/month, so we are sponging off the Service Committee again. . . .

November 25, 1946

. . . My, this last was an extravagant weekend—two performances of the Ballet Russe, when I had never seen a ballet before. It was so magnificent Saturday night that I decided we had to go on Sunday too. The whole theater gang followed. First there is the conception of the body, light as air, as miraculously balanced as if you could balance a triangle on one of its points, fluid as a river in its movements, yet strong as steel. It moves with the rhythm of music, it coordinates all its parts, it coordinates with all the other moving bodies about it and with the static ones too—the props. Then there is the color, dazzling, kaleidoscopic. Then there are the forms, all creations of freed imaginations; the costumes either subservient to the body, as in the old classical ballet—the men in tights, the women in bodices and frill skirts, or animated by the body, as in a ballet like *Scheherazade*, where Bakst has really outdone himself. Then there is the music, rhythmic and fluid because it is dance music, full of arresting innovation because it is partly representational. We saw a marvelous variety, the whole gamut. I was amazed at the breadth of it. . . . Now, this group is just a fraction of the total repertory of the ballets which they are equipped to perform, at, figuratively, a minute's notice. It gives us repertory theater people starting on our first play, a slight inferiority complex. And the skill, the training, practically from birth, the disciplines, the keeping in shape that the ballet takes! Here, I think, is integrity and devotion like you will find in no other art you can see in America today. . . .

. . . Now I am reading [Eric] Gill and [Frederic] Goudy on typography . . . and I am even being drawn and quartered here. Gill doesn't like machines and Goudy does, and I like both of them. I have told Marty that I'll lay out the Prisons issue of *Compass* after all. We are going to try to get Rayner (where I work) to print it. . . .

December 5, 1946

. . . Si and Marty came for a big duck dinner and mince pie [at Thanksgiving]. My, it was good to have this day away from the print shop! Dick, the veteran apprentice, has copped the music engraving because he came first. While I have managed to keep away from binding Spike Jones and Gene Autry, because I have had a lot of composition experience, setting up song covers like "My Lovely Hula Girl" and "If I Flew Blind to Paradise" in the standard format is most discouraging. So last Saturday I investigated the Grabhorn Press. I had gone by the building often on the way to the Friends' Center, and it had always intrigued me because it looked settled and industrialized. Then I had seen an exhibit of their books at the library, beautiful editions of everything from the Sermon on the Mount to D. H. Lawrence poems. Furthermore, Goudy, the leading American type designer, gave the Grabhorn Press a mention in the book I was reading, so I determined to go. . . . Robert Grabhorn, one of the brothers, was very cordial, suggested that I keep coming in, and maybe he'll have something for me to do around the first of the year. If I want to pursue fine printing this is certainly the best shop anywhere. What joy it will be to work on something I believe in, to know I am doing something which is beautiful both in what it is saying and in its typography, and to know that I am not just filling up the world with more crud. It is very easy to justify going on at the music press by pointing out the skills I am learning, but at the same time look at the sacrifice—of what I am producing from day to day, of my perception of beautiful things from day to day. . . .

December 14, 1946

. . . We have decided to set aside the Pirandello for a play in which we can get more body work and voice exercise. The Shaw [*Great Catherine*] is a natural. And suddenly I have a tremendous voice, where a month or two ago I could hardly get across the footlights. Well, it isn't very hard, for Patiomkin requires only bellowing, as you will see if you will read the play. . . .

January 12, 1947

. . . Marty has come back from his swing around the country bringing some
of the flavor of the East. . . . There was news of the people we were with last
spring in Portland, of the Dupres keeping house for the semanticist,
S. I. Hayakawa. Vlad is writing a recipe column for a paper, and Ibby is
doing Mrs. Alving, in six rehearsals, at the University of Chicago. News of
Pendle Hill, of Hedgerow, with the men back from the prisons, and pictures
of the Erles, Joe Gistirak, Dave Jackson—people with the highest ideals and
talents—Kem-toning [painting] tenements on the lower East Side of New
York. The readjustment looks pretty dismal. Bus is unable to play in New
York because of a union technicality, Joe is "through with theater," but still
pining for it. We can consider ourselves pretty lucky with a concrete project,
with decent places to live, with jobs that hold some promise.

Marty posed a question last night which has made us re-evaluate the
producing of *Great Catherine*; simply, "What will be the impression made by
this particular play?" To be sure, it has many of the elements we like in
theater, fun, a fusion of many arts, some exploration, but it hardly conveys a
serious approach. So Kermit suggested doing it in two weeks, instead of a
month, with word-of-mouth invitations instead of printed ones, no costumes
or set, coupling the performance with a discussion, and announce a reading
of one of the Lorca plays. So we do away with all the pretensions of a full-scale
production and let that wait until fall. I think this plan comes much closer
to our true feeling about the group and this play. We need more people and
a real "work-in-progress" production should do it.

January 28, 1947

. . . The gentlemen from Los Angeles came up again so it was a tremendous
weekend of parties, feasts, discussions, and laughter. Kemper, Tom Polk
Miller, Eshelman, the Jadikers . . . , the Rubins, and countless others were
on hand at Marty's on Saturday night, talking theater and old times. About
midnight, Everson, whom none of us had seen since camp, wandered in. He
has been keeping apart during the "readjustment" so there was some strain
and lack of communication, mixed with the usual reverence. He has found
himself a woman—another New Directions writer, in Berkeley, and so he has
abandoned the hermit's life up north. I think it's what he needed. Sunday,
from breakfast on, everyone was over here, roaring with laughter at [Joyce's
reading of] E. B. White's *Quo Vadimus*. . . .

I went out to Mills College last week at the suggestion of Ed Grabhorn to
see a Miss Rosalind Keep who has a wonderful press in a tremendous
eucalyptus grove behind the campus. She is retiring from the faculty this

summer and hopes to devote her full time to printing, even commercial work. Imagine it, a wisp of a woman, going into the printing business at the age of sixty-eight. Needless to say, she will need somebody to lift the chases and run the presses for her, which is where I might come in. The work she has done I had seen at Anna Brinton's about whom we talked very much. It is of high quality, but very traditional and fussy. This, coupled with it probably being a part-time job and not paying very much, makes me doubtful about its working out. But we'll see what develops. . . .

February 3, 1947

. . . The work-in-progress production last night went beautifully, with a very responsive audience of sixty-five or seventy, so that one of our purposes, the experience of audience participation, was very well fulfilled. The other purpose, to get more people to work with us, so that we can cast plays like Lorca's *The Shoemaker's Prodigious Wife*, and Synge's *Well of the Saints*, didn't work out so well. Plenty of people stayed for the discussion afterwards, but they were either deadheads or our own friends. There was a lot of vague talk about how to finance a repertory theater, but no solution to the problem of where to get people so that we will have something to offer. Henry Schnitzler, the son of the famous German author, Arthur Schnitzler, who heads the drama department at Cal, kept things to the point, though. He appears to be a splendid man, the sort of director we need if we are going to go ahead. He thinks he can steer some Cal. graduates to us, but it is doubtful whether he'll have time to direct. His criticism of the performance was that he missed the contrast between the staid English and the extravagant Russians, which is, after all, the point of the play. . . .

February 17, 1947

. . . We had an interesting gathering with some members of the cast of the all-negro play *Anna Lucasta* at Marty's the other night. Before we could talk of anything else, we had to clear our thinking on the place of the negro in the theater. We used a colored boy as a soldier in *Great Catherine*. But could we use him as the servant, John, who has an affair with the Count's daughter in Strindberg's *Miss Julie*? Certainly not. It would throw the focus of the play from the class problem to the miscegenation problem. Two of the *Anna Lucasta* people were hoofers who have been batting their heads against this wall for years. Why not whiten negroes just as Othello is usually played black-face? Isn't this a valid function of make-up? They told some fantastic stories of discrimination. Either they're just a shade too "dark" to play white men, or a trifle too light to play black men. We must have our stereotypes. It was *reductio ad absurdum* when Laura Bowman broke into a perfect Irish brogue.

March 4, 1947

. . . I have a new job, in an ordinary shop in the printing and financial district. The compositing is quite dull but working in the deep canyons with the streets full of quick, efficient life is very exciting. I like being a rebel in my sweater among all the business uniforms, and taking mental pot-shots at the stupidities they utter about the paintings when I eat lunch (65 cents only) at The Iron Pot, where the work of the Telegraph Hill artists is exhibited. . . .

Sometime in March a tiny apartment next to Marty's, on Haight Street, became vacant, and Adrian and I rented it and moved in. It was in an old Victorian house with one bathroom on each floor which had to be shared with the other apartment, but it was much closer to our work and rehearsals. The move also delivered us from the various irritations of our landlady, Mrs. Roark, who was snoopy and suspicious, and critical of every improvement we made to her dilapidated house.

At this time it was necessary, and exciting, to firm up our organization of the group, and choose a name. Adrian was to design and print mailing announcements and programs for the two nights of performances of the double bill of Chekhov plays, which we were to stage in the Friends' Center auditorium. We made up lists of possible names, discussed them pro and con ad infinitum and finally set a date for a deadline for the final choice. Chris Rambo, our company wit, unrolled a four-foot banner at the meeting, with THE INTER-PLAYERS lettered on it, and it was immediately accepted with joy. We were sure that the word expressed the concept of cooperation and mutual dependence which was at the heart of our theater philosophy.

A month later Adrian designed and printed our first mailing pieces on inexpensive red wrapping paper with the new name diagonally crossing the names of the eleven members of the company. The programs were printed in red and black on handsome strips of paper from the Grabhorn trimming pile.

312 Haight Street
March 11, 1947

. . . We plan to prepare several plays for performance the beginning of September. Dave Jackson, who directed *Aria da Capo* and *The Sea Gull* at Waldport, is arriving from New York the first of May, probably to direct Chekhov's *Three Sisters* (if we can find three sisters), Schnitzler of Cal. (University) might direct another, and probably Kermit will do the third, to make the short "season" on which we stand or fall. Our ad, a little typo-

graphical gem by me in the Bauhaus manner, appeared four days in the
Chronicle. We got three calls about it Friday—one from a man who had "a
yah with Cohnell." Fortunately, he didn't show up last night. The one who
did was a very facile reader and may be able to do Jean in Strindberg's
Miss Julie!

April 6, 1947
. . . The plans for the summer look better every day. Now Joe Gistirak, in
whom I have great faith, writes that he will be coming, probably the beginning
of June. As Marty said when he came back from the East, if we will only per-
sist, those who have the same vision but less initiative will one by one come
into the fold. . . .

May 2, 1947
Having just finished a new combination radio, filing cabinet and desk unit,
I finally have a decent place to write this long delayed letter. The other
reason I delayed was that I couldn't say when I would come east. First came
your letter saying you were now sailing the 25th of June, and then Texas City
blew up tossing all the tin into the Gulf of Mexico and I got laid off at the
smelter. (At least that was the reason the personnel manager gave.) Of course
this lay-off was very convenient for getting the set built and the announcements printed for the Chekhov plays, but it wasn't earning me any money
for going home. Furthermore the damn union took $10 out of my last pay
check, which was about all I would have saved out of that job. Labor always
gets it in the neck. So now I am basking in the luxury of being one of the
great unemployed, jobless, penniless, with no hope for another job, but
somehow still well-fed and busy as hell at things which mean something
to me. . . .
    A Soldier's Tale at Cal., directed by Schnitzler was almost the experience
it was when Krenek directed it at Hamline. Certainly the acting, with the
men back from the wars, was superior, but the music was not quite so arresting
as when Mitropoulos, in shirt sleeves, conducted his eight first-chair men. . . .
The other work, *The Trial of Lucullus* by the German, Bertold Brecht, was
made into an opera for the occasion, by Roger Sessions, but it fell flat. . . .
If we hadn't been in the middle of a row and sitting next to Darius Milhaud
we would have walked out. Schnitzler's staging was again fine, though
necessarily static because of the writing. If only he'll work with us this
summer! Scott and Eshelman came up for the event. We had a Sunday breakfast here that lasted until 5 p.m. Scott played the piano (we have rented one)
marvelously—all the English folk songs and the Brahms songs (I learned

them in Daltry's class) while we sang and sang. I'm not sure whether that or *A Soldier's Tale* was the best. My clarinet is being fixed next week, so music should begin to figure a little more in this life.

May 13, 1947

I have just been out to get the newspaper reviews, à la movies, but there weren't any. Probably the critic who came to last night's performance was too absorbed in explaining the plays to the Service Committee expeditor's five-year-old son, who chose that particular lap to watch things from. Anyhow the sharper critics like Everson, Pauline Kael of Brentano's, and Bob Stock, the center of the San Francisco Bohemians, found merit in certain aspects of the productions. It was amazing that *The Anniversary* held together at all, what with Terry Kilpatrick, a student at San Francisco State, doing the biggest role with one week's rehearsal, and Marty putting so much emphasis on comic details that the progressive distraction of the men by the women was often obscured. *The Boor* got fewer laughs than we expected, and than *The Anniversary*, but it was certainly very lively and got long applause.

I went to Ed Grabhorn with the program today. He thought it was a very interesting job, but still has no opening for me. . . .

Dave Jackson arrived yesterday, in time to scout our talent for the play he will direct. There was no trace of the morbidness of camp, and he is full of ideas, perceptions, and plays for the repertory. We are thinking of putting *Ghosts* and Chekhov's *The Sea Gull* in the repertory since most of the C.P.S. cast will be here. Add to these a couple of Strindberg or Lorca or Synge or Joyce or Cocteau or another Ibsen, and San Francisco will have a season like it has never had before, at least as far as we can find out. . . .

May 25, 1947

. . . With me and most of the others in the theater group out of jobs, we keep saying "since we believe in cooperation, why don't we start a business of our own" and so we dream up the most fantastic schemes. The latest is Si Miller's. He has hooked up with a man who has a fine recording studio, and plans to make albums of readings by Everson, Robert Duncan, and Henry Miller, to be sold by $10 advance subscription. My function in this is to design and execute the printing, which comes first. Idealistically, it is very nice to have Everson and Duncan on records (I'm not so sure about Miller), but recalling the trouble these poets have had peddling their books at twenty-five cents a copy, the records seem fantastic. . . .

The theater goes better—lots of new faces and good voices for the casting readings of *Heartbreak House* so that we are even getting a feeling of com-

petition. . . . David is handling the rehearsals with great intelligence
and enthusiasm. . . .

June 10, 1947

How wonderful to get a letter from you, Dad! I hope there will be many
more from Holland. It is certainly fine that you have the prospect of more
interesting work to come home to. I'm beginning to realize what that means
this week, after running in the harness of several dumb jobs during the winter,
for I have begun my own printing business. Of course it means that I work
twice as hard and long as I would for someone else, and that I dream type all
night, but I can't wait to get to the press in the morning. The machine is the
very one mentioned in the *Harper's* article ["The West Coast Cult of Sex and
Anarchy"] as the instrument of abortion of an anarchist little mag called
The Ark. The magazine has finally come out after a year and a half of printing,
and now the press is free for me. It stands in a tool shed behind one of the
big, old, palm-shaded mansions on O'Farrell Street, recently acquired by a
revolting hag who "squats at the door, the owner," like T. S. Eliot's Jew.
Being a thoroughly Bohemian crew, the *Ark* boys have neglected to pay the
rent, so she has extorted $13 from me plus $1.25 for electricity for the motor
I hitched to the press. But in turn, I gleaned a lot of beautiful paper from
the Grabhorns and already have run off two big jobs. . . .

There were some searching questions in your letter, Norm. I feel I have
answered most of them in my letters over the past few years. Of course I don't
advocate "communal societies," governments which are merely dispensers
of information on which people act according to their consciences, "self-
abnegation complete and utter," and mystical religion any more. I see the
folly of deciding anything for anybody but myself. But I still do value as the
greatest good absorption in creative activity. If the absorption is intense
enough many of the problems of ethics and government are taken care of—
you just don't have time to think about them. Of course this leaves me open
to Shaw's point that we must think about these things or else we can't
complain when conscription comes and the atom bombs start falling. In fact
I have come to the point of seeing the paradoxes and compromises in every
attempt at consistency. Creative activity for what? For the moment. But what
about beyond the moment? It is hard for me to feel any ultimate meaning in
things these days. So I go on the old assumptions: it is good to make people
think; it is good to recombine old materials and ideas to artistic effect; it is
good to be engaged in things which will last beyond one's life or interest; it is
good to extend oneself, to love, to be healthy, to fulfill one's physical existence. But the futility of it all in the face of millions of people going in and
out of the world each year as I get older, of the indiscriminate crushing steps

of nature, death, and nations, of the riddle of why I am I, seeing all this happening, comes over me again and again. There is beauty in the rose, but no satisfaction in its mystery. . . .

June 19, 1947

A bon voyage for your sailing! I wish I had a better picture of what is happening with you. Are you driving straight down to New York with Norm the day before you sail? . . .

The wind is howling off the Pacific tonight between our windows and the blinking lights of Nob Hill. I get a sudden sense of the smallness and aloneness of myself and this city pushed to the edge of a continent, in the face of this great enveloping wind and the thousands of miles it will blow before it blows itself out. And I think of the west winds which will blow in the rigging of your ship the thousands of miles until you get to some city on the edge of another continent. And what puts you there and me here, when ten years ago we would have been together and twenty years ago we were together? There are forces within us that drive us and pick us up and shake us like this tremendous wind. For a second, like tonight, they let us drop and we see what has happened, and then they start blowing again. Who can say what they are or where they blow? And what could we have done or should we have done to stop them? So you sail, and I sit here thinking of you. . . .

I hope you have a wonderful trip. All my love goes with you.

[c. June 27, 1947]

. . . I was over at Daliel's bookstore the other day talking to one Berg who knows a lot about publishing and has ideas for reprints of classics that I might do in between jobs. He got to showing me various beautifully printed books they have around. The one that impressed me most, mainly because of its large, bold, well designed type, was an excerpt from Joyce's *Finnegan's Wake*, "The Mime of Nick, Mick" and somebody else. I was amazed to see that it had been put out by The Servire Press, The Hague, and according to the colophon, was printed on the presses of G. J. Thieme at Nymegen. If you get to The Hague, I wish you would look up this press. . . .

July 14, 1947

. . . We had the first full-length rehearsal of *Heartbreak House* last night. Everyone had fine sections, so that David was quite optimistic about making a mid-August date. The play runs three and a half hours, so people will get their money's worth. It looks like we'll get the Friends' Center after all. My own part in the play is not very enjoyable. I am discovering that to get to the "source," you have to go through the whole mental process of the character you are playing at the speed he would go through it. And not once, but every night. So it becomes a really exhausting discipline, one in which I am having little success.

I got not only the Brahms sonatas but also the Hindemith sonata for my birthday and I have been playing them several hours each day. . . .

July 21, 1947

. . . I have felt closer to Holland this week because I have been trying to identify that typeface in the James Joyce book. It occurred to me that as long as I was going to buy some type it should be one I was really enthusiastic about, especially if it were Dutch and imported. After much research, I suspect it is Grotius. To make sure I am writing the Servire Press about it. By the way, who was Grotius?

I am beginning the printing for the plays now that we have decided on dates and place. We can have the Friends' Center for $175 for twelve nights. Our plays will run four weekends, ending September 14. . . . I am getting to be like all printers on the matter of estimates and promises, so that I now have a policy of giving figures far above and beyond what I think. Then, if things take less time and cost less than expected the customers think I am wonderful. Several good size orders should come in soon from S.F. State College, the Jewish Community Center, and some gift shops. If I could carry these along through the school year, it would be a lot better than dish-washing. . . .

July 29, 1947

. . . The play productions and the presses are rolling. We had a fine meeting with George Barati, cellist in the San Francisco Symphony, who had made sketches for music for another production of *Don Perlimplin* and wants to do guitar and clarinet music for this one. Furthermore he wants to write some-thing [for clarinet] for the shepherd scene in *Aria da Capo*. When I saw him at a performance of another Lorca play at Mills last night, he said he had already written something.

I have done the first run on the Coffield book, gotten an order for another book of poems, and an order to design and print cards for Robert M. Kasper, the leading modern furniture store, plus all the printing for the plays. I wish I had a typeface that expressed my taste better than the beautiful but too feminine Centaur which I just bought. Maybe I'll call on you to get me Grotius if it's available and that's what it is.

August 25, 1947

Finally an evening at home, Schubert songs at the piano, the kitty sleeping through it all. The repertory has opened, all the technical things are done, so now we can rest. We had very good houses (about a hundred) for the first two nights and everything went well. I didn't even miss a note in the *Pastorale* I play through four times as background for the shepherd scene in *Aria*, which is a good thing since the composer George Barati, a cellist in the Symphony, was there. The nice thing is that we still have another opening to look forward to, *Heartbreak House*, on Friday, but we are getting skeptical about the audience staying since it runs until 12:30. I guess it will be easier to serve coffee between acts than to cut it. Our Los Angeles contingent will be up for the weekend, so we can look forward to lots of art talk, wit, and music, besides the plays.

In September 1947, Adrian registered at the University of California, Berkeley, in the School of Architecture. He carried on his job and theater printing in the backyard shed, and began commuting to Berkeley for classes. During the Christmas vacation he traveled across the country with some fellow students and spent two weeks with his parents in Middletown. Soon after his return in January 1948, while he was drawing a scale model of the gate to the Japanese Tea Garden in Golden Gate Park for a class assignment, Jack Stauffacher happened along, and in their conversation Adrian found that Jack had more work in his print shop than he could handle. He began to seriously consider dropping the architecture studies to work with Jack at the Greenwood Press.

November 2, 1947

... To answer your questions: No, I certainly don't use the University printing equipment. The U.C. Press is the largest and most modern plant I have ever seen; it does very fine work and, in fact, is the only real publisher on the Coast, with a list etc. and an output of one edition a month. I don't know Johnston's book but I've been reading Updike's two volume *Printing Types* until I find the sans serif which we used so much at Waldport very cold and dull. I have discovered the marvelous Rare Book Room at the Library and go there every Wednesday, sometimes with Everson. They have the four greatest printed books in the world, the Kelmscott Chaucer, the Doves Bible, the Ashendene Dante, and the Nash Dante, Bruce Rogers Bible or Grabhorn Whitman, no one can decide. As an entity, I like the Kelmscott (William Morris) Chaucer the best. It has the love of the materials—rich ink, handmade paper, all through it. And this is what I feel implicit in the Grotius type—a black letter that will take punch, but full of air so that you get the paper woven through it. The type I have is more beautiful in its forms, but lacks these qualities. Of course now that the local type founders have the 72 pt. (1 inch) letters which I used to head the *Merchant of Venice* program for the Bay Theater, it is hard to resist, and I suppose I'll stick to it. At any rate, it is the Morris tradition of thinking of the book in tactile terms that Everson and I would like to perpetuate. I would like to add the principles of painting and layout—i.e., the meaningful relationship by placement of text and illustration—so that we have something which is beautiful and various as paintings and at the same time restrained by and in the nature of printing. Somewhere along the line I feel the text being lost sight of, and this must not be allowed to happen. And the printer must still discriminate between what is good and bad text and know what kind it is to give it the proper setting— the argument I started with Grabhorn a year ago and was told that if I could tell, my place wasn't in printing. But I still believe it. . . .

January 11, 1948

. . . [Jack] Stauffacher, being nobody's fool, isn't quite ready to take me into his business this minute. He is not quite recovered from the painful surgery of dismissing his last partner, a nice young fellow, who, unfortunately, had no passion whatsoever for book-making. For the moment he wants to work on his own. But it is clear he will need me. And I, him. If I could live on designing alone I would turn over my jobs to him, but I still need to make wages, so I'll be on my own a little while longer. I do plan to take another crack at the Grabhorns, but have little hope. Your little paragraphs from Elbert Hubbard were reassuring, probably more for you than for me. I am not completely reconciled to not being in the author's chair. While I forget about him in my present passion for type, he still exists, and I sometimes can't see why he has to be somebody else than me.

I feel the need for vigorous anti-war writing more and more. Last night I dreamt some people were passively accepting the inevitability of another war, saying "It will be nice to remount," as they mounted contraptions made of machine guns and bayonets as if they were horses. I shouted with all the passion of belief, "No! War is wrong!" And they said, "Why?" And I said even more passionately, "Because war doesn't *do* anything!" So one of them got off his contraption and threw the bayonet on the ground and said simply, "O.K." And then I had a vision of an anti-war poem over-printing a Japanese woodblock print—a sample of purposeful beauty, of art and propaganda mixing as some might sneer. But through my passionate statements I had the feeling that I might be wrong about war, that my statements might be just blind passion. And I wondered if belief has any worth in this world, if it isn't always blind to the relativity and eventual meaninglessness of life. What a curse this ability to see the other side of things is! How can I ever act positively? Or why should I? ...

January 25, 1948

... As you gather, nothing has materialized with Stauffacher, who is not quite over the disappointment of his last partner. I have been seeing him almost daily, however, between job hunting, and we have been talking spiritedly of publishing. Jack has been raving about Eric Gill, the passionate Catholic sculptor, wood-block cutter, type designer, etc. who wrote many essays on the necessity for every workman being an artist, and Jack now wants us to print Gill's powerful anti-war essay "And Who Wants Peace?" This makes Jack the easiest (and only) convert to pacifism I ever had, and plays beautifully into my hand, since (as you could tell from my dream) I have long wanted to mix art and propaganda. I imagine we'll use an imported hand-made paper, large type set according to Gill's typographic principles, and sell copies for the cost of the materials. This will be good practice for our magnum opus, Thoreau's *Walden*, which will match the Grabhorn's Whitman.

February 17, 1948

This is a very good night for me to be writing you because what I have been waiting for to happen ever since I came back here, has happened. Stauffacher and I agreed today that I should go to work with, or more properly for him, since he will be paying me a salary, beginning Monday. We were in at the paper company today choosing a paper for the book we will begin printing, a sort of theological text for Stanford University by one Spiegelberg, called *The Religion of No Religion*. It will be similar in format to a book Jack did for this man before, so the printing will be a routine matter but fine experience. One of us will make up the forms (linotype, already set) while the other runs the Colt's Armory press. It will run 500 copies, 128 pages. Paper will cost $100. Thank God Jack has capital. This is such an elevation from my lowly status in a basement, without equipment, way out in the Mission District, that I can't wait 'til Monday. Jack has a fine sunny shop in the top of one of the printing buildings in the center of all the typesetters, paper houses, and seafood depots (fabulous stenches), the real San Francisco, two Colt's presses capable of the finest work, oodles of leads, slugs, furniture and type. Our approach to printing is amazingly the same, though his critical judgment is entirely intuitive while mine is pretty intellectual. And he is such a "character" with his black beard and intense eyes, completely forthright and honest. It is hard to believe he wasn't a C.O. Perhaps he is too well adjusted for that. I just hope this relationship works out and that we can do great work.

Furthermore the Bay Theater wanted my estimates on all their printing today since they are big stuff now, 700 each night last weekend, purely on a publicity basis. This will mean stationery, posters, announcements and programs for a show a month. They like my idea of doing broadsides for the program à la *Merchant of Venice*, which should be satisfying and creative. On Jack's presses it should be a cinch. . . .

February 29, 1948

I have begun to think that your wish that I be as happy as I was in my youth is rapidly coming true. This last week has been sheer delight. I wake up hours before arising in anticipation of going to work. I come home ecstatic with the events of the day. Jack is a prince to work with. He is just incompetent and untutored enough so that I get a sense of equality and really being useful in his shop. His childlike enthusiasm and integrity almost bring tears to my eyes. Twice already we have made errors in the book which we caught only after the pages were run off. It has been fascinating to watch his mind work—back and forth—over whether to do it over again. Of course we always do though it means a loss of $10 worth of paper plus all the work. He must have money behind him because, I am sure, he never made any in printing and because he never balks at any expense or at my asking $50 a week. If we can get over making mistakes, however, I think we will do some great printing and make some money to boot. I set as much type as we had for the Eric Gill anti-war essay and it looks fine. Finally we got samples of handmade papers from England and France, stuff so beautiful you want to eat it, so it looks like the Gill essay is going through. . . .

March 8, 1948

Life continues rich and merrie at the Greenwood Press. I bounce out of bed at the crack of dawn and compose a typographical anthem:

Jackie boy!
Master.
Print ye well?
Very well.
Hey down, Ho down, derry, derry down,
Among the Wood so Green-o!

. . . I still feel as a child in my attitudes, and printing is a childish occupation anyway: playing with letter blocks, fitting them in with wooden blocks, pounding them with hammers, squeezing them in presses—but I must have grown up at sometime, and when I contemplate the body of printing I have done in the past year, there seems no reason why I can't do something great within the next five. . . .

May 2, 1948

If I don't write, don't think something has happened to me. I merely get so absorbed in this supercharged aesthetic atmosphere that events, the usual provocation for letters, don't matter (don't happen!), life becomes a state of being, a letter would be simply the same old reflection of that state, the days fly by, and I don't write. I'll admit though that something did happen last week. We came to a final agreement on the first page of the Eric Gill essay after a hundred different set-ups, printed a few proofs on handmade paper, and it was magnificent! Now we are debating whether to damp the sheets to achieve "that dense, lustrous black," in Everson's words, or to achieve it with impression as Grabhorn does. Also we mailed out 400 of the enclosed announcements and had three orders in the mail the next morning. I don't think we'll save the world with this book, but we'll certainly establish ourselves as heirs of the great tradition of San Francisco fine printing. Next we'll embark on a little Gandhi for practice, using the same format, and then start setting up Thoreau's *Walden*. You probably wonder if there is really any point to using expensive handmade paper. There are aesthetic reasons—a fine piece of paper is like a fine piece of cloth. There are practical reasons: printing is a preservative art and we want the words we are setting up to last in perfect form, as for example the Gutenberg Bible has lasted.

Of course this kind of work is meaning expanding relationships with people and the world of art. One's work in any art form has bearing on and draws sustenance from every other. So now where Everson and I talked only poetry at camp we can talk both poetry and its expression in printing. And the whole realm of book illustration, the artists, and the work they have done in other media opens out. Eric Gill, whom I admired mainly as a writer, now is revealed as an extremely sensitive wood engraver, illustrator, and type designer, as well as sculptor, the profession for which he wanted most to be known, so that we can print his essay with double confidence. And then there is the finest of all printing, Japanese woodblock printing, which opens out all Japan, so that I am now reading a whole series of books on that unique culture. Saturday afternoon Jack and I went out to the leading local bibliophile's house (Albert Sperisen) to look at his collection. He is the art director of one of the big advertising agencies and has sunk most of his money as well as a very discriminating taste into his library. Of course it was completely dazzling to us and we left reeling. Every word we uttered, he had a book for it. The Eric Gills were the greatest revelation—exquisite book after book, plus lots of original engravings. He, by the way, was rather overwhelmed by our Eric Gill page—thought it was completely in the spirit of the master. There is of course a danger in this: we lose sight of the purpose of books in making them beautiful. But if the words are good enough they can stand a tremendous amount of artful treatment, craftsmanship, and repetition. It is still my purpose to make people read less better, instead of more faster. . . .

1720 Baker Street
September 26, 1948

The great housewarming is already over—seventy punch glasses washed, rafts of flowers arranged in everything that could conceivably hold water, all the presents put in their appropriate places. It was wonderful to have your blessing and benediction on our marriage. My mind goes whirling on all kinds of fancies about things we would see and do if you came out here, or how it would be if we came east. So much seems possible now. It was all very simply accomplished at City Hall. I of course, printed the announcements, rather a unique experience. They have been sent to all the parents and teachers in Joyce's nursery school and to old friends in the East. The housewarming invitations served both purposes for our friends here. They are so elegant I am surprised everyone didn't bring Spode dinnerware and Steuben glass. . . . The house was magnificent for the party, mainly because of Joyce's energy and taste. People who should know have said it is the most wonderful combination of colors they have ever seen in an interior. It certainly has an atmosphere of warmth and vitality, and at the same time, repose and elegance, though looks like, or was in fact, bought in a store.

The prospects for my coming east don't look so good. Joyce's friend in L.A. who was going to drive in November, has now lost her job and won't have the money. The ads in the paper that say you can fly to New York for $88 continue to intrigue me, but who's got $88? I didn't get paid for three weeks because there just wasn't any money, mainly because of my reluctance to go out selling and because Jack just doesn't. The minute I went out selling we got plenty of business. But I certainly long sometimes for the East, especially now that a sniff of fall has penetrated this fog-walled atmosphere. This apartment is very wonderful but I realize it is still so new it doesn't have any of the qualities that things get when they have been lived with for years. I would certainly like to browse through the eastern graphic arts circles, the libraries, publishing houses and fine presses. The Meriden

Gravure Company is the first collotype process plant in the country—collotype being the best method for reproducing illustrations and seeing it, or even working there would be an education. In other words I am coming to see more and more that all you people in the East must be living there for some reason other than a lack of desire to make fresh starts. But maybe you will come out here before I can get back. We would certainly go to Yosemite. I got John Muir's guide book out of the library and would print it as magnificently as the Gill if there was a financier. And San Francisco is the marvelous place to show people around in. When Joyce's father and stepmother came out this spring there seemed no end of things to do. So be thinking about it. Much love from *us both.*

October 11, 1948

The lovely Dutch calendar you gave me has been performing a very worthy function, namely scheduling an itinerary for an eastern hegira! It says here that we are to arrive in Middletown on Friday, November 12, and I guess it will happen! The idea is to put a down-payment on a good car with a loan from Joyce's brother, and sell it when we get back, if we can't afford to keep it. How long we'll be able to stay in Middletown is conditioned by the fact that we want to see the Grand Canyon, Joyce's folks in Atlanta, New York, and the farm in the Catskills, plus ten little theaters and twenty-two fine presses in the space of a month. According to the schedule, we have seven nights in Middletown, but one of those we'd like for a circuit of New England—Boston, Concord, Cummington, and Northampton. We plan to spend an overnight with Norm at Antioch or wherever he's working, and Thanksgiving with Vlad and Ib Dupre, old C.P.S. friends, in Chicago. As Joyce is writing to her daddy, it's too bad there aren't a few pleats taken in this continent, so that we could spend a week in each of the nostalgic spots. But the itinerary has worked out remarkably, if only we can stick to it. At the press we'll have just finished Gordon Onslow-Ford's book on his paintings, for the Museum, and I'll be back again to take care of the Christmas rush, I hope. The Interplayers will survive. Saturday we look for a car. What a day! What a trip! Joyce will add a note of eager anticipation.

Much love,
Adriaantje

EPILOGUE

The gathering of the C.P.S. friends in San Francisco, the organization of the theater, and the beginning of Adrian's career seems the right place to end our story. The war was over. The tide was turning. Creation, rather than destruction, was emerging everywhere. Many minds were turning away from rejection and resistance toward adjustment and construction. A few of the conscientious objectors organized the first listener-sponsored radio station on the West Coast. Even the TIME-LIFE Library of America in Neil Morgan's *The Pacific States* (1967), stated, "In postwar San Francisco there was . . . some of the creative excitement of past decades. Much of the revival, particularly in poetry, was in the hands of Quakers and other conscientious objectors who had been held in a camp at Waldport, Oregon, during World War II. Like the military they had visited San Francisco on leave and settled there. . . . Experimental theater came to life in San Francisco, with one group, The Interplayers, moving *in toto* from the Waldport camp. . . ."

Our theater was launched and sailing! For some twenty years, weathering many storms and some changes of crew with every voyage, it rode the billows, until it went on tour and finally sank in 1968. I had been among those at the helm until the mid-sixties when I began performing with other theaters, and Adrian was busy designing for presses across the country, printing, teaching, lecturing, and writing.

In 1957 Adrian gathered together the overprints of theater programs and announcements of the first ten years, with his commentary, and tipped them into a book he printed and published, *Printing for Theater*. It was a sumptuous folio, which I edited, and that was the beginning of our collaboration on books: scholarly works about the history of printing, children's books that I wrote and illustrated, and the bibliography of his work, *The Work and Play of Adrian Wilson*, published in 1983. In that same year Adrian was awarded a MacArthur Prize Fellowship with a generous five-year stipend.

In 1986 we celebrated forty years of our intimate partnership that began at Waldport. We continued warm friendships through the years with many of the characters in this story, and have heard or read news of some of the others.

By coincidence in the catalogue of *Fall 1984 New Books* of the University of California Press, in which the publication of our work, *A Medieval Mirror: Speculum Humanae Salvationis 1324-1500*, was announced, there was a description of a book entitled *The Foundations of Psychoanalysis*, by Adolf [sic] Grünbaum, one of the Wesleyan "heretics" of the earliest letters. He is a Professor of Philosophy and Psychiatry at the University of Pittsburgh.

Clayton and Barbara James settled in the Northwest and practiced their arts; Clayton's sculpture in clay, wood, concrete, and bronze has been exhibited throughout the West.

Martin Ponch continued work in the theater, at first with The Interplayers, and later directed and acted in several companies in California. His teaching career in drama and English to the foreign-born, in the San Francisco Community College District, spanned a period of twenty-one years.

Vlad and Ibby Dupre, now settled in Bethesda, Maryland, have six children and five grandchildren. After many years of college teaching in psychology and sociology, Vlad was president of the National Training Institute for Applied Behavioral Science from 1970 to 1975. Since then he has developed a private practice in psychotherapy, specializing in families. As well as raising a family, Ibby has taught a Head Start program and directed a cooperative nursery school. She has recently gained a master's degree in social work and is now working for an addiction program in a hospital.

Bob Harvey continued painting and writing but made his living in electronics. He and Manche Langley married and had two daughters.

Broadus (Bus) Erle founded the New Music Quartet in New York, which traveled throughout the country and recorded many disks. He became concertmaster of the Tokyo Symphony, and later was on the music faculty of Yale University.

Kermit Sheets, one of the founders of The Interplayers, continued as director and actor for several years. In 1948 he set up the Centaur Press with James Broughton, with whom he also made a number of films. He became general director of the San Francisco Playhouse Repertory Company, was for ten years a director of The Lighthouse for the Blind, and now writes fiction. He is married to Jane Steckle, actress and painter.

Kemper Nomland returned to Los Angeles and practiced architecture in his father's firm. He designed several houses that Jerry Rubin built on property he bought right after the war in Marin County, California. Jerry and Jan set up their weaving studio there, but after a time, Jerry became manager of the landscape architecture firm of Lawrence Halprin, and following that, he devoted himself to the cooperative movement.

Bill Jadiker returned to his plumbing business and developed into a very successful general contractor in Los Angeles, where he built a number of buildings, some in collaboration with the Nomland architecture firm.

Tom Polk Miller and Isabel Mount married and established their joint architecture firm in Denton, Texas, where they have had distinguished careers. In 1982 they received the Community Arts Recognition Award, given annually by the Greater Denton Arts Council for enhancement of community life through achievement in the arts. Isabel has received citations for architectural work in historic restoration, and Tom has been honored for long service in the cause of civil liberties.

Bill Eshelman completed two graduate degrees in California and began a career that was almost evenly split between librarianship and publishing. For fourteen years he was librarian at Los Angeles State College, then at Bucknell University. While in California he was editor of the quarterly journal of the state library association preceding his ten years as editor of the *Wilson Library Bulletin*, a national journal for the profession. Following this he was president of The Scarecrow Press, which specializes in books for libraries. Among these are two relating to William Everson, a bibliography, and a collection of his prefaces and afterwords. Esh has now retired and set up a press in Ohio, where his wife, Pat Rom, is the director of library services for the College of Wooster.

The Night Is Where You Fly, a book of poems by Glen Coffield, was printed by Adrian, and published in 1949 by the Centaur Press. Coffield for many years issued mimeographed folders of his poems and a periodical that included the writing of others, but to our knowledge no other hardbound volumes appeared.

William Everson is the author of dozens of books of poetry and criticism, and he has lectured and read throughout the country, for some years as Brother Antoninus, but after he withdrew from a religious order, under his own name. He was Poet in Residence at the Santa Cruz campus of the University of California from 1971 to 1982, and there established the Lime Kiln Press. In 1986 Adrian printed and published Everson's *In Medias Res: Canto One of an Autobiographical Epic*.

Adrian died in 1988. His last work was the design of the four volumes of *The Collected Poetry of Robinson Jeffers* for Stanford University Press. It is a fitting culmination of his intense interest in Jeffers.

Joyce Lancaster Wilson
San Francisco, May 1989

INDEX

Two Against the Tide has been printed from Monotype Ehrhardt on acid-free paper and produced in an edition of 850 copies at the press of W. Thomas Taylor. An additional 60 copies have been printed on Frankfurt cream mouldmade paper and bound in quarter linen with handmade paste-paper sides by BookLab in Austin, Texas. The calligraphy is by Jerry Kelly.